IPv6 DEPLOYMENT AND MANAGEMENT

T0176635

IPv6 DEPLOYMENT AND MANAGEMENT

By

MICHAEL DOOLEY
TIMOTHY ROONEY

IEEE
COMMUNICATIONS
SOCIETY

IEEE PRESS

IEEE Press
Series On
Network
Management

WILEY

Library of Congress Cataloging-in-Publication Data:
Rooney, Tim.
  IPv6 deployment and management / Timothy Rooney, Michael Dooley.
    pages cm
  ISBN 978-1-118-38720-7 (pbk.)
 1. TCP/IP (Computer network protocol)   2. Internet addresses.   I. Title.
  TK5105.585.R66 2013
  004.6'2068—dc23

                                        2012041248

Printed in the United States of America

10 9 8 7 6 5 4 3 2

Michael would like to dedicate this book to his parents

Timothy would like to dedicate this book
in memory of his mother, Kathryn
"Kitty" Rooney

CONTENTS

ACKNOWLEDGMENTS

We would both like to thank Vint Cerf for the introduction to this book; we are humbled and honored. We would also like to thank Thomas Plevyak, our series editor at IEEE Press, as well as Michael Vincent and Jeff Schmidt for their time spent reviewing drafts of this book and providing extremely useful feedback and comments.

From Michael: I would also like to thank my family, my wife Suzanne, my son Michael, and my daughter Kelly, for all their love and support and allowing me not to be distracted at home while I was working on this book. And I can't forget my puppy Bailey as well, who nudged me at every opportunity to pet her instead of letting me write. I would also like to thank the following individuals who are my friends and coworkers. I have had the pleasure to work with some of the best and brightest people in the world, and I am truly blessed. In no particular order, I thank Karen Pell, Steve Thompson, Greg Rabil, John Ramkawsky, Alex Drescher, Brian Hart (aka Billy Bond), Bob Lieber, David Cross, and Al Hilton. I would also like to acknowledge the original Quadritek leadership team that I had the privilege to work with as we helped to define and create the IP Address Management market back in the early years, specifically including Arun Kapur, Keith Larson, and Leah Kelly. And a special thanks to Joe D'Andrea whose leadership has had a profound impact on my life and my career.

From Timothy: I would also like to thank my family, my wife LeeAnn, and my daughters Maeve and Tess, for their love and support during the development of this book! I would also like to thank the following individuals with whom I have had the pleasure to work and from whom I have learned tremendously about communications technologies and IPv6: Greg Rabil, John Ramkawsky, Andy D'Ambrosio, Alex Drescher, David Cross, Marco Mecarelli, Brian Hart, Frank Jennings, and those I have worked with at BT Diamond IP, INS, and Lucent. From my formative time in the field of networking at Bell Laboratories, I thank John Marciszewski, Anthony Longhitano, Sampath Ramaswami, Maryclaire Brescia, Krishna Murti, Gaston Arredondo, Robert Schoenweisner, Tom Walker, Ray Pennotti, and especially Thomas Chu.

INTRODUCTION

Nearly 14 years have passed since RFC2460 was published, specifying the IPv6 packet format. Authored by Steve Deering and Bob Hinden, this document represented nearly 8 years of debate beginning in the early 1990s over how the Internet's 32-bit IPv4 address space could be expanded. There were four proposals for what was called "IPng" for IP next generation. I won't catalog them here except to say they varied dramatically in their functionality. There was even a fifth proposal to adopt the OSI connectionless networking protocol format (CLNP) that provoked howls of outrage from many passionate engineers in the Internet Engineering Task Force (IETF) where this problem was near the top of the agenda.

After all the debate, the cochairs of the IPng Working Group, Deering and Hinden, recorded the results in December 1998 and submitted them as RFC 2460 to the Internet Engineering Steering Group (IESG) for release to the RFC editor. Many of us hoped there would be an immediate effort to implement this protocol. There was great concern that the rate of consumption of the Internet address space was accelerating during the period now known as the "dot-boom." New Internet companies were popping up like mushrooms after a spring rain. But at the same time that the IPng debates were taking place, another effort to restrain IPv4 address consumption, through reinterpretation of the bits of the address structure, was in full swing. The so-called classless interdomain routing system made much more efficient use of address space by allowing any bit boundary in the address structure to mark the dividing line between "network" and "host." In addition, the concept of autonomous system (AS) was introduced through which to associate indicators (masks) illustrating where this boundary lay. The Border Gateway Protocol was revised to take into account the masks marking network and host extents in the address format. Together with rules to guide very conservative IPv4 address allocations by the Regional Internet Registries, the rate of consumption of IPv4 address space was substantially curtailed. So much so that the pressure to implement IPv6 generally dissipated.

Network address translation (NAT) functionality was also introduced to allow multiple devices using private IP address numbering to share a single public address space. Port numbers were used in the NAT boxes to map to/from public addresses and the private addresses associated with individual devices in a local network. This practice attracted cable and telecommunications providers who were offering Internet service because they could now maximize the number of devices that could share one "public" IP address. This improved the absolute number of customers they could sign up to be subscribers to their Internet service.

These various practices actually stretched the use of IPv4 addresses until February 2011 when the Internet Assigned Numbers Authority (IANA), operating under the auspices of the Internet Corporation for Assigned Names and Numbers, announced that it had exhausted the supply of IPv4 addresses at the source of its allocation. The Regional Internet Registries (ARIN, LACNIC, RIPE-NCC, AFRINIC, APNIC) still had allocations but APNIC soon exhausted its supply in April 2011 and RIPE-NCC has announced that it has exhausted its supply in September 2012. A market for IPv4 address space has formed but it cannot possibly solve the real need.

The "Internet of Things" is upon us. Mobiles using LTE for data transfer will need end-to-end communication capability. The same may be said for set-top boxes, sensor devices, Internet-enabled automobiles, countless household and office appliances, and, eventually, personal devices that may even be embedded or attached in some way to our bodies. The only sensible solution is to implement IPv6 addressing capability *in parallel* with IPv4. We cannot simply "throw a switch" to convert every device on the Internet from IPv4 to IPv6 addressing. The transition will take years.

This long transition leads to the need for very thoughtful design and implementation of control and management systems that can deal with both IPv4 and IPv6 operating concurrently in the network and in many devices. We cannot even try to form enclaves that are IPv4 only or IPv6 only for "simplicity." Devices that are mobile or portable will regularly encounter both IPv4 and IPv6 and mixed environments. There is also a very good chance that areas of the Internet will be IPv6 only for lack of IPv4 address space. Complex environments involving NATted IPv4 and end-to-end IPv6 will also be encountered. It is no wonder that a book of this kind, written by Michael Dooley and Timothy Rooney, will be needed on every Internet engineer's bookshelf (or in his laptop or pad or mobile, cloud client, and digital reader).

Configuration and network management are hard. Dealing with them in a mixed IP packet format environment is even harder. Error messages will be generated for both protocols even if a common fault, for example, a fiber cut, is the proximate cause. Network management systems will need to become much smarter about filtering, correlating, and sorting various error and status or warning messages emerging from a mixed IP addressing environment. The mere fact that the packet headers are potentially larger in IPv6 will create the potential for fragmentation or at least complicate the discovery of the minimum packet size needed to avoid fragmentation of blockage. These are just a few of the questions that need answering. Any system architect preparing to cope with a dual-stack environment will find this book a useful companion and source of advice.

It is not too late to start implementation but it is surely timely. The rest of this decade will see major changes and extensions to the Internet in many dimensions, not the least of which is a massive increase in the number of devices that can be attached and referenced in the system.

Some ISPs have been heard to say "customers are not asking for IPv6" as an excuse to delay implementation. From where I sit, customers should have to know nothing about IPv6. They should have a reasonable expectation that their ISPs will implement dual stack without their asking. It is irresponsible not to move rapidly to deployment of dual stack before there is no more IPv4 address available, even through NAT mechanisms. We must complete the transition to a fully connected IPv6 network as soon as possible. This does not mean we have to abandon the use of IPv4, only that we need connectivity as complete with IPv6 as we have had with IPv4—and we need it now.

Vint Cerf

VP and Chief Internet Evangelist Google

CHAPTER 1

IPv6 DEPLOYMENT DRIVERS

1.1 THE INTERNET: A SUCCESS STORY

The Internet has come a long way. Invented in the late 1960s as a resilient interconnected network of networks for the U.S. Department of Defense, it has evolved into a global communications phenomenon. With the invention of the World Wide Web by Tim Berners-Lee, defining the hypertext linking of information over a network such as the Internet through the use of a web browser, this innovation of simple point-and-click user interface brought the Internet out of government and science laboratories and into ordinary people's lives. Email was the second key Internet application that contributed to the widespread adoption of Internet services during the mid-1990s. Today's Internet users generally find this ubiquitous availability of wide variety of information and applications indispensable in their day-to-day lives. If popular Internet applications like Facebook, YouTube, Twitter, Google, Blogger, shopping, and news sites, and even good old email were suddenly rendered unavailable, most people would not know what to do with themselves!

But the abundance of information and applications on the Internet is not universally available worldwide today. Figure 1-1 illustrates the statistics reported by Internet World Stats indicating the penetration of Internet users as a percentage of overall population in various regions of the world as of mid-2012. Just over one-third of the world's population has access to and use the Internet from work, home, mobile, or wireline. Penetration in North America is highest among the measured regions at more than 78% with Europe second at 63%. Among the Asian population, penetration is only about 28%.

Looking at the same data from a raw numbers perspective, Figure 1-2 illustrates the distribution of Internet users throughout the world. Comparing Figures 1-1 and 1-2, note that while Internet penetration in Asia is less than 28%, the number of users in Asia tops 1 billion, representing 45% of global Internet users, estimated at 2.4 billion by Internet World Stats.

With worldwide penetration of Internet users at just 34%, there seems to be plenty of room for an expanding Internet population. And with the likelihood of multiple devices required per user, this expansion will create accelerated demand for Internet Protocol (IP) addresses. But what circumstances would facilitate such expansion? A recent study by the World Bank concluded that in low- and middle-income countries, for every 10% increase in Internet penetration, the country's average economic growth increases by 1.12% as measured by gross

IPv6 Deployment and Management, First Edition. By Michael Dooley and Timothy Rooney.
© 2013 by The Institute of Electrical and Electronics Engineers, Inc. Published 2013 by John Wiley & Sons, Inc.

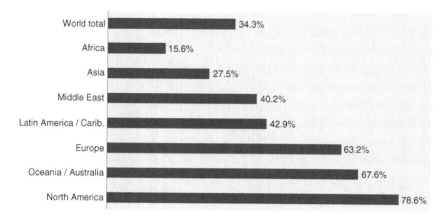

Figure 1-1. Internet penetration by region [1].

domestic product (GDP) [2]. A 10% increase in broadband penetration yields an average GDP increase of 1.38%. The report also extols other socio-economic benefits for broadband deployment including higher employment, expanding entrepreneurial opportunities, providing social contacts, and delivering public information-based services. While some governments may desire to restrict free access to certain content or applications, the economic correlation to Internet growth is difficult to ignore.

And trends leading up to the present time indicate strong growth over the last decade. Figure 1-3 illustrates growth in Internet users and penetration. These appear to be directly proportional. The compound annual growth rate (CAGR) over this time period, by region, is represented in Table 1-1 and averaged 18% worldwide.

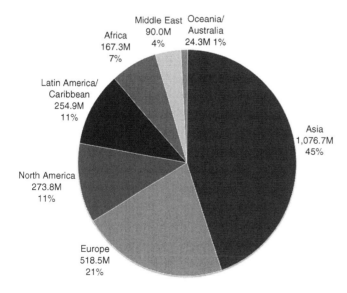

Figure 1-2. Worldwide Internet users by region [1].

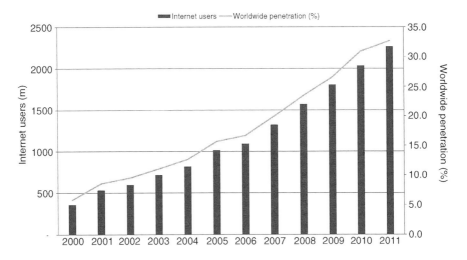

Figure 1-3.   Internet users history [1].

The number of content providers or "producers" on the Internet as measured by the number of new websites is also growing at an increasingly rapid rate according to Netcraft [3], an Internet research and security services firm. As of June 2012, the total number of discovered unique website hostnames reached nearly 700 million, while active (non-template, based solely on domain registration) sites approached 200 million as shown in Figure 1-4. Both metrics have increased at an accelerated rate over the past two years. New organizations beyond some point in time desiring to operate their own websites or hosting providers will eventually only have access to IPv6 address space for publishing web content.

1.1.1 Supply-Side Issues

Given this history of sustained growth of Internet users and content suppliers, the relatively modest penetration rates, and the economic benefits of broadband deployment and Internet access, it's reasonable to predict that Internet user and producer

TABLE 1-1. Worldwide Internet User Growth per Region

Internet users (M)	2000	2011	CAGR (%)
Africa	4.5	139.9	37
Asia	114.3	1016.8	22
Europe	105.1	500.7	15
Middle East	3.3	77.0	33
North America	108.1	273.1	9
Latin America/Caribbean	18.1	235.8	26
Oceania/Australia	7.6	23.9	11
Worldwide total	361.0	2267.2	18

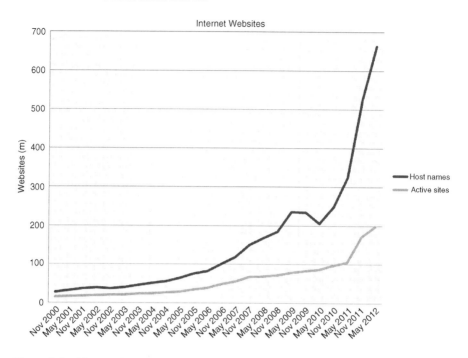

Figure 1-4.   Measured quantity of Internet websites [3].

demand will continue to grow. Unfortunately, the currently available capacity of IPv4 addresses to support this growth is insufficient. With IPv4 address space depleted, for all intents and purposes, the only Internet Protocol available to support this demand is IPv6.

When the Internet Assigned Names and Numbers Authority (IANA) announced, on February 3, 2011, that it had allocated its last remaining IPv4 address space to the Regional Internet Registries (RIRs), that day was the beginning of the end of the Internet as we know it. Figure 1-5 illustrates the IP address space "food chain," with IANA allocating base address blocks to RIRs. IANA is a department within the Internet Corporation for Assigned Names and Numbers (ICANN), which itself is a not-for-profit public-benefit corporation with participants from around the world. IANA is the centralized coordinating body for Internet domain names managing the Domain Name System (DNS) root and several other top-level domains, Internet number resources (IP addresses), and protocol assignments (protocol-specific parameters, e.g., Dynamic Host Configuration Protocol (DHCP) option number assignments).

The RIRs are organizations responsible for allocation of address space within their respective global regions from their corresponding space allotments from IANA:

- AfriNIC (African Network Information Centre)—Africa region
- APNIC (Asia-Pacific Network Information Centre)—Asia-Pacific region
- ARIN (American Registry for Internet Numbers)—North America region including Puerto Rico and some Caribbean Islands

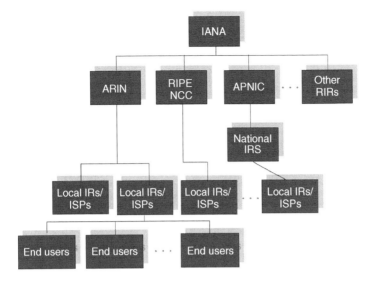

Figure 1-5. The IP address space hierarchy [4].

- LACNIC (Regional Latin-American and Caribbean IP Address Registry)—Latin America and some Caribbean Islands
- RIPE NCC (Réseaux IP Européens Network Coordination Centre)—Europe, the Middle East, and Central Asia.

The RIR system was established with the following goals for IP address allocation to National Internet Registries, Local Internet Registries (LIRs), and Internet Service Providers (ISPs):

- *Uniqueness.* Each IP address must be unique worldwide for global Internet routing.
- *Aggregation.* Hierarchical allocation of address space assures proper routing of IP traffic on the Internet. Without aggregation, routing tables become fragmented which could ultimately create tremendous bottlenecks within the Internet.
- *Conservation.* With IPv4 in particular but also for IPv6 space, address space needs to be distributed according to actual usage requirements.
- *Registration.* A publicly accessible registry of IP address assignments eliminates ambiguity and can help when troubleshooting. This registry is called the *whois* database. Today, there are many whois databases, operated not only by RIRs but also by LIR/ISPs for their respective address spaces.
- *Fairness.* Unbiased address allocation based on true address needs and not on long-term "plans."

Despite efforts to extend the lifetime of IPv4 through technologies such as Network Address Translation (NAT) and Classless Inter-Domain Routing (CIDR) as well as RIR policies enabling sales and transfers of IPv4 address space, eventually the RIRs will each allocate their last vestige of IPv4 address space to their constituents. The ISPs then in turn will eventually exhaust their IPv4 resources for distribution to their customers, generally enterprise businesses. The APNIC and RIPE NCC RIRs have already exhausted their respective IPv4 space.

1.1.2 Internet at a Crossroads

So what does all this mean? When IPv4 address space runs out among the ISPs within a given RIR's region, any new organization requiring IP address space or existing organizations requiring supplemental IP address space in that region will, by necessity, receive an IPv6 address space allocation. As new organizations initiate web presences, they will be accessible only by IPv6. As new "IPv6-only" organizations join the web, the composition of the Internet itself will slowly change from the homogeneous IPv4 Internet available today to a mixed IPv4/IPv6 Internet in the future. How quickly and to what levels this IPv6 density within the Internet will rise is uncertain.

The growth in number of IPv6-only users is expected to surface initially in Asia. The economies of major Asian countries, particularly China and India, have grown more rapidly in recent years than the rest of the world according to the International Monetary Fund [5] as illustrated in Figure 1-6. From 2000 through 2011, the average annual GDP growth in China was 10.2% and India was 7.1%, while the world average was 2.7%. This in turn has led to rising disposable incomes and government infrastructure investment in communications technologies such as broadband and wireless. Point Topic Ltd estimated that nearly half of the world's broadband net additions for the first half of 2012 were in Asia [6]. Point Topic's report also mirrored that of Internet World Stats, which reported that while Asia boasts the most Internet users at over one billion, its Internet penetration rate is below the world average (33%) at 26%.

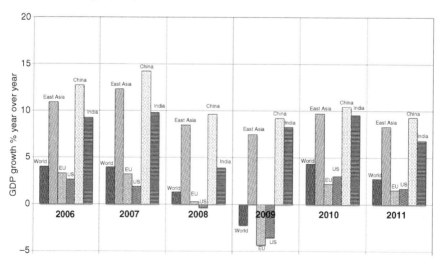

Figure 1-6. GDP growth 2006–2010 [7].

Though growth slowed during 2012, the rate of subscriber growth remains strong, stimulating many service providers in the region and throughout the world to implemente translation gateways, tunnel brokers, or similar technologies, which we'll describe in Chapter 3. Depending on the selected approach, these technologies allow service providers to support customer premises equipment (CPE) configured with IPv4 or IPv6 addresses with the ability to access IPv4 or IPv6 Internet destinations. Service providers will need to support customer access to both protocols to avoid subscribers complaining that should IPv4 subscribers be unable to access IPv6-only content and IPv6 subscribers be unable to access IPv4-only content.

1.1.3 Which Internet Are You On?

This is precisely what is at stake with today's current crossroads on the Internet. At this point, perhaps you're wondering what IPv6 deployment in Asia has to do with you. Quite simply, *the ubiquity of the Internet is at stake*. If every organization with ample IPv4 space continues to manage an IPv4-only Internet presence, then this growing IPv6-only population will be unable to reach them. Conversely, these IPv4-only users will be unable to reach IPv6-only Internet content. Unfortunately, there is no inherent conversion of IPv4 packets into IPv6 packets and vice-versa, so launching an IPv6 packet at an IPv4 web server will result in a dropped packet before it gets to the web server. Hence a bifurcated Internet could evolve along the lines of the two network layer versions. This would be most unfortunate, let alone short sighted.

Not only is Internet ubiquity at stake in terms of providing a global network for everyone, communications, commerce, collaboration, and recreation, but competitiveness and leadership position in the world are also at stake. The RIPE NCC publishes a periodically updated graph [8] indicating the percentage of BGP ASNs that advertise an IPv6 prefix among their advertisements. The Border Gateway Protocol (BGP) is the routing protocol on the Internet backbone, and each autonomous system number (ASN) represents an organization. During 2012, all regions experienced more than a 32% increase in the number of IPv6 Internet routes. About 15% of the organizations (ASNs) worldwide as of the time of this writing have obtained IPv6 address space and have implemented it at least externally for reachability. If your competition is among these and the new market emerging, particularly in the Asia region, how quickly will you be able to respond? Supporting an ongoing worldwide web presence is a key consideration for IPv6 deployment.

1.2 EMERGING APPLICATIONS

In addition to IPv4/IPv6 Internet ubiquity, a class of emerging applications that leverage IPv6 features promises to revolutionize daily life. These "smart" applications, while technically supportable via IPv4, are expected to require high mobility, plentiful address space, and the ability to autoconfigure IP addresses based on current network location, all features not as efficiently supportable by IPv4. While most features invented for IPv6 were ported back into IPv4, providing relatively close feature parity, expanded address space is certainly a unique advantage of IPv6. But other improvements include improved mobility with more efficient routing, address autoconfiguration, efficient packet routing with fragmentation performed on the network perimeter, and improved routing performance with the simplified IPv6 header structure.

There's no argument regarding address capacity given the sheer size of IPv6 address space. Address autoconfiguration and improved mobility support in particular also provide key features to satisfy the demands for continuing Internet growth, driven primarily by increased proliferation of mobile devices. But these capabilities also create an environment for a new class of applications where remote sensors, for example, can monitor, detect, and report to centralized applications for processing. This nascent class of applications are based on machine-to-machine communications or M2M, which defines an architecture and method for machines communicating with each other to collect and aggregate massive amounts of "big data" information, ultimately for human consumption.

Figure 1-7 illustrates the basic M2M architecture. Starting from the bottom of the figure, application-specific sensors are deployed which report monitoring status updates via an aggregator to an M2M gateway. The set of sensors that are deployed, for the purpose of monitoring a particular object, comprise an M2M area network. An aggregator may be deployed to receive and process updates from the set of sensors within the M2M area network. In some cases, sensors may communicate directly to the M2M gateway and in other cases, the aggregator may be another sensor or device such as a cell phone that relays sensor messages to the M2M gateway.

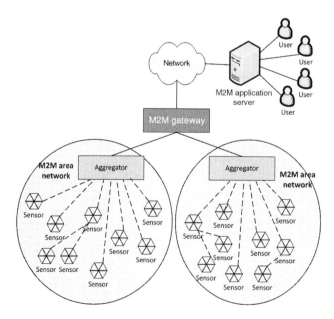

Figure 1-7. Basic M2M architecture.

The M2M gateway forwards the aggregated sensor information to an M2M application server, which processes message updates for presentation to an application's user. The M2M application server may also analyze reported sensor data to generate alerts or to proactively notify users of certain detected events. This "value-added" processing capability is critical to pre-process what could be inputs from millions or billions of deployed sensors into an actionable prioritized view of the monitored element(s).

With decreasing size, cost, and power consumption, M2M sensor devices can be manufactured for a wide variety of functions in support of corresponding applications. M2M sensors communicate via wireless to each other, to an aggregator or a gateway to provide updated sensor information to the application for analysis. From an IP layer perspective, RFC 6568 [9] defines "design and application spaces for IPv6 over low-power wireless personal area networks (6LoWPANs)." The 6LoWPAN architecture aligns well with M2M, where LoW-PAN nodes map to sensors and local controller nodes map to M2M aggregators. The gateway interface traverses a LoWPAN border router at the IP layer in the 6LoWPAN architecture.

M2M and 6LoWPAN technology opens new markets for service providers as well as sensor and application developers to expand offerings to utilities, municipalities, healthcare organizations, and many more. Some example M2M and 6LoWPAN applications include:

- *Smart Applications.* Provides a centralized view of yet unrealized volumes of data for more intelligent resource management and customer service such as:

  ○ *Smart Grid.* Dynamic matching of electricity, water, gas, etc., supply with demand, reducing resource waste, and saving consumers on utility bills.

  ○ *Smart Cars.* Diagnostic and usage sensors within an automobile for performance reporting, troubleshooting and customer notification of worn components, and recommended service check-ups as well as automated crash detection and reporting.

  ○ *Smart Homes.* Remote monitoring of premises, remote control of power, heating/cooling, lighting, entertainment, and access.

- *Municipal and Industrial Surveillance and Monitoring.* Physical access control and monitoring, environmental monitoring for extreme conditions (e.g., natural disaster, fire, floods), structural monitoring, and traffic monitoring.

- *Field Applications.* Fleet management, dispatch, and vehicle telematics.

- *Healthcare.* Remote monitoring of a patient's vital signs, diagnostics and medication administration, "body area networks," monitoring of storage environments, e.g., for plasma, organs.

- *Industrial.* Factory line monitoring, diagnostics, resource control, supply chain management, process monitoring, and control leveraging improved accessibility that wireless provides.

- *Military.* Battlefield ad hoc networks with various soldier sensors reporting status updates to military command.

These applications and others like them generally require deployment of hundreds, thousands, or even millions of sensor devices whose measurements and status information must be communicated to a centralized application server for processing and presentation. The M2M architecture supports them with a common approach for network access, reliable communications, security, and centralized management.

Given the potential quantities of M2M devices, it's logical to surmise that IPv6 represents the logical network layer protocol to be "designed in" to provide plenty of capacity with room for growth, especially as new M2M applications emerge, while obviating the need to upgrade to IPv6 later on. The autoconfiguration feature is beneficial for M2M applications as well because as sensors are deployed and "awaken" from power saving sleep mode, they may determine their linked network via router advertisements and derive an Interface ID to create an IPv6 address. After successfully completing the duplicate address detection process, the address can be considered active[1]. Ultimately the selection of IPv6 as the protocol of choice lies with relevant applications of standards groups, and many have included IPv6 support as well as IPv4.

1.3 IPv6 BUSINESS CASE

Each organization needs to determine, for itself, if, when, and how it should deploy IPv6. There are many approaches with corresponding levels of effort along the continuum from "do nothing" to "full IPv6 deployment." For those who are skeptical about whether IPv6 deployment is necessary, we'd recommend at least scoping out an order of magnitude estimate of effort required to implement IPv6, should some Internet event or news inspire a call from the leaders of your organization to deploy IPv6 quickly. We'll describe this high-level process. Then, should you decide to move forward, the requisite deeper discussion begins in Chapter 4. This initial exercise, however, is beneficial in helping you understand what would need to be done and roughly how long it would take you to move forward with deployment quickly.

There's no denying that the Internet continues to expand both in terms of users and content producers. This expansion by necessity will dilute the nearly 100% IPv4 Internet density to an increasingly hybrid Internet. It's not overly difficult to support both IPv4 and IPv6 in order to retain Internet ubiquity for your organization. But it's also not trivially simple. Deploying IPv6 requires analysis of your current IPv4 network, scoping IPv6 deployment, identifying upgrades or modifications to network equipment, applications or end user devices, and managing the project to completion. The intent of this book is to help you along and through this process.

To begin the process, you'll likely need to justify the resource allocation. Capital outlay and expense payments, to embark on an IPv6 deployment project or even the discovery and assessment phases of the project to fully define the expected

---

[1] We'll discuss address states in more detail in Chapter 2.

costs to a high degree of confidence, will need to be determined. Access to existing network and computing system documentation can help you estimate costs for discovery and assessment alone or the entire deployment.

In terms of the upside, which is measured by increased revenue, lower costs, and/or reduced lost sales, the following should be analyzed with respect to your business:

- Sustained or increased revenue growth especially if you are a service provider who relies on IP connectivity.

- Universal Internet presence if your organization offers products or services to consumers around the world. The opportunity cost of not deploying IPv6 is that IPv6 "eyeballs" will never reach your site. As Internet growth is fueled over time by IPv6 users, these incremental prospects will be lost. Conversely your internal users will be unable to access their IPv6 Internet resources.

- Competitive advantage or parity, which can have amplified impacts if you're in a technology related industry.

- As more employees bring their (your) own devices ("BYOD") to work, many current and future portable devices will be IPv6-ready. Many leading operating systems already support IPv6 by default. If you work with partners who have only IPv6 address space, you may need to support IPv6 at least for such connections.

- Network visibility of IPv6 traffic, given end user device IPv6 support. Awareness and visibility to native or tunneled IPv6 traffic as well as external probes or attacks using IPv6 is necessary from a network security perspective.

- Supporting emerging applications that leverage unique IPv6 features, especially for mobility and autoconfiguration.

- Creating an interesting and challenging work environment for IT or operations teams. As we shall see, managing an IPv4/IPv6 network is certainly more challenging than managing a single protocol network, but this can be rewarding for employees' knowledge and career growth.

- Supporting IPv6 due to regulatory or legal requirements.

You may want to qualify the opportunity cost based on Internet IPv6 density. For example, once the percentage of IPv6 users and websites on the Internet exceeds 20%, this may represent a sufficiently large population to justify IPv6 deployment to communicate with the full Internet including those among the 20%. This is a decision your organization needs to make. But whether that density is 1% or 99%, it behooves you to have in hand a plan to initiate the IPv6 deployment project at the appointed time.

The basic project authorization process is summarized in Figure 1-8 and starts with defining the objectives for the project. One or more of the upside items presented above may serve as objectives for your deployment and may help focus the scope of your deployment. With your objectives, scope, high-level assessment based on network documentation, and the steps outlined in this book, you should be able to estimate high-level resource costs and timeframes. Depending on your

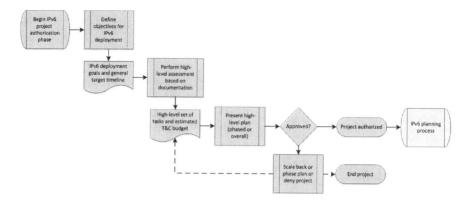

Figure 1-8. Basic authorization process.

organization, the expected level of detail required for project approval may vary. Or you may seek approval merely for the discovery and assessment phase, then revisit the overall deployment project approval thereafter.

Assessing your network, identifying gaps, and creating a project plan are advisable for immediate or deferred execution based on your decision criteria. The overall deployment process described in this book follows five basic steps as depicted in Figure 1-9. We've discussed the authorization process in this chapter, which requires a basic definition of the goals, scope, plan, costs, and benefits of IPv6 deployment. We focus much of the remainder of this book on the next phase, the planning phase, which is critical for a smooth deployment with minimal surprises. We dedicate a chapter to each to four core planning aspects: network and computing infrastructure assessment and planning, IP address planning, security, and network management planning. Effective planning leads to the deployment phase which includes an initial testing and verification process followed by production deployment.

Once in production, management of your IPv4/IPv6 network requires similar processes over managing IPv4 alone, though with a few modifications and additions. At some point perhaps in the distant future, IPv4 will be retired. It's hard to imagine this at this point in time, but some day it will happen, though probably not for another two decades.

Before we embark on detailing the core aspects of the planning process, it makes sense to first understand IPv6 itself and technological strategies for implementing IPv6 within an IPv4 network. We'll discuss these topics in the next two chapters, then follow that with chapters covering the planning, deployment, and management processes.

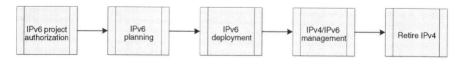

Figure 1-9. Basic overall process.

CHAPTER 2

IPv6 OVERVIEW

Internet Protocol version 6[1] is an evolution from version 4 but is not inherently compatible with version 4[2]. This incompatibility drives the need to take action to deploy IPv6 on top of or beside IPv4. Chapter 3 describes several IPv4/IPv6 co-existence techniques. The primary objective for version 6 was essentially to redesign version 4 based on the prior 20 years' experience with IPv4. Real-world application support that had been added to the IPv4 protocol suite over the years was designed into IPv6 from the outset. This included support for security, multicast, mobility, and autoconfiguration.

The most striking difference in the evolution from IPv4 to IPv6 is the tremendous expansion of the size of the IP address field. Whereas IPv4 uses a 32-bit IP address field, IPv6 uses 128 bits. A 32-bit address field provides a maximum of 2^{32} addresses or 4.2 billion addresses. A 128-bit address field provides 2^{128} addresses or 340 trillion trillion trillion addresses or 340 undecillion[3] (3.4×10^{38}). To put some context around this tremendously large number, consider that this quantity of IP addresses:

- Averages to 5×10^{28} IP addresses per person on Earth based on a 6.5 billion population.
- Averages to 4.3×10^{20} IP addresses per square inch of the earth's surface.
- Amounts to about 14 million IP addresses per nanometer to the nearest galaxy, Andromeda, at 2.5 million light years.

As with IPv4, not every single address will necessarily be usable due to subnetting inefficiencies, but a few undecillion of wasted addresses won't have much impact on overall address capacity! Beyond this seemingly incomprehensible number of IP addresses, there are a number of similarities between IPv6 and IPv4. For example, at a basic level, the "IP packet" concept applies equally well for IPv6, as IPv4 in terms of the concept of the packet header and contents, as does the basic concept of protocol layering, packet routing, CIDR allocations, use of Internet Control Message Protocol (ICMP), multicast addressing, and more.

---

[1] IP version 5 was never implemented as an official version of IP. The version number of '5' in the IP header was assigned to denote packets carrying an experimental real-time stream protocol called ST, the Internet Stream Protocol. If you'd like to learn more about ST, please refer to RFC 1819 [10].

[2] Portions of the information in this chapter are based on material in [11].

[3] We're using the American definition of undecillion of 10^{36}, not the British definition which is 10^{66}.

IPv6 Deployment and Management, First Edition. By Michael Dooley and Timothy Rooney.
© 2013 by The Institute of Electrical and Electronics Engineers, Inc. Published 2013 by John Wiley & Sons, Inc.

2.1   IPv6 KEY FEATURES

The Internet Engineering Task Force (IETF) attempted to develop IPv6 as an evolution of IPv4. The evolutionary strategy in migrating from IPv4 to IPv6 was intended to enable IPv6 to provide many new features while building on the foundational concepts that made IPv4 so successful. Key IPv6 features include:

- Expanded addressing—128 bits hierarchically assigned with address scoping (e.g., local link vs. global) to improve scalability.
- Routing—strongly hierarchical routing, supporting route aggregation.
- Performance—simple (unreliable, connectionless) datagram service.
- Extensibility—new flexible extension headers provide built-in extensibility for new header types and more efficient routing.
- Multimedia—flow label header field facilitates quality of service (QoS) support.
- Multicast—replaces broadcast and is compulsory.
- Security—authentication and encryption are built-in though no longer inherently required.
- Autoconfiguration—stateless and stateful address self-configuration by IP devices.
- Mobility—mobile IPv6 support with improved routing to/from roaming networks.

2.2   THE IPv6 HEADER

The IPv6 header layout is shown in Figure 2-1. While the size of both the source and destination IP address fields quadrupled over that of the IPv4 header, the overall IP header size only doubled. The fields in the IPv6 header are as follows:

Version. The Internet Protocol version, 6 in this case.

Traffic Class. This field is analogous to the IPv4 type of service/differentiated services (DS) header field and indicates the type or priority of traffic in order to request corresponding routing treatment.

Flow Label. Identifies the "flow" of traffic between a source and destination to which this packet belongs as set by the source. This is intended to enable efficient and consistent routing treatment for packets within a given communications session.

Payload Length. Indicates the length of the IPv6 payload, which is the portion of the packet after the base IPv6 header, in octets. Extension headers, if included, are considered part of the payload and are counted within this length parameter.

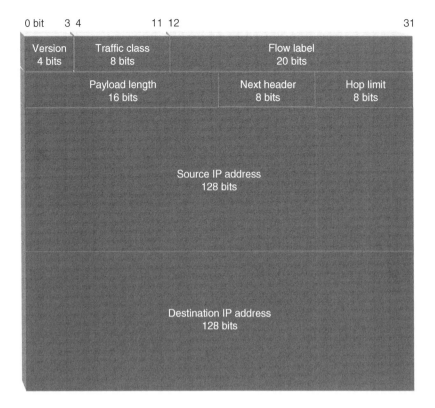

Figure 2-1. IPv6 header [12].

> *Next Header.* This field indicates the type of header that follows this IP header. This may be an upper layer protocol header (e.g., TCP, ICMPv6) or an extension header. The extension header concept enables specification of source routing, fragmentation, options, and other parameters associated with the packet only when they are necessary, not as overhead on all packets as in IPv4. Parameter value encodings are the same as those assigned for the IPv4 Protocol header field [13].

> *Hop Limit.* Analogous to the IPv4 Time to Live (TTL) field, this field specifies the number of hops over which this packet may traverse before being discarded. Each router decrements the value of this header field upon forwarding the packet.

> *Source IP Address.* The IPv6 address of the sender of this packet.

> *Destination IP Address.* The IPv6 address of the intended recipient(s) of this packet.

2.2.1 IPv6 Extension Headers

The Next Header field in the IPv6 header provides a means to minimize IPv6 header overhead while also enabling concatenation of headers for various purposes as needed.

Figure 2-2.   IPv6 extension headers.

This concatenation is illustrated in Figure 2-2, with the main IPv6 header on the left indicating a next header value of 0, the hop-by-hop header, which itself is followed by the authentication header, then the TCP header and finally upper layer payload.

Header types are to be prioritized in specific order to minimize the requirements and resources on the part of routers along the path of a packet to deeply analyze IPv6 headers. Every node along the path of an IPv6 packet, including routers, is required to examine if present, the hop-by-hop options, routing header, and shim6 header. As such the required ordering of defined IPv6 extension headers is given in Table 2-1.

TABLE 2-1.   IPv6 Extension Header Ordering

Order if present	Header type	Next header code
1	Basic IPv6 header described above	N/A
2	Hop-by-hop options—must be examined by each node along the path of the packet	0
3	Destination options—parameters intended for processing by the first destination that appears in the basic header destination address field plus subsequent destinations listed in the Routing header	60
4	Routing header—initially defined for source routing (type 0 routing header) which has since been deprecated; type 1 not used and type 2 is for mobility	43
5	Shim6 multi-homing header—used to provide connectivity continuity in multi-homed environments (connections to multiple ISPs)	140
6	Fragmentation header—information about this packet which is being sent in multiple parts (fragments)	44
7	Authentication header—provides an Integrity Check Value (ICV) for the packet to authenticate its integrity and origin	51
8	Encapsulating security payload (ESP)—provides a mix of security services for the packet including data origin authentication, data integrity, anti-replay with sequence number integrity, and limited confidentiality (encryption)	50
9	Mobility header—mobile IPv6 information	135
10	Destination options—parameters intended for processing only by the final destination of the packet	60
Upper layer	TCP—Transmission Control Protocol	6
	UDP—User Datagram Protocol	17
	ICMPv6—Internet Control Message Protocol for IPv6	58

New extension headers may be specified through the IETF RFC process, though the IETF recommends adding new hop-by-hop extension options to the existing hop-by-hop header specification and destination options to the existing destination header. This will reduce the risk of packets being dropped due to an unrecognized newly defined Next Header value in the IPv6 header due to security policies.

2.3 IPv6 ADDRESSING

Three types of IPv6 addresses have been defined. Like IPv4, these addresses apply to interfaces, not nodes. Thus, a printer with two interfaces would be addressed by either of its interfaces. The printer can be reached on either interface, but the printer node does not have an IP address per se[4]. Of course, for end users attempting to access a node, DNS can hide this subtlety by enabling a host name to map to one or more interface addresses.

Unicast. The IP address of a single interface. This is analogous to the common interpretation of an IPv4 host address (non-multicast/non-broadcast/32-bit IPv4 address).

Anycast. An IP address for a set of interfaces usually belonging to different nodes, any one of which is the intended recipient. An IP packet destined for an anycast address is routed to the nearest interface (according to routing table metrics) configured with the anycast address. The concept is that the sender doesn't necessarily care which particular host or interface receives the packet, but that one of those sharing the anycast address receives it. Anycast addresses are assigned from the same address space from which unicast addresses have been allocated. Thus, one cannot differentiate a unicast address from an anycast address by sight. Anycast addresses are often used to provide *closest routing to the intended service*, such as for DNS servers by using a shared IP address. This provides benefits in simplifying client configuration, by having it always use the same [anycast] IP address to query a DNS server (regardless of where on your network the client is connected).

Multicast. An IP address for a set of interfaces typically belonging to different nodes, all of which are intended recipients. This of course is similar to IPv4 multicast. Unlike IPv4, IPv6 does not support broadcasts. Instead, applications that utilized broadcasts in IPv4, such as DHCP, use well-known (i.e., pre-defined) DHCP multicast group addresses in IPv6.

A device interface may have multiple IP addresses of any or all address types. IPv6 also defines a link-local address scope to uniquely identify interfaces attached to a particular link, such as a LAN. Additional scoping can be

---

[4] Many router and server products support the concept of a "box address" via a software loopback address. This loopback address, not to be confused with the 127.0.0.1 or ::1 loopback addresses, enables reachability to any one of the device's interfaces.

administratively defined per site or per organization, for example, as we'll discuss later in this chapter.

2.3.1 Address Notation

Recall that IPv4 addresses are represented in dotted decimal format where the 32-bit address is divided into four 8-bit segments, each of which are converted to decimal, then separated with "dots." If you thought remembering a string of four decimals was difficult, IPv6 will make life a little tougher. IPv6 addresses are not expressed in dotted-decimal notation; they are represented using a colon-separated hexadecimal format. Jumping down to the bit level, the 128-bit IPv6 address is divided into eight 16-bit segments, each of which is converted into hexadecimal, then separated by colons. Each hexadecimal "digit" represents four bits per mapping of each hex digit (0-f) to its 4-bit binary mapping below. Each hex digit corresponds to four bits with possible values of:

0 = 0000	4 = 0100	8 = 1000	c = 1100
1 = 0001	5 = 0101	9 = 1001	d = 1101
2 = 0010	6 = 0110	a = 1010	e = 1110
3 = 0011	7 = 0111	b = 1011	f = 1111

After converting a 128-bit IPv6 address from binary into hex, IPv6 groups sets of four hex digits and separates them with colons. We'll use the term *nibble* to represent a grouping of 4 bits or a single hex digit and the term *sedectet* to refer to a grouping of four hex digits or 16 bits. Thus, we have eight sedectet values separated by colons, rendering an IPv6 address appearing as in Figure 2-3.

Instead of dealing with four decimal values, each between 0 and 255, separated by dots in IPv4, IPv6 addresses consist of up to eight sedectet values, each between 0000 and ffff, separated by colons. There are two acceptable abbreviations when writing IPv6 addresses. First, leading zeroes within a sedectet, that is, between colons, may be dropped. Thus, the address of Figure 2-3 could be abbreviated:

2001 : db8 : 5f62 : ab41 : 0 : 0 : 0 : 801

The second form of abbreviation is the use of a double colon to represent one or more consecutive sets of zero sedectets. Using this form of abbreviation, the address above can be further abbreviated as:

2001 : db8 : 5f62 : ab41 :: 801

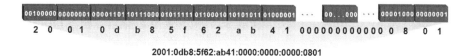

2001:0db8:5f62:ab41:0000:0000:0000:0801

Figure 2-3. IPv6 address: binary to hexadecimal.

Note that only one double colon may be used within an address representation. Since there are always eight sedectet segments in the address, one can easily calculate how many of them are zero with one double-colon notation; however it would be ambiguous with more than one.

Consider the address: 2001:db8:0:56fa:0:0:0:b5. We could abbreviate this address as either:

2001 : db8 :: 56fa : 0 : 0 : 0 : b5   *or*   2001 : db8 : 0 : 56fa :: b5

We can easily calculate that the double colon denotes one sedectet (8 total minus 7 nibbles shown) in the first case and three (8 minus 5 shown) in the second notation. If we attempted to abbreviate this address as 2001:db8::56fa::b5, we could not unambiguously decode this, as it could represent any of the following possible addresses:

2001 : db8 : 0 : 56fa : 0 : 0 : 0 : b5
2001 : db8 : 0 : 0 : 56fa : 0 : 0 : b5
2001 : db8 : 0 : 0 : 0 : 56fa : 0 : b5

Thus, the requirement holds that only one double colon may appear in an IPv6 address. The correct abbreviation according to RFC 5952, *A Recommendation for IPv6 Address Text Representation* [14], shortens the longest stretch of zero sedectets or the first of many equal-sized segments yielding 2001:db8:0:56fa::b5 as the proper abbreviated form for our example. Incidentally, RFC 5952 also stipulates use of lower-case hex digits.

You may notice IPv6 addresses suffixed with a percent sign followed by some digits or text, as in `fe80::9848:a87:e2f1:6d42%11` or `fe80::9848:a87: e2f1:6d42%eth0`. The percent sign delimits the IPv6 address from its *scope zone* or sometimes referred to as "scope ID" or "zone." The scope ID value is defined by the local host's operating system to identify the network topological scope of the address, namely, interface-local, link-local, global, or administratively defined. For example, the scoped IPv6 address just illustrated could define an interface local scoped link-local address. The format and association of zones with topology is administratively defined based on the device's operating system.

2.3.2 Address Structure

The IPv6 address is segmented into three fields:

1. The global routing prefix is analogous to an IPv4 network number and is used by routers to forward packets to router(s) locally serving the network corresponding to the prefix. For example, a customer of an ISP may be assigned a /48-sized global routing prefix and all packets destined to this customer would contain the corresponding global routing prefix value. In this case, $n = 48$ per Figure 2-4. When denoting a network, the global routing prefix is written, followed by slash, then the network size, called the prefix length. Assuming our example IPv6 address, 2001:db8:5f62:ab41::801, resides within a /48

Figure 2-4.   IPv6 address structure [15].

global routing prefix, this prefix address would be denoted as 2001:
db8:5f62::/48. Notice that the "network slash prefix length" CIDR notation
used in IPv6 is analogous to that used in IPv4. And as with IPv4, the network
address is denoted with zero-valued bits beyond the prefix length (bits 49-128
in this case) as denoted by the terminating double colon.

2.   The subnet ID provides a means to denote particular subnets within an
organization. Our ISP customer with a /48 would use 16 bits for the subnet
ID, providing 2^{16} or 65,534 subnets. In this case, $m = 16$ per Figure 2-4. This
leaves $128 - 48 - 16 = 64$ bits for the interface ID.

3.   The interface ID denotes the interface address of the source or intended
recipient for the packet. As we'll discuss a bit later, the global unicast address
space that has been allocated for use so far requires a 64-bit interface ID field[5].

One of the unique aspects of this IPv6 address structure in splitting a network ID
consisting of the global routing prefix and subnet ID, from an interface ID, is that a device
can retain the same interface ID independently of the network to which it is connected,
effectively separating "who you are", your interface ID, from "where you are," your
network prefix. As we'll see, this convention facilitates address autoconfiguration,
though not without privacy concerns. But we're getting a little ahead of ourselves, so let's
jump back up a level and consider the IPv6 address space allocated so far by the Internet
addressing authority, the Internet Assigned Numbers Authority (IANA).

2.3.3   IPv6 Address Allocations

The address space that has been allocated so far by IANA is indicated in Table 2-2
and is discussed in the ensuing text. These allocations represent less than 14% of the
total available IPv6 address space.

2.3.3.1   ::/3—Reserved Space   Address space prefixed with $[000]_2$ is currently
reserved by the IETF. Addresses within this space that have unique meaning include
the unspecified (::) address and the loopback (::1) address. The *IP Version 6
Addressing Architecture* specification, RFC 4291 [15], requires that all unicast
IPv6 addresses, except those within this address space (i.e., beginning with::/3
($[000]_2$)) must utilize a 64-bit interface ID field, and this interface ID field must
utilize the modified EUI-64[6] algorithm to map the interface's layer 2 or hardware
address to an interface ID. Thus, addresses within the::/3 address space can have any

---

[5] Except point-to-point inter-router links which may use one bit for each end or a 127-bit network prefix
[16].
[6] EUI-64 refers to the 64-bit Extended Unique Identifier defined by the IEEE. We'll cover the modified
EUI-64 algorithm later in this chapter.

TABLE 2-2.   IPv6 Address Allocations [17]

IPv6 prefix	Binary form	Relative size of IPv6 space	Allocation
0000::/3	000	1/8	Reserved by IETF— The "unspecified address" (::) and the loopback address (::1) are assigned from this block
2000::/3	001	1/8	Global unicast address space
4000::/3	010	1/8	Reserved by IETF
6000::/3	011	1/8	Reserved by IETF
8000::/3	100	1/8	Reserved by IETF
a000::/3	101	1/8	Reserved by IETF
c000::/3	110	1/8	Reserved by IETF
e000::/4	1110	1/16	Reserved by IETF
f000::/5	1111 0	1/32	Reserved by IETF
f800::/6	1111 10	1/64	Reserved by IETF
fc00::/7	1111 110	1/128	Unique local unicast
fe00::/9	1111 1110 0	1/512	Reserved by IETF
fe80::/10	1111 1110 01	1/1024	Link local unicast
fec0::/10	1111 1110 11	1/1024	Reserved by IETF
ff00::/8	1111 1111	1/256	Multicast

length interface ID field, unlike the remainder of the IPv6 unicast address space, which must utilize a 64-bit interface ID field.

2.3.3.2   2000::/3—Global Unicast Address Space

The global unicast address space allocated so far, 2000::/3, represents 2^{125} or 4.25×10^{37} IP addresses. Given the 64-bit interface ID requirement defined in the aforementioned IPv6 addressing architecture (RFC 4291), the global unicast address format as formally defined in RFC 3587 [18] is shown in Figure 2-5.

The first three bits are $[001]_2$ to indicate global unicast address space. The following 45 bits comprise the global routing prefix, followed by the 16 bit subnet ID and 64 bit interface ID, respectively. Current guidelines call for ISPs allocating /48 networks to their customers, thereby assigning global routing prefixes to customers. Each customer may then define up to 65,534 subnets by uniquely assigning values within the remaining 16-bit subnet ID field for each subnet.

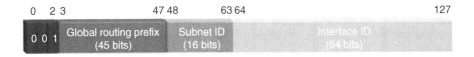

Figure 2-5.   Global unicast address format [18].

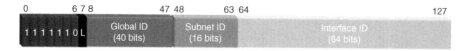

Figure 2-6. Unique local address format [19].

2.3.3.3 fc00::/7—Unique Local Address Space   The unique local address (ULA) space, defined in RFC 4193 [19], is intended to provide locally assignable and routable IP addresses, usually within a site. RFC 4193 states that "these addresses are not expected to be routable on the global Internet." Thus, while not as stringent as RFC 1918 in defining private IPv4 address space, the unique local address space is essentially private address space, providing "local" addressing with a high probability of still being globally unique. The format of unique local address space is given in Figure 2-6.

The first seven bits, bits 0-6, are $[1111\ 110]_2 = \text{fc00::/7}$, which identifies a unique local address. The eighth bit, the "L" bit is set to "1" if the global ID is locally assigned; setting the "L" bit to "0" is currently undefined, though the Internet community (IETF) has discussed enabling this setting for globally unique local addresses, assignable through Internet Registries. The 40-bit global ID field is intended to represent a globally unique prefix and must be allocated using a pseudo-random algorithm, not sequentially. In either case, the resulting /48 prefix comprises the organization's ULA address space, from which subnets can be allocated for internal use. The subnet ID is a 16-bit field to identify each subnet, while the interface ID is a 64-bit field.

An example pseudo-random approach to deriving a unique global ID as described in RFC 4193 recommends computing a hash[7] of:

- The current time as reported by a Network Time Protocol (NTP) server in 64-bit NTP format.
- Concatenated with an EUI-64 interface ID of an interface on the host performing this algorithm.

The least significant (right-most) 40 bits of the result of the hash operation is then populated as the global ID.

2.3.3.4 fe80::/10—Link Local Address Space   Link local addresses are used only on a particular link, such as an Ethernet link; packets with link local destination addresses are not routed. That is, packets having link local addresses will not reach beyond the corresponding link. These addresses are used for address autoconfiguration and neighbor discovery, which will be discussed shortly. The format of link local addresses is given in Figure 2-7.

The fe80::/10 link local prefix is followed by 54 zero bits and the 64-bit interface ID.

---

[7] A hash is created by performing a mathematical operation on the data to be hashed and a random value. A particular mathematical algorithm, the Secure Hash Algorithm 1 or SHA-1 is required in this case.

Figure 2-7. Link local address format [15].

2.3.3.5 ff00::/8—Multicast Address Space

Multicast addresses identify a group of interfaces typically on different nodes. Think of multicast addresses as a scoped broadcast. All multicast group members share the same Group ID and hence all members will accept packets destined for the multicast group. An interface may have multiple multicast addresses; that is, it may belong to multiple multicast groups. The basic format of IPv6 multicast addresses is given in Figure 2-8.

The prefix ff00::/8 identifies a multicast address. The next field is a 4-bit field called "Flags." The format of the multicast address is dependent on the value of the Flags field. The scope (also affectionately referred to as "scop") field indicates the breadth of the multicast scope, whether per node, link, global, or other scope values defined below. The value of the flags and scope fields can fortunately be easily discerned by looking at the address as the third and fourth hex digit within the address, respectively, as we'll summarize a bit later.

Flags   The Flags field is comprised of four bits, which we'll discuss starting from right to left [15]:

0	R	P	T

- The T bit indicates whether the multicast address is of transient nature or is a well-known address assigned by IANA. The T bit is defined as follows.

T = 0—this is an IANA-assigned well-known multicast address. In this case, the 112-bit multicast address is a 112-bit Group ID field (Figure 2-9).

IANA has assigned numerous Group IDs so far[8]. For example, Group ID = 1 means all nodes within the associated scope (defined by the scope field), Group ID = 2 refers to all routers within the scope, etc. The scope field is defined below, but example well-known multicast addresses are:

- ff01::1 = all nodes on this link
- ff02::2 = all routers on this link

Figure 2-8. Multicast address format [15].

---

[8] Please refer to http://www.iana.org/assignments/ipv6-multicast-addresses for the latest assignments.

Figure 2-9. Multicast address with Flag T = 0.

- ff05::1 = all nodes on this site
- ff05::2 = all routers on this site
- ff0e::2 = all routers on the Internet
  - T = 1—this is a temporarily assigned or transient multicast address. This can be an address assigned for a specific multicast session or application. An example might be ff12::3:f:10.

The P bit indicates whether the multicast address is comprised partly of a corresponding unicast network prefix or not. The P bit is defined[9] as follows:

- P = 0—this multicast address *is not* assigned based on the network prefix. The format of a multicast packet with P = 0 is as described above (i.e., when T = 0), with the 112-bit Group ID field.

- P = 1—this multicast address *is* assigned based on the network prefix of the unicast subnet address "owning" the multicast address allocation. This enables allocation of multicast space associated with allocated unicast space for simpler administration. If P = 1, the T bit must also be set to 1. The corresponding format of a multicast packet is as in Figure 2-10.

When P = 1, the scope field is followed by eight zero bits (Reserved), an 8-bit Prefix Length field, a 64-bit Network Prefix field, and a 32-bit Group ID field. The Prefix Length field represents the prefix length of the associated unicast network address. The Network Prefix field contains the corresponding unicast network prefix, while the Group ID is the associated multicast Group ID.

For example, if a unicast prefix of 2001:db8:b7::/48 is allocated to a subnet, a corresponding unicast-based multicast address would be of the form: ff3*s*:0030:2001:db8:b7::*g*, where

- ff = multicast prefix
- 3 = [0011]$_2$, i.e., P = 1 and T = 1

Figure 2-10. Multicast address with Flag P = 1 [15].

---

[9] The definition of the P bit is documented in RFC 3306 [20].

- $s =$ a valid scope as we'll define in the next section
- $00 =$ reserved bits
- $30 =$ prefix length in hex $= [0011\ 0000]_2 = 48$ in decimal, the prefix length in our example
- 2001:db8:b7:0 = 2001:0db8:00b7:0000 = 48 bit network prefix in the 64-bit Network Prefix field
- and $g =$ a 32-bit Group ID.

A special case of this format occurs with $P = T = 1$ when the Prefix Length field $=$ FF and $s \leq 2$. In this case, instead of the Network Prefix field consisting of the unicast network address, this field will be comprised of the interface ID of the respective interface. The interface ID used must have passed the duplicate address detection process, which is discussed later in this chapter, to assure its uniqueness. In this special case, the scope field must be 0, 1, or 2, meaning of interface-local or of link-local scope. This *link-scoped multicast address* format is defined as an extension of the IPv6 addressing architecture via RFC 4489 [21].

The R bit within the Flags field enables specification of a multicast rendezvous point (RP) which enables multicast group would-be subscribers to link in temporarily prior to joining the group permanently. If the R bit is set to 1, the P and T bits must also be set to 1. When $R = 1$, the multicast address is based on a unicast prefix, but the RP interface ID is also specified. The format of the multicast address when $R = 1$ is identical to the case when $R = 0$ and $P = 1$ with the exception that the Reserved field is split into a 4-bit Reserved field and a 4-bit Rendezvous Point interface ID (RIID) field (Figure 2-11).

- The IP address of the RP is identified by concatenating the Network Prefix of corresponding Prefix Length with the value of the RIID field. For example, if an RP on the [unicast] network is 2001:db8:b7::6, the associated multicast address would be ff7s:0630:2001:db8:b7:g, where $s =$ a valid scope defined below and $g =$ a 32-bit Group ID.
- The explicit breakdown of this address is as follows:
- ff = multicast prefix
- $7 = [0111]_2$, i.e., $R = 1$, $P = 1$ and $T = 1$
- $s =$ a valid scope defined below
- $0 =$ reserved bits
- $6 =$ RIID field, to be appended to the Network Prefix field.

Figure 2-11. Multicast address with Flag $R = 1$.

- $30 = $ prefix length in hex $= [0011\ 0000]_2 = 48$ in decimal, the prefix length in our example
- $2001:db8:b7:0 = 2001:0db8:00b7:0000 = 48$ bit network prefix in the 64-bit Network Prefix field.
- and $g = $ a 32-bit Group ID.
- The first Flag bit is reserved and is set to 0.

2.3.3.6 *Multicast Flags Summary* Who thought multicast addressing could be so complicated? But as is typically the case, with complexity comes flexibility! To summarize, the net result of the above bit stipulations yields the following valid values of the Flags field as currently defined. Since the Flags field immediately follows the first eight "1" bits, we denote the "effective prefix" of these first eight bits followed by the valid 4-bit Flags field (Table 2-3).

Scope The scope field identifies, naturally enough, the scope or "reach" of the multicast address. This is used by routers along the multicast path to constrain the reach of the multicast communications with the corresponding scope. Note that scopes other than interface-local, link-local, and global must be administratively defined within the routers serving the given scope in order to enforce the corresponding reach constraint.

2.3.3.7 *Special Case Multicast Addresses*
Solicited Node Multicast Address One form of multicast address that each node must support is the solicited node multicast address. This address is used for duplicate address detection and to resolve the link layer address of a given host as part of the neighbor discovery protocol (neighbor solicitation message). The solicited node multicast address is formed by appending the low-order (rightmost) 24 bits of the solicited node's interface ID to the well-known ff02::1:ff00:0/104 prefix (multicast scope = link).

For example, let's say a node wishes to resolve the link layer address of the device (interface) with IP address: 2001:db8:4e:2a:3001:fa81:95d0:2cd1. Using the

TABLE 2-3. Multicast Flags Summary

Flags (binary)	Effective prefix	Interpretation
0000	ff00::/12	Permanently assigned 112-bit Group ID scoped by 4-bit scope field
0001	ff10::/12	Temporarily assigned 112-bit Group ID scoped by 4-bit scope field
0011	ff30::/12	Temporarily assigned unicast prefix based multicast address
0111	ff70::/12	Temporarily assigned unicast prefix based multicast address with rendezvous point interface ID
All other Flags values	—	Undefined

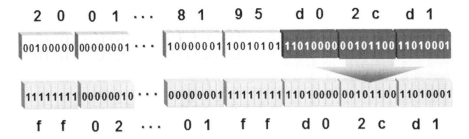

Figure 2-12. Solicited node multicast address derivation [15].

low-order 24-bits, d02cd1 in hex, the device would address its request to ff02::1: ffd0:2cd1 (Figure 2-12).

2.3.4   Internet Control Message Protocol for IPv6 (ICMPv6)

The Internet Control Message Protocol (ICMP) is part of the IPv4 protocol used to feed information back to IP nodes regarding network errors, diagnostics, and resource constraints. ICMPv6 is the corresponding protocol for IPv6 [22]. It provides similar functions but is also instrumental in the operation of core IPv6 features including neighbor discovery, mobile IPv6, and multicast router discovery. As we will discuss, neighbor discovery is an integral IPv6 function supporting router discovery, layer 2 address discovery, address autoconfiguration, duplicate address detection, and neighbor unreachability detection. As such, ICMPv6 is an integral part of IPv6, though messages are encoded as an upper layer protocol, with ICMPv6 being assigned an IPv6 header "Next Header" code of 58. The format of ICMPv6 messages is displayed in Figure 2-13.

Table 2-4 illustrates currently assigned ICMPv6 Type and associated Code parameter values [23]. Type values 1-4 represent error messages while values 128-255 are for informational and diagnostic messages (Table 2-5).

Let's take a closer look at some of the IPv6 features that utilize ICMPv6.

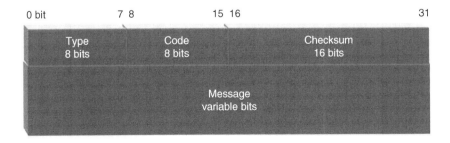

Figure 2-13.   ICMPv6 message structure.

TABLE 2-4.   Multicast Scope Field Interpretation

Scope field			
Binary	Hex	Meaning (scope)	Description
0000	0	Reserved	Reserved
0001	1	Interface-local	Scope consists of a single interface on a node and is useful only for loopback transmission
0010	2	Link-local	Scope is only the link on which the multicast packet is transmitted
0011	3	Reserved	Reserved
0100	4	Admin-local	Scope is limited to the smallest scope administratively configured. This is not based on physical connectivity or other multicast related configuration
0101	5	Site-local	Scope is limited to the site as administratively defined
0110-0111	6-7	Unassigned	N/A
1000	8	Organization-local	Scope consists of multiple sites within one organizational entity as administratively defined
1001-1101	9-D	Unassigned	N/A
1110	E	Global scope	Scope is unlimited
1111	F	Reserved	Reserved

2.3.5   IPv6 Ping

As with the familiar "ping" utility of IPv4, IPv6 supports an analogous function, typically run on a command line as "ping6" versus "ping." This feature utilizes ICMPv6 type 128 for an outbound ping6, or "echo request," while ICMPv6 type 129 serves as the "echo reply" message.

2.3.6   Multicast Listener Discovery

The Multicast Listener Discovery (MLD) feature enables a router to identify the presence of multicast listeners on its directly attached links, that is, nodes configured to listen on multicast addresses, as well as corresponding multicast address(es). Identification of multicast hosts and addresses enables the router to route and deliver multicast IPv6 packets accordingly. The router uses a link local IPv6 address as its source IPv6 address when sending MLD queries on a given link. The first version of MLD, referred to as MLDv1 was defined in RFC 2710 [24]. The second version, MLDv2 [25] is compatible with MLDv1 and adds source filtering, that is, enabling a multicast listener to express interest in multicast packets from a specific source IPv6 address. Four MLD message types are defined, each having a corresponding ICMPv6 type value:

- Multicast Listener Query (type value = 130)—enables the router to query for listeners:

TABLE 2-5.   ICMPv6 Type and Code Values

Type		Code	
Value	Meaning	Value	Meaning
0	Reserved		
1	Destination unreachable	0	No route to destination
		1	Communication with destination administratively prohibited
		2	Beyond scope of source address
		3	Address unreachable
		4	Port unreachable
		5	Source address failed ingress/egress policy
		6	Reject route to destination
		7	Error in source routing header
2	Packet too big	0	
3	Time exceeded	0	Hop limit exceeded in transit
		1	Fragment reassembly time exceeded
4	Parameter problem	0	Erroneous head field encountered
		1	Unrecognized next header type encountered
		2	Unrecognized IPv6 option encountered
5–99	Unassigned		
100–101	Private experimentation		
102–126	Unassigned		
127	Reserved for expansion of ICMPv6 error messages		
128	Echo request	0	
129	Echo reply	0	
130	Multicast listener query	0	
131	Multicast listener report	0	
132	Multicast listener done	0	
133	Router solicitation	0	
134	Router advertisement	0	
135	Neighbor solicitation	0	
136	Neighbor advertisement	0	
137	Redirect message	0	
138	Router renumbering	0	Router renumbering command
		1	Router renumbering result
		255	Sequence number reset
139	ICMP node information query	0	The data field contains an IPv6 address which is the subject of this query
		1	The data field contains a name which is the subject of this query or is empty (No-Op)
		2	The data field contains an IPv4 address which is the subject of this query

TABLE 2-5. (*Continued*)

Type		Code	
Value	Meaning	Value	Meaning
140	ICMP node information response	0	A successful reply—the data field may or may not be empty
		1	The responder refuses to supply the answer—the data field will be empty
		2	The Qtype of the query is unknown to the responder—the data field will be empty
141	Inverse neighbor discovery solicitation message	0	
142	Inverse neighbor discovery advertisement message	0	
143	Version 2 multicast listener report	0	
144	Home agent address discovery request message	0	
145	Home agent address discovery reply message	0	
146	Mobile prefix solicitation	0	
147	Mobile prefix advertisement	0	
148	Certification Path Solicitation Message		
149	Certification path advertisement message		
150	ICMP messages utilized by experimental mobility protocols		
151	Multicast router advertisement		
152	Multicast router solicitation		
153	Multicast router termination		
154	FMIPv6 message (fast mobile IPv6 handovers)	0, 1	Reserved
		2	Router solicitation for proxy advertisement (RtSolPr)
		3	Proxy router advertisement (PrRtAdv)
		4, 5	Deprecated and unavailable for assignment
155	RPL control message (tentatively assigned for "routing protocol for low power and lossy networks")		
156–199	Unassigned		
200–201	Private experimentation		
255	Reserved for expansion of ICMPv6 informational messages		

     ○ General query—enables the router to learn which multicast addresses have listeners.

     ○ Multicast address specific query—determines whether a particular multicast address has any listeners.

     ○ Multicast address and source specific query—for MLDv2 only, determines whether a particular multicast address of a given source address(es) has any listeners.

- Multicast Listener Report (type value = 131)—enables a multicast listener to reply to a router query indicating its desire to receive so-addressed multicast packets.
- Multicast Listener Done (type value = 132)—allows a multicast listener to announce that it has finished listening to a given multicast addressed transmission. This message is send to the link-scoped all-routers multicast address, ff02::2.
- Multicast Listener (v2) Report (type value = 143)—used by MLDv2 hosts to inform link-attached routers of its multicast listening state, for example, to which addresses it is listening or is not listening.

2.3.7 Multicast Router Discovery

The multicast router discovery (MRD) process is defined to enable identification of routers actively engaged in multicast routing and to enable switches to determine which switch ports should be bridged in multicast communications. As such MRD packets are intended to be link-local with a hop limit of "1." MRD for IPv6 utilizes three ICMPv6 message types:

- Multicast Router Advertisement (ICMPv6 type = 151)—a router periodically advertises or responds to solicitations using this message sent to the "All-Snoopers" multicast address (ff02::6a) to advertise its participation in multicast forwarding.
- Multicast Router Solicitation (ICMPv6 type = 152)—enables a node to solicit a multicast router advertisement message for MRD.
- Multicast Router Termination (ICMPv6 = 152)—sent by a router to indicate it is on longer engaged in multicast message forwarding.

2.3.8 Neighbor Discovery Protocol

The neighbor discovery protocol (NDP) in IPv6 provides several key network operational functions.

- NDP enables a node to discover routers serving its attached link and corresponding IPv6 prefix(es) configured on the link.
- NDP provides a redirect function to direct a node to a better first hop router (or locally attached host).

- Stateless address autoconfiguration (SLAAC) leverages NDP for automated IPv6 host address derivation.
- Duplicate address detection (DAD) enables a node to identify if another node on the subnet is configured with the same address it intends to use.
- A node uses NDP for address resolution, to identify other IPv6 nodes on the subnet and to identify their link layer addresses.
- NDP supports node unreachability detection, which applies to detecting unreachable neighbors, that is, unreachable nodes on the same link.

Discovery of routers enables IPv6 nodes to automatically identify routers on the subnet, negating the need to configure a default gateway manually within the device's IP configuration. Router discovery enables a device to identify the network prefix(es) and corresponding prefix length(s) assigned to the link, as well as other parameters such as the availability of address assignment and domain name services. This information is indispensable for address autoconfiguration.

The router discovery process entails each router periodically sending advertisements on each of its configured subnets indicating its IP address, its ability to provide default gateway functionality, its link layer address, the network prefix(es) served on the link including corresponding prefix length and valid address lifetime, as well as other configuration parameters.

The router advertisement also indicates whether a DHCPv6 server is available for address assignment or other configuration. The M bit (managed address configuration flag) in the router advertisement indicates that DHCPv6 services are available for address and configuration settings. The O bit (other configuration flag) indicates that configuration parameters other than the IP address are available via DHCPv6; such information may include which NTP servers to query for devices on this link. The interpretation of the M and O bits are summarized in Table 2-6.

Nodes can also solicit router advertisements using Router Solicitation messages, addressed to the link local routers multicast address (ff02::2). A summary of ICMPv6 type codes for each of these neighbor discovery messages follows:

- Router solicitation (ICMPv6 type = 133)—enables a host to request routers to generate router advertisements immediately.
- Router advertisement (ICMPv6 type = 134)—routers use this message type to advertise their presence and available prefix information periodically or in response to a router solicitation message.

TABLE 2-6. Router Advertisement M and O bits

Flag	O bit = 0	O bit = 1
M bit = 0	No DHCPv6 services are available	DHCPv6 services are available for configuration information only, not address assignment
M bit = 1	DHCPv6 services are available for address assignment and configuration information	DHCPv6 services are available for address assignment and configuration information

- Neighbor solicitation (ICMPv6 type = 135)—enables a host to determine the link layer address of an on-link neighbor and to perform duplicate address detection.
- Neighbor advertisement (ICMPv6 type = 136)—sent by a host in response to a neighbor solicitation or upon link layer address change.
- Redirect (ICMPv6 type = 137)—send by a router to inform link hosts of a better first hop for a given destination. The better first hop may be another router or an on-link host whose address is within a prefix that was not advertised as on-link, for example.

2.3.9 Secure Neighbor Discovery (SEND)

The Secure Neighbor Discovery (SEND) Protocol adds digital signatures to neighbor discovery messages to reduce the risk of falsified responses especially on ad hoc networks. Hosts using SEND must be configured with a trust anchor, which enables the host to certify a router on its network and a private/public key pair. The node using SEND attaches a cryptographically generated address (CGA) as an NDP option in its messages. The CGA is derived using the host's private/public key pair. A 64-bit hash of the public key (and some auxiliary parameters) is created and the CGA is generated using the 64-bit subnet prefix and the 64-bit public key hash. The corresponding private key can be used to sign NDP messages, and the corresponding digital signature is added within the RSA Signature NDP option parameter. While an attacker can create SEND messages using a self-derived key pair, he/she cannot impersonate another IPv6 node on the subnet.

Identities of routers are further verified using certificates which bind a router identity with a public key, which is then compared with public keys (trust anchors) configured on the host. Two additional ICMPv6 message types are defined for this purpose:

- Certification Path Solicitation (ICMPv6 type = 148)—a host issues this message to a router to request its certification path to one of the host's configured trust anchors.
- Certification Path Advertisement (ICMPv6 type = 149)—a router issues this message in respond to a certification path solicitation to provide its certificate (s) and/or trust anchor(s) in the form of fully qualified DNS domain name (FQDN) or X.501 name.

2.3.10 Inverse Neighbor Discovery

Inverse neighbor discovery (IND) defines the process of resolving an IPv6 address associated with a known link layer address. Similar in concept to "inverse ARP," IND enables layer 2 network resolution of layer 3 information, for example, for frame relay networks. IND also utilizes ICMPv6:

- Inverse Neighbor Discovery Solicitation (ICMPv6 type = 141)—requests the IPv6 address corresponding to the provided target link layer address.

- Inverse Neighbor Discovery Advertisement (ICMPv6 type = 142)—response to an IND solicitation including a list of one or more IPv6 addresses for the interface identified by the target link layer address.

2.3.11 Router Renumbering

The concept of router renumbering seeks to make renumbering networks as simple and automated as individual host address autoconfiguration. Defined in RFC 2894 [26], router renumbering uses "prefix control operations" within ICMPv6 messages (ICMPv6 type = 138) to instruct a router (or multiple routers when sent via multicast) to add a new IPv6 prefix or to delete or change a configured prefix. Prefix information includes the prefix address, length, and associated address lifetime values and flags. Given the sheer power to renumber a network remotely, routers are required to apply security policies to router renumbering messages to authenticate the sender and verify message integrity. Message sequence numbers are also used to prevent replay attacks.

2.3.12 Node Information Query

The node information query message enables solicitation of host name and IPv6 and IPv4 address information from an IPv6 host. If you think this sounds like an overlap with what DNS already provides, you're correct. However, according to RFC 4620 [27], this mode of resolution "is currently limited to diagnostic and debugging tools and network management." And instead of querying a DNS server for this information, a query is issued to the node information query address.

Node Information Query messages are sent using ICMPv6 and addressed normally with a destination IPv6 address or by using the node information query multicast address. Use of this link-scoped multicast address format enables an IPv6 address to be formed based only on the host name of the intended recipient; if the IPv6 address is already known and host name information is requested, the IPv6 address itself may be used as the destination address. When IP address information is being requested for a known host name, the canonical host name[10] is hashed using the 128-bit MD-5 algorithm, and the first 24-bits resulting from the hash are appended to the ff02::2:ff00:0/104 prefix. Each node receiving a message addressed to this node information query address compares the last 24 bits in the address with the first 24 bits of a hash of its own host name; if it matches, the recipient will reply with the requested information.

The node information query messages are as follows:

- Node Information Query (ICMPv6 type = 139)—enables a node to query for information regarding another node based on a provided IPv6 address, IPv4 address or host name.
- Node Information Response (ICMPv6 type =140)—enables a node to respond with requested information or to refuse such information (Figure 2-14).

---

[10] The "canonical hostname" is technically the first "label" in the fully qualified domain name in lowercase characters which is generally is the intended destination hostname.

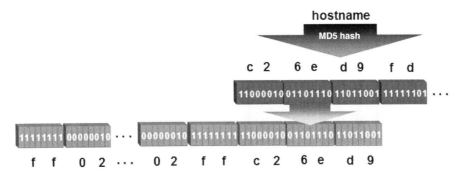

Figure 2-14. Solicited node information query address.

2.4 IPv6 ADDRESS AUTOCONFIGURATION

One of the major advertised benefits of IPv6 is the ability for devices to automatically configure their own IPv6 address that will be unique and relevant to the subnet to which it is presently connecting[11]. This behavior is governed by the settings of the managed (M) and other (O) bits in router advertisements as discussed in the NDP section. There are three basic forms of IPv6 address autoconfiguration:

Stateless. This process is "stateless" in that it is not dependent on the state or availability of external assignment mechanisms, for example, Dynamic Host Configuration Protocol for IPv6 (DHCPv6). The device attempts to configure its own IPv6 address(es) without external or user intervention.

Stateful. The stateful process relies solely an external address assignment mechanism such as DHCPv6. The DHCPv6 server would assign the 128-bit IPv6 address to the device in a manner similar to DHCP for IPv4 operation.

Combination Stateless and Stateful. This process involves a form of stateless address autoconfiguration used in conjunction with stateful configuration of additional IP parameters. This commonly entails a device autoconfiguring an IPv6 address using the stateless method, then utilizing DHCPv6 to obtain additional parameters or options such as which Network Time Protocol servers to query for time resolution on the given network.

At the most basic level, stateless autoconfiguration of an IPv6 address involves concatenating the address of the network to which the device is connected (where you are) and the device's interface ID (who you are). Let's first consider how the device determines the address of the network to which it is connected.

---

[11] Note that some IPv4 protocol stacks, such as those provided with Microsoft Windows 2000 and XP, among others, perform address autoconfiguration utilizing the IPv4 "link local" address space, 169.254.0.0/16.

2.4.1   Modified EUI-64 Interface Identifiers

Once a node identifies the subnet to which it is attached, it may complete the address autoconfiguration process by formulating its interface ID. The IPv6 addressing architecture stipulates that all unicast IPv6 addresses, other than those beginning with binary $[000]_2$ must use a 64-bit interface ID derived using the modified EUI-64 algorithm. The "unmodified" EUI-64 algorithm entails concatenating the 24-bit organizational unique identifier (OUI) issued by the IEEE to each network interface hardware manufacturer (e.g., the initial 24 bits of an Ethernet address) with a 40-bit extension identifier. For 48-bit Ethernet addresses, the company identifier portion of the Ethernet address (first 24 bits) is followed by a 16-bit EUI label, defined as hexadecimal `fffe`, followed by the 24-bit extension identifier, that is, the remaining 24 bits of the Ethernet address.

The modification required to create a modified EUI-64 identifier calls for inverting the "u" bit (universal/local bit) of the company identifier field. The "u" bit is the seventh most significant bit in the company identifier field. Within an Ethernet MAC address, when u=1, the MAC address is locally administered address, that is, assigned by a network administrator, where when u=0, the MAC address is a universally administered address, that is, assigned by the NIC manufacturer ultimately from the IEEE. The motivation [15] for inverting the "u" bit is to make it easier for network administrators to manually define interface IDs, enabling incremental counting, for example, ::1, ::2, ::3, etc. instead of ::200:0:0:1, ::200:0:0:2, ::200:0:0:3, etc. which would be required to indicate that the address is locally administered (u=1). Thus the algorithm for a 48-bit MAC address is to invert the "u" bit and insert the hexadecimal value `fffe` between the company identifier and the interface identifier. This is illustrated in the following example using a MAC address of AC-62-E8-49-5F-62. The resulting interface ID is ae62:e8ff:fe49:5f62 (Figure 2-15).

For non-Ethernet MAC addresses, the algorithm calls for use of the link layer address as the interface ID, with zero padding (from the "left"). For cases where no

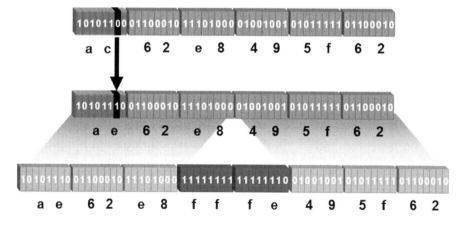

Figure 2-15.   Modified EUI-64 interface ID example [28].

link layer address is available, for example, on a dial up link, a unique identifier utilizing another interface address, a serial number, or other device-specific identifier is recommended.

While the modified EUI-64 algorithm streamlines autoconfiguration, it also creates a static interface ID that could enable simple identification of a given device of a known MAC address, with the ability to "track" the device. RFC 4941 [29] defines privacy extensions for derivation and variation of randomized interface IDs to address this concern.

The interface ID may not be unique, especially if not derived from a unique 48-bit MAC address. Thus the device must perform duplicate address detection (DAD) prior to committing the new address. Prior to completing the DAD process, the address is considered tentative.

2.4.2 Duplicate Address Detection (DAD)

DAD is performed using the neighbor discovery protocol, which entails the device sending an IPv6 Neighbor Solicitation packet to the IPv6 address it just derived (or obtained from DHCPv6) in order to identify a pre-existing occupant of the IP address. After a slight delay, the device also sends a Neighbor Solicitation packet to the solicited node multicast address associated with this address as well.

If another device is already using the IP address, it will respond with a Neighbor Advertisement packet, and the autoconfiguration process will stop; that is, manual intervention or configuration of the device to use an alternate interface ID is required. If a Neighbor Advertisement packet is not received, the device can assume uniqueness of the address and assign it to the corresponding interface. Participation in this process of Neighbor Solicitation and Advertisement is required not only for autoconfigured addresses but even for those statically defined or obtained through DHCPv6.

IPv6 addresses have a lifetime during which they are valid. In some cases the lifetime is infinite, but the concept of address lifetime applies to both DHCPv6 leased addresses as well as autoconfigured addresses. This is useful in easing the process of network renumbering. Routers are configured with and advertise a *preferred* lifetime and a *valid* lifetime value for each network prefix in their Router Advertisement messages. IP addresses that have successfully proven unique through the DAD process described above can be considered either preferred or deprecated. In either state, the address is valid, but this differentiation provides a means for upper layer protocols (e.g., TCP, UDP) to select an IP address that will likely not change during the ensuing session (Figure 2-16).

A device refreshes the preferred and valid time with each Router Advertisement message in accordance with the values advertised. When time expires on a preferred prefix, the associated address(es) will become deprecated, though still valid. Thus the deprecated state provides a transition period during which the address is still functional but should not be used to initiate new communications. Once the valid lifetime of the address expires, the address is no longer valid for use. Should a subnet be reassigned a different network prefix, the router can be configured to advertise the new prefix, and devices on the network would undergo the autoconfiguration process using the new prefix as the lifetime of the old prefix expires.

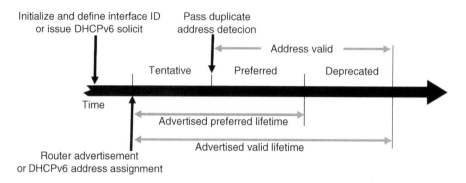

Figure 2-16.   IPv6 address lifetimes. *Source:* Based on [30].

2.5   MOBILE IPv6

IPv6 mobility support, or Mobile IPv6, enables an IPv6 node to communicate seamlessly while moving from link to link. This means that upper layer transport and application layer communications remain intact despite a changing underlying network, data link and physical layer network. Certainly when changing link attachment, for example, when moving from a 4G wireless service to a local WiFi network, which implies an IPv6 prefix change, the mobile device must, by necessity, change its IPv6 address. This changeable IPv6 address which is associated with the current network attachment is referred to as the *care-of address*.

Each mobile IPv6 device also has a "fixed" IPv6 address known as its *home address*. When the device is "home" or not roaming, IPv6 traffic routes normally to and from the device using its home address. When the device roams, it obtains a care-of address using stateless or stateful address autoconfiguration based on its then-current location and point of network attachment. The mobile node then registers its care-of address with its *home agent*, a mobile IPv6-configured router serving the link on which the mobile node's home address resides. When the mobile host is home, the home agent routes IPv6 packets to it just as would a normal router, on its serving link as shown in Figure 2-17. When the mobile host is roaming, the home agent intercepts IPv6 packets destined for the mobile host's home address and tunnels them to the mobile host using its care-of address.

Communications between the mobile host and another host (*correspondent node*) may ensue in one of two ways. Using the tunneling approach mentioned above,

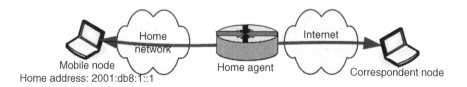

Figure 2-17.   Mobile IPv6 with mobile at home.

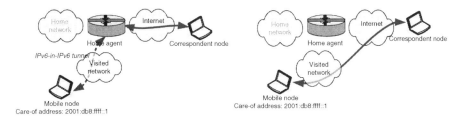

Figure 2-18. Mobile IPv6 with mobile roaming.

IPv6 packets may be communicated directly to the home address, where they will be intercepted by the home agent and tunneled to the mobile host; return traffic would follow the same route, reaching the correspondent node by way of the home agent. This is depicted on the left side of Figure 2-18.

Generally, this "triangular routing" process is inefficient and can lead to resource overload on the home agent. A more efficient direct communications mode between the mobile node and correspondent node as shown on the right of Figure 2-18. This more efficient routing process is available as long as the correspondent node supports the mobile IPv6 protocol, including the mobility extension header. The mobility header is used to carry messages between the mobile and correspondent nodes to verify care-of and home address association, direct routability and to communicate binding updates as the mobile host continues to move. We'll discuss the details of this in the context of message security in Chapter 6.

In addition to extension headers, Mobile IPv6 utilizes five ICMPv6 message types:

- Home Agent Address Discovery Request (ICMPv6 type = 144)—allows a mobile node to initiate dynamic home agent discovery. Addressed to the well-known home-agents anycast address (discussed in the next section) for the mobile's home address prefix, this allows the mobile to identify a home agent on its home network, for example, if a home agent was reconfigured while it's been roaming.

- Home Agent Address Discovery Response (ICMPv6 type = 145)—reply from a home agent in response to a home agent address discovery request to identify its unicast address in the capacity of the mobile's home agent.

- Mobile Prefix Solicitation (ICMPv6 type = 146)—enables a mobile to gather prefix information about its home network, for example, in the event of a home network reconfiguration.

- Mobile Prefix Advertisement (ICMPv6 type = 147)—a home agent can communicate current home network prefix information using this message.

- Mobile IPv6 fast handover messages (ICMPv6 type = 154)—this message type is used both by a mobile node to stimulate routers to send proxy router advertisements and for proxy routers to provide such advertisements for fast mobile handover. Service providers commonly implement such proxies to reduce air interface overhead and improve networking efficiencies.

2.6 RESERVED SUBNET ANYCAST ADDRESSES

RFC 2526 [31] defines the format for reserved subnet anycast addresses. These addresses are used by IPv6 devices to route packets to the nearest device of a particular type on a specified subnet. For example, a reserved subnet anycast address can be used to send packets to the nearest mobile IPv6 home agent on a specified subnet. Since the global routing prefix and subnet ID are specified within this address type, it enables a node to locate the nearest node of the desired type on that subnet.

The format of the address takes on one of two forms based on whether the subnet prefix requires formulation of the interface ID field in modified EUI-64 format. Recall that all global unicast addresses other than those beginning with $[000]_2$ must utilize 64-bit interface IDs formulated based on the interface's link layer address and the modified EUI-64 algorithm described previously.

1. If the EUI-64 algorithm is required, the reserved subnet anycast address is formulated by concatenating the following fields:

    o 64-bit global routing prefix and subnet ID.

    o 57 bits of all 1s except the seventh bit in this sequence (the 71st bit from the beginning, counting left-to-right), which is 0. This seventh bit corresponds to the "u" bit (universal/local bit) of the company identifier field in the hardware address when applying the EUI-64 algorithm. This bit is always zero in this particular scenario to represent the "local" setting of the bit.

    o 7-bit anycast ID. RFC 2526 defines a single anycast ID of hex 7e for the mobile IPv6 home agent anycast address. Other anycast ID values are reserved, though IANA may assign additional anycast IDs based on future IETF RFC publications (Figure 2-19).

2. If EUI-64 is *not* required based on the global routing prefix and subnet ID, then the network prefix length is arbitrary at *n* bits, followed by 121-*n* 1 bits, followed by the 7-bit anycast ID (Figure 2-20).

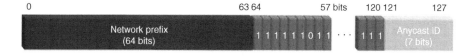

Figure 2-19. Reserved subnet anycast address format when EUI-64 is required [31].

Figure 2-20. Reserved subnet anycast address format when EUI-64 is not required [31].

2.7 REQUIRED HOST IPv6 ADDRESSES

RFC 4294 [32] summarizes the requirements for IPv6 nodes, a device that implements IPv6, and for IPv6 routers. In terms of required addresses, all IPv6 nodes must be capable of recognizing the following IPv6 addresses for itself:

- The loopback address (::1).
- Its link local unicast address (fe80::<interface ID> as configured via autoconfiguration).
- The all-nodes multicast address (ff0s::1 where $s =$ scope).
- Unicast and anycast addresses configured automatically or manually on each interface.
- The solicited node multicast address for each of its unicast and anycast addresses.
- Multicast addresses for each multicast group to which the node belongs.

A router node is required to support the above addresses plus the following addresses:

- The subnet-router anycast address (<subnetwork prefix>::/128, that is interface ID $= 0$s) except on /127 point-to-point router links.
- The all-routers multicast address (ff0s::2 where $s =$ scope).
- Anycast addresses configured on the router.

Other device types such as DHCP and DNS servers must recognize scoped multicast addresses corresponding to Group IDs assigned by IANA (i.e., when Flags $= 0$).

2.8 IPv6 ROUTING

IPv6 dynamic routing operates the same way as IPv4 routing, using a longest-prefix matching algorithm. Major routing protocols have been updated to support communication of IPv6 prefixes/routes. In addition to manually configured static routes for IPv6 destinations, interior gateway protocols with IPv6 support include:

- OSPFv3—Open Shortest Path First
- Integrated IS-ISv6—Intermediate System-Intermediate System
- RIPng—Next Generation Routing Information Protocol
- Cisco EIGRP—Enhanced Interior Gateway Routing Protocol.
- BGP, Border Gateway Protocol, the *de facto* exterior gateway protocol also supports IPv6 in version 4 and above.

CHAPTER **3**

IPv4/IPv6 Co-Existence Technologies

Every organization planning to deploy IPv6 must consider managing IPv4 and IPv6 together. This holds true even for "greenfield" networks where such organizations have the luxury of deploying a single protocol IPv6 network. The issue stems back to our discussion in Chapter 1 about the increasingly hybrid complexion of the global Internet. Assuming an organization desires to connect to the "ubiquitous Internet," both IPv4 and IPv6 connectivity must be supported for some time.

The Internet community recognized early on the requirement for IPv4/IPv6 interoperability, given the lack of an inherent compatibility. In fact, the Internet Engineering Task Force (IETF) has specified over 20 different methods for IPv4/IPv6 interoperability, offering no shortage of choices. But with so many choices it may be difficult to decide which technology(ies) is best for your network. In this chapter, we will highlight the myriad defined IPv4/IPv6 co-existence technologies and discuss the salient features and advantages of each to help you decide where a given technology choice makes the most sense.

From a general perspective, the set of IPv4/IPv6 co-existence technologies can be organized into three categories:

- *Dual Stack.* Implementation of both IPv4 and IPv6 protocols on network devices.
- *Tunneling.* Encapsulation of an IPv6 packet within an IPv4 packet for transmission over an IPv4 network or vice-versa.
- *Translation.* IP header, address, and/or port translation such as that performed by host, gateway or network address translation (NAT) devices.

Some service providers' dual protocol strategies involve a combination of technologies from multiple categories as we'll discuss later in this chapter. Enterprise deployments may likewise require implementation of multiple technologies to accommodate phased deployments or partner networks for example. The most common approach envisioned for enterprises is dual stack.

IPv6 Deployment and Management, First Edition. By Michael Dooley and Timothy Rooney.
© 2013 by The Institute of Electrical and Electronics Engineers, Inc. Published 2013 by John Wiley & Sons, Inc.

3.1 DUAL STACK

The dual stack approach consists of implementing both IPv4 and IPv6 protocol stacks on devices requiring access to both network layer technologies, including routers, other infrastructure devices, application servers, and end user devices. Such devices are configured with both IPv4 and IPv6 addresses, and they may obtain these addresses via methods defined for the respective protocols as enabled by administrators.

Implementations may vary with dual stack deployment with respect to the scope of the stack which is common versus what is unique to each IP version. Ideally, only the network layer would be dualized, using a common application, transport, and data link layer. This is the approach implemented in Microsoft Vista and 7, as opposed to the XP implementation, which utilized dual transport and network layers, requiring in some cases, redundant configuration of each stack. Other approaches may span the entire stack, down to the physical layer requiring a separate network interface for IPv6 versus IPv4. This approach, while contrary to the benefits of a layered protocol model, may be intentional and even desirable, especially in the case of network servers with multiple applications or services, some of which intentionally support only one version or the other.

3.1.1 Implementing Dual Stack

Deployment of dual-stacked devices sharing a common physical network interface implies the operation of both IPv4 and IPv6 over the same physical link. This is depicted from a physcial view and logically in Figure 3-1. After all, Ethernet and other layer 2 technologies support either IPv4 or IPv6 payload, thanks to protocol layering. Dual-stacked devices require routers supporting such links to be dual stacked as well, or that both an IPv4 router and an IPv6 router are link-connected. The following techniques are defined to assign IPv4 and IPv6 addresses to a given device:

- For infrastructure devices such as routers and switches as well as Internet-accessible devices like web or email servers both the IPv4 and IPv6 address

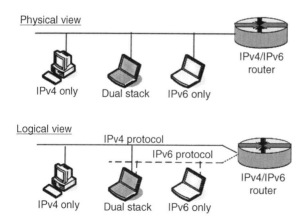

Figure 3-1. Dual-stacked network perspectives [28].

may be manually configured locally on the device. This provides deterministic address persistence. If addresses were to change on these devices, then corresponding DNS resource records (A and AAAA types) would have to change as well.

- For non-infrastructure devices, static addressing may also be applied or dynamic addressing may be used. Dynamic IPv4 addressing is most commonly implemented using Dynamic Host Configuration Protocol (DHCP). DHCP's IPv6 equivalent, DHCPv6 may be used to dynamically assign the host's IPv6 address, as may stateless address autoconfiguration (SLAAC) or a combination of DHCPv6 and SLAAC. Note that assignment of the IPv4 address is an independent process from that of the IPv6 address; there is no DHCP combination that could assign both an IPv4 address and an IPv6 address in one transaction. And one may configure one address using static methods and the other via DHCP for example.

While it's generally anticipated that routers would be among the first IP elements to be upgraded to support both protocols, RFC 4554 [33], an informational RFC, describes an innovative approach to support an overlay configuration using VLANs without requiring immediate router upgrades. This approach relies on VLAN tagging to enable layer 2 switches to broadcast or trunk the Ethernet frames containing IPv6 payload to one or more IPv6 capable routers. By upgrading one router to support IPv6, for example, the gateway to an IPv6 network (Internet), the switch ports to which its interfaces are connected can be configured as the "IPv6 VLAN." Other IPv6 or dual-stacked devices could then be configured as members of the IPv6 VLAN, and multiple such VLANs could be likewise configured. An example of this deployment is displayed in Figure 3-2.

3.1.2 Which Address Is Used?

After you've configured selected devices with both an IPv4 and an IPv6 address, how can you influence which protocol is used? RFC 6724 [34] specifies algorithms for selecting source and destination addresses, respectively, for IPv6 devices when not specified by the upper layer application[1]. When the application does not specify the address, it will generally use the getaddrinfo() sockets API call to its TCP/IP stack to obtain a set of destination IP addresses. Hence if your laptop is dual stacked, when you enter a "www" web address, the web browser uses getaddrinfo() to get a destination IP address or set of addresses. The address selection algorithm defined in RFC 6724 is used by getaddrinfo() to place in priority order the IP addresses returned to the application to select the destination address. The source address is generally selected by the network layer (e.g., among those configured on your laptop) to initiate a connection to the selected destination address.

---

[1] When entering an IP address to open an ftp session, for example, this destination address would be used (assuming an address of the corresponding protocol version is configured on the source device).

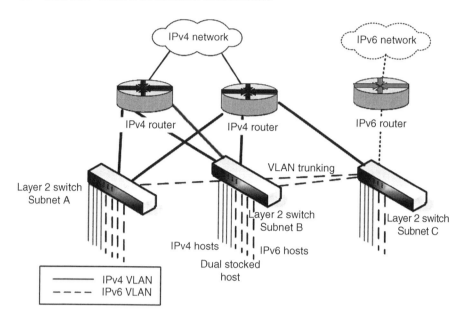

Figure 3-2. Dual stack deployment using VLANs [33].

Address selection is based on several inputs: a device's configured addresses, the state of each (e.g., preferred vs. deprecated), the scope of each (e.g., unique local address (ULA) vs. public) as well as addresses returned via A and AAAA type DNS queries. The addresses are selected from this candidate set of addresses by choosing the highest preference or best fit from a policy table, implemented within the TCP/IP stack of the device, which is generally built into the device's operating system. The policy table is structured as a longest matching prefix table, with each prefix configured with an associated preference value and label as shown in Table 3-1.

Destination addresses returned from DNS are ordered with respect to their respective precedence values; the higher the precedence, the higher in the list an address appears. Source addresses are likewise prioritized according to precedence

TABLE 3-1. Address Selection Policy Table [34]

Prefix	Precedence	Label	Interpretation
::1/128	60	0	Loopback address
::/0	40	2	IPv6 address
::ffff:0:0/96	30	3	IPv4 address (IPv4-mapped)
2002::/16	20	4	6to4
2001::/32	10	5	Teredo
fc00::/7	50	1	ULA
::/96	1	10	IPv4-compatible (deprecated)
fec0::/10	1	11	Site local (deprecated)
3ffe::/16	1	12	6bone (phased out)

though a source address with a matching label value for a destination address is preferred above others. So for example, if a DNS query resolves to a ULA address and the source device also has a ULA address of matching prefix, the corresponding source and destination address fields in the IPv6 header will be so populated with these ULA addresses. Given the ordering of the policy table above in descending order of precedence, the order shown is generally the preferred order: use loopback if matching, a ULA address, an IPv6 address, then an IPv4 address, 6to4, then a Toredo address. The remaining three entries show a precedence value of "1," meaning they are discouraged. From an IPv4/IPv6 co-existence perspective, clearly IPv6 is favored over IPv4 according to the default policy table.

Another factor influencing IPv4 or IPv6 connection is implementation of "happy eyeballs dual stack," defined in RFC 6555 [35]. The normal process for establishing a connection (by TCP or by the application) is to serially cycle through addresses returned from the address selection process just described. The happy eyeballs approach seeks to reduce potential connection delays, with such an approach when an initial IPv6 connection fails, then a subsequent IPv4 connection succeeds. This is done by first attempting a connection using IPv6, assuming an IPv6 address ranks highest in the address selection process; then after a short delay on the order of 300 ms, initiate a connection attempt to the highest IPv4 address returned through the selection process. In this manner, if the IPv6 connection fails, the wait to establish an IPv4 connection is minimized and application performance suffers only slightly. This approach works if the given host domain name to which the connection is attempted, for example, www.ipamworldwide.com, is published in DNS with an A and a AAAA record. So it's recommended[2] that dual stack host domain names be published with both record types, instead of using an "ipv6" identifier such as "ipv6. ipamworldwide.com."

3.1.3 DNS Considerations

Considering the foregoing discussion regarding the IPv6 host policy table, DNS clearly plays a crucial role in encouraging IPv6 traffic for dual stack hosts. Publishing AAAA and A records for such hosts with the same host domain name will enable source devices to connect via IPv6 whenever possible. As a matter of fact, DNS is crtical to the proper operation of every transition technology discussed in this chapter; after all, it provides the vital linkage between end user naming, for example, website address at the application layer and the destination IP address, whether IPv4 or IPv6 at the network layer. And with IPv6 addressing, users may find it difficult entering the IPv6 address at the application layer. End users attempting to access a dual-stacked device will query DNS, which can be configured by administrators with an A resource record corresponding to the node's IPv4 address and a AAAA resource record corresponding to its IPv6 address. The owner

---

[2] During initial implementation and testing, a separate host domain name for the IPv6 address is actually a good practice to work out any connectivity issues. But once proven in, the IPv6 unique host name can be eliminated and the AAAA owner changed to that of the common host domain name.

field of the resource record may have the same or different host domain name corresponding to the device as per the following example.

```
dual-stack-host.ipamworldwide.com. 86400 IN A 10.200.0.16
dual-stack-host.ipamworldwide.com. 86400 IN AAAA 2001:db8:2200::a
```

This example illustrates that the host, dual-stack-host.ipamworldwide.com, is reachable via IPv4 or IPv6. Dual-stacked devices attempting to reach this host will first attempt to connect via IPv6. Failing success, IPv4 will be attempted.

Resolution of IP-address-to-host domain names should also be configured in DNS within the appropriate .arpa domain. The PTR resource record corresponding to the IPv4 address, listed first, is placed into the appropriate in-addr.arpa zone file, while the IPv6 PTR record must be configured in the appropriate ip6.arpa zone file. The "appropriate" zone file depends on DNS administration policies within the organization. Some organizations with centralized DNS administration may provision all IPv4 PTR records in one in-addr.arpa zone file and all IPv6 in one ip6.arpa zone file. Others may delegate DNS responsibility to every subnet administrator, yielding a reverse zone file for every subnet! Most organizations however end up somewhere in between with a modest number of zone files to manage. Regardless of the number of zone files, resource records for each host generally need to be configured.

```
16.0.200.10.in-addr.arpa. 86400 IN PTR dual-stack-host.
ipamworldwide.com.
a.0.0.0.0.0.0.0.0.0.0.0.0.0.0.0.0.0.0.0.0.0.0.2.2.8.b.
d.0.1.0.0.2.ip6.arpa. 86400 IN PTR dual-stack-host.
ipamworldwide.com.
```

A dual stack node itself should be able to support receipt of A and AAAA records during its own DNS resolution processing and communicate with the intended destination using the address and protocol corresponding to the returned record(s) in accordance to its address selection policy table. In terms of the IP version used in the transport of DNS queries and answers, RFC 3901 (Internet Best Current Practice 91) [36] recommends that each recursive DNS server should support IPv4-only or dual-stack IPv4/IPv6. The RFC also recommends that every DNS zone should be served by at least one IPv4-reachable authoritative DNS server. These recommendations were set forth to provide backward compatibilty for IPv4-only resolvers which will be around for quite some time. So if you plan to implement dual stack on a subset of your network, DNS servers should be included within that subset.

3.1.4   DHCP Considerations

The mechanism for using DHCP under a dual stack implementation is simply that each stack use its corresponding version of DHCP. That is, to obtain an IPv4 address, use DHCP(v4); to obtain an IPv6 address or prefix, use DHCPv6. However, additional configuration information is provided by both forms of DHCP, such as which DNS or NTP server to use. The information obtained may lead to incorrect behavior on the client, depending on how the information from both servers is merged together. For example, if DNS server addresses are provided by both DHCP transactions, preferences of IPv4, IPv6, or mixed preference ordering cannot be conveyed. This remains an ongoing area of concern, as documented in RFC 4477 [37], but the current standard is to use a DHCP server for IPv4 and a DHCPv6 server for IPv6, possibly implemented on a common physical server.

3.2 TUNNELING APPROACHES

The second major IPv4/IPv6 co-existence category is tunneling, and a wide variety of tunneling technologies have been developed to support IPv4 over IPv6 and IPv6 over IPv4 tunneling. These technologies are generally categorized as *configured* or *automatic*. Configured tunnels are pre-defined, whereas automatic tunnels, also referred to as "softwire tunnels," are created and torn down on the fly. We'll discuss these two tunnel types after reviewing some tunneling basics.

In general, tunneling of IPv6 packets over an IPv4 network entails prefixing an IPv6 packet with an IPv4 header. This enables the tunneled packet to be routed over an IPv4 routing infrastructure; the IPv6 packet is simply considered payload within the IPv4 packet (Figure 3-3). The entry node of the tunnel, whether a router or host, performs the encapsulation. The source IPv4 address in the IPv4 header is populated with that node's IPv4 address and the destination address is that of the other tunnel endpoint. The protocol field of the IPv4 header is set to 41 (decimal) indicating an encapsulated IPv6 packet. The exit node or tunnel endpoint performs decapsulation to strip off the IPv4 header and routes the packet as appropriate to the ultimate destination via IPv6.

3.2.1 Tunneling Scenarios for IPv6 Packets Over IPv4 Networks

Using this basic tunneling approach, a variety of scenarios based on tunnel endpoints have been defined. Probably the most common configuration is a router-to-router tunnel, depicted in Figure 3-4, which is the most common approach for configured tunnels.

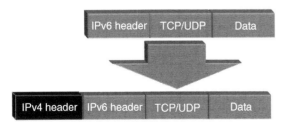

Figure 3-3. IPv6 over IPv4 tunneling [28].

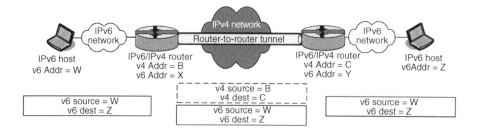

Figure 3-4. Router-to-router tunnel [28].

In this figure, the originating IPv6 host on the left has IPv6 address of W (for simplicity and brevity for now). A packet[3] destined for the host on the far end of the diagram with IPv6 address of Z is sent to a router serving the subnet. This router, with IPv4 address of B and IPv6 address of X, receives the IPv6 packet. Configured to tunnel packets destined for the network on which host Z resides, the router encapsulates the IPv6 packet with an IPv4 header. The router uses its IPv4 address (B) as the source IPv4 address and the tunnel endpoint router, with IPv4 address of C as the destination address as depicted by the dashed rectangle beneath the IPv4 network in the center of Figure 3-4. The tunneled packets are routed like "regular" IPv4 packets to the destination tunnel endpoint router. This endpoint router decapsulates the packet, stripping off the IPv4 header and routes the original IPv6 packet to its intended destination, Z.

Another tunneling scenario features an IPv6/IPv4 host, capable of supporting both IPv4 and IPv6 protocols, tunneling a packet to a router, which in turn decapsulates the packet and routes it natively via IPv6. This flow and packet header addresses are shown in Figure 3-5. The tunneling mechanism is the same as in the router-to-router case, but the tunnel endpoints are different.

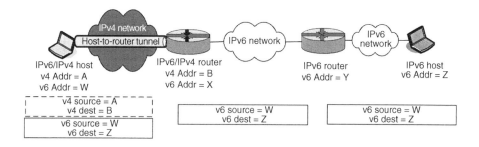

Figure 3-5. Host-to-router tunneling configuration [28].

---

[3] This packet is crudely identified in the figure as the solid-line rectangle beneath the originating host displaying the packet's IPv6 source address of W and destination address of Z. The tunnel header is shown as the dotted-line rectangle in this and subsequent tunneling figures.

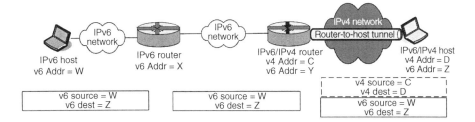

Figure 3-6. Router-to-host tunnel configuration [28].

The router-to-host configuration is also very similar, as shown in Figure 3-6. The originating IPv6 host on the left of the diagram sends the IPv6 packet to its local router, which routes it to a router closest to the destination. The serving router is configured to tunnel IPv6 packets over IPv4 to the host as shown in the figure.

The final tunneling configuration is one that spans end-to-end, from host-to-host. If the routing infrastructure has not yet been upgraded to support IPv6, this tunneling configuration enables two IPv6/IPv4 hosts to communicate via a tunnel as shown in Figure 3-7.

3.2.2 Tunnel Types

As mentioned, tunnels are either configured or automatic. Configured tunnels, such as 6in4 tunnels, are pre-defined by administrators in advance of communications. In the scenarios described above, manual configuration of the respective tunnel endpoints is required to configure each device regarding when to tunnel IPv6 packets, that is, based on destination, along with other tunnel configuration parameters that may be required by the tunnel implementation.

An automatic tunnel does not require tunnel pre-configuration, though enablement of tunneling configuration may be required. Tunnels are created based on information contained within the IPv6 packet, such as the source or destination IP address. The following automatic tunneling techniques are described in this section:

- *6to4.* Automatic tunneling technique based on a particular global address prefix and associated global (public) IPv4 address; 6to4 can be useful for

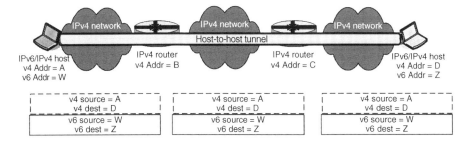

Figure 3-7. Host-to-host tunnel configuration [28].

interconnecting several remote sites within an enterprise network over an IPv4-based MPLS network, for example, though connection failure rates when connecting to Internet sites has been measured in the 10–25% range [38].

- *ISATAP*. Automatic host-to-router, router-to-host, or host-to-host tunneling based on a particular IPv6 address format with inclusion of an embedded IPv4 address.

- *6over4*. Automatic host-to-host tunneling using IPv4 multicast.

- *Tunnel Brokers*. Automatic tunnel setup by a server acting as a tunnel broker in assigning tunnel gateway resources on behalf of hosts requiring tunneling.

- *Teredo*. Automatic tunneling through NAT firewalls over IPv4 networks, though measured Internet connection failure rates have been measured on the order of 40–45% of connection attempts [38].

- *Dual Stack Transition Mechanism (DSTM)*. Enables automatic tunneling of IPv4 packets over IPv6 networks.

3.2.2.1 6to4 6to4 is an IPv6 over IPv4 tunneling technique that utilizes a particular IPv6 address format to identify 6to4 packets and to tunnel them accordingly. The address format consists of a 6to4 prefix, 2002::/16, followed by a globally unique IPv4 address for the intended destination site or host if host/router-to-host tunneling applies. This concatenation forms a /48 prefix as per Figure 3-8.

The unique IPv4 address shown in this example 192.0.2.131 represents the public IPv4 address of the 6to4 router or host terminating the 6to4 tunnel. The 48-bit 6to4 prefix serves as the global routing prefix, and a Subnet ID can be appended as the next 16 bits, followed by an Interface ID to fully define the IPv6 address. A host engaged in 6to4 tunneling must encapsulate and decapsulate its IPv6 payload within an IPv4 packet (i.e., append the IPv4 header) while a router can route IPv6 packets over an IPv4 network in a similar manner as routing warrants. Routers with 6to4 tunneling support (6to4 routers) must be employed, and IPv6 hosts that are to send/receive data via 6to4 tunnels must be configured with a 6to4 address and are considered 6to4 hosts.

Let's consider an example: two sites containing IPv6 hosts desire to communicate and are interconnected via 6to4 routers connected to a common IPv4 network, for example, the Internet. In Figure 3-9, the IPv4 addresses of the routers' IPv4 interfaces facing the Internet are 192.0.2.130 and 198.51.100.1, respectively. Transforming these IPv4 addresses into 6to4 addresses, we arrive at 2002:c000:282::/48

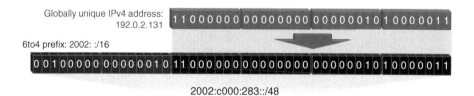

Figure 3-8. 6to4 address prefix derivation [39].

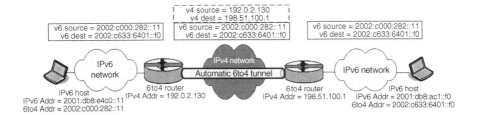

Figure 3-9.   6to4 tunneling example [39].

and 2002:c633:6401::/48, respectively. Each /48 block can be advertised on the Internet from each site and can be allocated (carved up) within the respective organizations down to the /64 subnet level for each subnet requiring IPv6 host connectivity over the IPv4 Internet or other IPv4 private network. Our 6to4 host on the left has Subnet ID = 0 and Interface ID = 11 for simplicity. Thus, this host's 6to4 address is 2002:c000:282:1::11. Similarly, the 6to4 host at the other (right) site resides on subnet ID = 0 and interface ID = f0, resulting in a 6to4 address of 2002: c633:6401::f0.

The AAAA and PTR resource records corresponding to these 6to4 addresses should also be added to DNS within the appropriate domains. When tunneling through the Internet, the destination AAAA and PTR records are maintained by each organization managing the corresponding 6to4 devices and resolution may require traversal down each domain subtree. The AAAA record follows normal "forward domain" resolution, but the PTR record is less straightforward. Since the PTR domain tree is based on the corresponding IPv6 address, which in the 6to4 case is "self-configured" by an organization based on its IPv4 address space and not by an upstream IPv6 address registry, the ip6.arpa delegation is unlinked from an authoritative upstream domain parent. A special registrar was established to handle delegations from the 2.0.0.2.ip6.arpa zone: the Number Resource Organization (NRO). Our administrators for the ip6.arpa domain corresponding to the 2002: c000:282::/48 prefix in our example would register the 2.8.2.0.0.0.0.C.2.0.0.2.ip6. arpa zone with 6to4.nro.net along with corresponding authoritative name servers.

Getting back to the packet flow, when our host on the left wishes to communicate with the host on the right, a DNS lookup would resolve to its 6to4 address (2002:c633:6401::f0), perhaps among several other answers. Based on a label match in its policy table, the sending host will use its 6to4 address (2002: c000:282::11) as the source and the destination 6to4 address as the destination. When this packet is received by the 6to4 router on the left, this router will encapsulate the packet with an IPv4 header using its (source = 192.0.2.130) and the other 6to4 router's (destination = 198.51.100.1) IPv4 addresses, respectively. The destination 6to4 router receiving the packet would decapsulate it, removing the IPv4 header, and route the packet to the 2002:c633:6401::/64 network to the destination 6to4 host.

6to4 can provide an efficient mechanism for IPv6 hosts to communicate over IPv4 networks. As IPv6 networks are incrementally deployed, *6to4 relay routers*, which are IPv6 routers that also support 6to4, can be used to relay packets from hosts on "pure" IPv6 networks to IPv6 hosts via IPv4 networks, essentially serving as

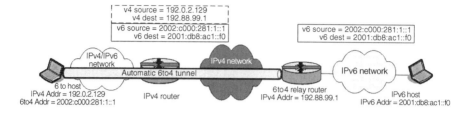

Figure 3-10. 6to4 host communicating with a native IPv6 host [39].

gateways between the IPv6 Internet and 6to4 hosts or routers. This enables 6to4 hosts to communicate with hosts on IPv6-only networks and vice versa.

The same addressing and tunneling scheme applies, however, the 6to4 host or router requires knowledge of 6to4 relay routers to map global unicast (native) IPv6 addresses to a 6to4 address for tunneling. There are three ways these relay routers can be configured:

1. Configure routes to destination native IPv6 networks with the 6to4 relay router as the next hop.

2. Utilize normal routing protocols, enabling the 6to4 relay router to advertise routes to IPv6 networks. This scenario would apply when advertising routes to migrated or internal IPv6 networks. If the pure IPv6 network in Figure 3-10 is the "IPv6 internet," the following default route option is likely a better alternative.

3. Configure a default route to the 6to4 relay router to reach IPv6 networks. This scenario may apply where an IPv6 Internet connection is reachable only through a IPv4 network internally to the organization and few or no pure IPv6 networks exist within the organization[4].

In walking through Figure 3-10, we have a 6to4 host on an IPv4/IPv6 network on the left of the diagram with a 6to4 address that is based on its configured public IPv4 address (192.0.2.129). This host must also be configured with routes or a default route for outgoing IPv6 packets using an advertised Internet 6to4 relay router IPv6 address or the well-known 6to4 anycast address, 192.88.99.1. This host desires to communicate with a native IPv6 host with IP address 2001:db8:ac1::f0 on an IPv6-only network on the right side of the figure. This IPv6 address is returned within a AAAA resource record response from a DNS server when queried for the IP address of the destination host.

Thus our 6to4 host on the left formulates an IPv6 packet using its 6to4 address as the source IP address and the destination host's IPv6 address as the destination. The host then tunnels this packet over IPv4 using its unique IPv4 address as the source and the corresponding 6to4 relay router IPv4 address as the destination. Upon

---

[4] A variant on this scenario calls for the definition of the default route next hop as the 6to4 relay router anycast address for IPv6 networks. This variation supports the scenario with multiple 6to4 relay routers. RFC 3068 defines an anycast address for 6to4 relay routers: 2002:c058:6301::/48. This address corresponds to the IPv4 address of 192.88.99.1. This variant is also illustrated in Figure 3-10.

arrival of the packet at the 6to4 relay router, the relay router routes to the destination 2001:db8:ac1::/48 network. In the reverse direction, use of the original source's 6to4 address as the destination IPv6 address would inform the 6to4 relay router that this packet requires 6to4 tunneling to the corresponding destination host.

3.2.2.2 ISATAP Intra-Site Automatic Tunneling Addressing Protocol (ISATAP) is an experimental protocol providing automatic IPv6 over IPv4 tunneling for host-to-router, router-to-host, and host-to-host configurations. ISATAP IPv6 addresses are formed using an IPv4 address to define its Interface ID. The Interface ID is comprised of::5efe:w.x.y.z, where w.x.y.z is the dotted decimal IPv4 notation. So an ISATAP interface ID corresponding to 192.0.2.131 is denoted as::5efe:192.0.2.131. The IPv4 notation provides a clear indication that the ISATAP address contains an IPv4 address without having to translate the IPv4 address into hexadecimal. This ISATAP Interface ID can be used as a normal interface ID in appending it to supported network prefixes to define IPv6 addresses. For example, the link-local IPv6 address using the ISATAP Interface ID above is fe80::5efe:192.0.2.131.

Hosts supporting ISATAP are required to maintain a *potential router list* (PRL) containing the IPv4 address and associated address lifetime timers for each router advertising an ISATAP interface. ISATAP hosts solicit ISATAP support information from local routers via router solicitation over IPv4. The solicitation destination needs to be identified by the host by prior manual configuration, by looking up the router in DNS with a host name of "isatap," or using a DHCP vendor-specific option indicating the IPv4 address(es) of the ISATAP router(s). The DNS technique requires administrators to create resource records for ISATAP routers using the isatap host name.

An ISATAP host encapsulates the IPv6 data packet with an IPv4 header as shown in Figure 3-11, using the IPv4 address corresponding to the chosen router from the PRL.

ISATAP hosts can autoconfigure their ISATAP Interface IDs using configured IPv4 addresses, whether the IPv4 address is defined statically or is obtained via DHCP. Microsoft XP and 2003 server perform such autoconfiguration if configured with IPv6. Microsoft Vista and 7 clients and Windows 2008 servers support ISATAP autoconfiguration by default. The ISATAP interface ID is appended to a 64-bit global network prefix and subnet ID provided by solicited ISATAP routers in their router advertisements.

Following Figure 3-11, the host on the left of the diagram identifies the destination host's IP address, in this case an IPv6 address, using DNS. An IPv6 packet

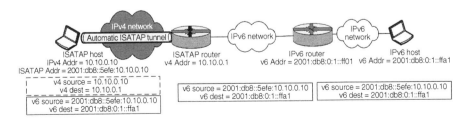

Figure 3-11. ISATAP host-to-router example [39].

would be formed by the host, using its ISATAP IPv6 address as its source address, and the destination IPv6 host address as the destination address. This packet is encapsulated in an IPv4 header, thereby forming an automatic tunnel. The tunnel source address is set to the ISATAP host's IPv4 address, the destination address is set to the ISATAP router's IPv4 address, and the protocol field in the IP header is set to decimal 41, indicating an encapsulated IPv6 packet. The ISATAP router need not be on the same physical network as the host, and the tunnel can span a generic IPv4 network (zero or more hops) between the host and the ISATAP router. The ISATAP router strips off the IPv4 header and routes the remaining IPv6 packet to the destination host using normal IPv6 routing.

The destination host can respond to the originating host using the originating host's ISATAP address. Since the ISATAP address contains a globally unique network prefix/Subnet ID, the destination packet is routed to the serving ISATAP router. Upon processing the Interface ID, the local ISATAP router can extract the IPv4 address of the destination host and encapsulate the IPv6 packet with an IPv4 header to the original host. Similarly, the native IPv6 host to the right of Figure 3-11 could have initiated the communication to the ISATAP host. Going from right to left, the ISATAP router in this case would initiate the ISATAP tunnel to the host.

Host-to-host ISATAP tunnels, similar to that displayed in Figure 3-7, can be initiated by ISATAP hosts residing on an IPv4 network, where a link-local (same subnet) or global network prefix can be prefixed to each host's ISATAP interface ID. In Figure 3-7, IPv6 addresses W and Z would represent ISATAP addresses formed from IPv4 addresses A and D, respectively.

3.2.2.3 6over4 6over4 is an automatic tunneling technique that leverages IPv4 multicast. IPv4 multicast is required and is considered a *virtual link layer* or *virtual Ethernet* by 6over4. Because of the virtual link layer perspective, IPv6 addresses are formed using a link-local scope (fe80::/10 prefix). A host's IPv4 address comprises its 6over4 Interface ID portion of its IPv6 address. For example, a 6over4 host with IPv4 address of 192.0.2.85 would formulate an IPv6 interface ID of::c000:255, and thus a 6over4 address of fe80::c000:255. 6over4 tunnels can be of the form host-to-host, host-to-router, and router-to-host, where respective hosts and routers are configured to support 6over4. IPv6 packets are tunneled in IPv4 headers using corresponding IPv4 multicast addresses. All members of the multicast group receive the tunneled packets, thus the analogy of virtual link layer and the intended recipient strips off the IPv4 header and processes the IPv6 packet. As long as at least one IPv6 router also running 6over4 is reachable via the IPv4 multicast mechanism, the router can serve as a tunnel endpoint and then route the packet via IPv6.

6over4 supports IPv6 multicast as well as unicast, so hosts can perform IPv6 router and neighbor discovery to locate IPv6 routers. When tunneling IPv6 multicast messages, for example, for neighbor discovery, the IPv4 destination address is formatted as 239.192.Y.Z, where Y and Z are the last two bytes of the IPv6 multicast address. Thus an IPv6 message to the all-routers link-scoped multicast address, ff02::2, would be tunneled to IPv4 destination 239.192.0.2. The Internet Group Membership Protocol (IGMP) is used by 6over4 hosts to inform IPv4 routers of multicast group membership so routers can forward multicast packets to them.

3.2.2.4 Tunnel Brokers Tunnel brokers provide another technique for automatic tunneling over IPv4 networks. The tunnel broker manages tunnel requests
from dual stack clients and tunnel broker servers, which connect to the intended IPv6
network. Dual stack clients attempting to access an IPv6 network can optionally be
directed to a tunnel broker web portal for entry of authentication credentials, to
authorize use of the broker service. The tunnel broker may also manage certificates
for authorization services. The client also provides the IPv4 address for its end of the
tunnel, along with the desired FQDN of the client, the number of IPv6 addresses
requested, and whether the client is a host or a router.

Once authorized, the tunnel broker performs a number of tasks to broker
creation of the tunnel:

- assigns and configures a tunnel server and informs the selected tunnel server of
  the new client;
- assigns an IPv6 address or prefix to the client based on the requested number of
  addresses and client type (router or host);
- registers the client FQDN in DNS;
- informs the client of its assigned tunnel server and associated tunnel and IPv6
  parameters including address/prefix and DNS name.

Figure 3-12 illustrates the client–tunnel broker interaction at the top of the
figure, and the resulting tunnel between the client and the assigned tunnel server
below. RFC 5572 [40] formalizes the Tunnel Setup Protocol (TSP) to promote
common tunnel setup messages and component interactions.

Teredo Tunneling through firewalls that perform NAT can be challenging if not
impossible by design. Teredo is a tunnel broker technology that enables NAT traversal
of IPv6 packets tunneled over UDP over IPv4 for host-to-host automatic tunnels. Teredo
incorporates the additional UDP header in order to facilitate NAT/firewall traversal.
Many NAT/firewall devices will not allow traversal of IPv4 packets with the packet
header protocol field set to 41, which is the setting for tunneling of IPv6 packets as
mentioned previously. The additional UDP header further "buries" the tunnel to enable
its traversal through NAT/firewall devices, most of which support UDP port translation
(Figure 3-13).

Teredo is defined in RFC 4380 to provide "IPv6 access of last resort" due to its
overhead and will be used less and less as 6to4-enabled or IPv6-aware firewall routers
are deployed. Teredo requires the following elements as shown in Figure 3-14:

- Teredo client,
- Teredo server,
- Teredo relay.

The Teredo tunneling process starts with a Teredo client performing a
qualification procedure to discover a Teredo relay closest to the intended destination
IPv6 host and identify the type of NAT firewall that is in place. The Teredo relay is
the Teredo tunnel endpoint serving the intended destination host. Teredo hosts must

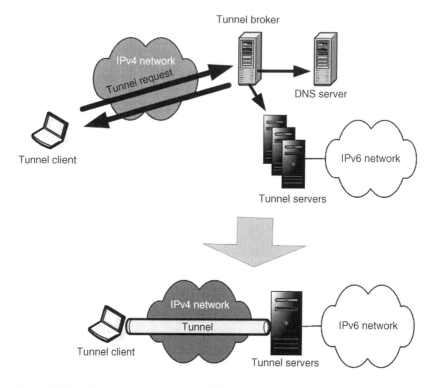

Figure 3-12. Tunnel broker interaction [39].

be pre-configured with Teredo server IPv4 addresses to use, which help establish Teredo connections.

Determining the closest Teredo relay entails sending an IPv6 ping (ICMPv6 echo request) to the destination host. The ping is encapsulated with a UDP and IPv4 header and sent to the Teredo server, which decapsulates it and sends the native ICMPv6 packet to the destination. The destination host's response will be routed via native IPv6 to the nearest (routing-wise) Teredo relay, then back to the originating host. In this manner, the client determines the appropriate Teredo relay's IPv4 address and port by virtue of its IPv4 and UDP [tunnel] headers. Figure 3-14 illustrates the case with a Teredo client communicating to a native IPv6 host.

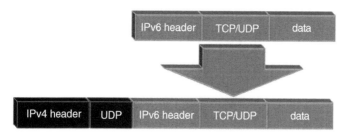

Figure 3-13. Teredo tunnels add UDP then IPv4 headers [41].

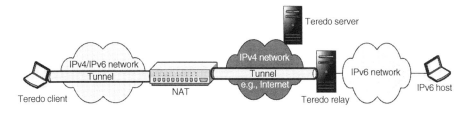

Figure 3-14. Teredo client to IPv6 host connection [39].

NAT Types In its initial incarnation, Teredo was designed to address traversal of cone and selected port-restricted NAT types. However, RFC 6081 defines Teredo extensions that greatly expands the set of NAT types supported for traversal as highlighted in Table 3-2 as specified in RFC 6081 [42]:

where:

- Yes = Supported by the initial Teredo specifications (RFC 4380).
- SNS = Supported with the Symmetric NAT Support Extension.
- SNS+UPnP = Supported with the Symmetric NAT support extension and the Universal Plug and Play (UPnP) Symmetric NAT extension.
- SNS+PP = Supported with the Symmetric NAT support extension and the Port-Preserving Symmetric NAT extension.
- SNS+SS = Supported with the Symmetric NAT support extension and the Sequential Port-Symmetric NAT extension.
- No = No support.

To communicate using Teredo, the NAT must be "initialized" to properly map the source and destination addresses corresponding to those within the NAT. To complete the mapping within the NAT of the internal host communicating with the destination host, a *bubble packet* is sent by the Teredo client to the destination host. A bubble packet is an IPv6 header with no payload, itself encapsulated in the Teredo tunnel IPv4/UDP header. It enables the NAT to complete the mapping of internal and external IP addresses and internal and external port numbers.

Generally the bubble packet is sent directly from the source Teredo client to the destination host. But if the destination host is also behind a firewall, the bubble packet may be discarded since this is an unsolicited external packet. In this case, the Teredo client times out and sends the bubble packet via the Teredo server, which is identified by the intended destination Teredo-formatted IPv6 address, which encodes the Teredo IPv4 address. The Teredo server then forwards the packet over a Teredo tunnel to the destination host, which has its own IPv4 address also encoded in the Teredo IPv6 address.

Assuming the destination host is also a Teredo client, it will receive the packet, having been initialized by a prior ping it sent to this Teredo server during client configuration. The destination host will then respond to the originating host directly, completing the NAT mapping (on both sides). Figure 3-15 illustrates this scenario with two Teredo clients communicating via a common Teredo relay.

TABLE 3-2. NAT Types Supported by Teredo Extensions [43]

Source NAT \ Destination NAT	Cone	Address-restricted	Port restricted	UPnP port restricted	UPnP port symmetric	Port-pres. port-sym.	Seq. port-symmetric	Port-symmetric	Address-symmetric
Cone	Yes	Yes	Yes	Yes	SNS	SNS	SNS	SNS	SNS
Address-restricted	Yes	Yes	Yes	Yes	SNS	SNS	SNS	SNS	No
Port-restricted	Yes	Yes	Yes	Yes	No	SNS+PP	SNS+PP	No	No
UPnP port-restricted	Yes	Yes	Yes	Yes	SNS + UPnP	No	No	No	No
UPnP port-symmetric	SNS	SNS	No	SNS + UPnP	SNS + UPnP	No	No	No	No
Port-preserving port-symmetric	SNS	SNS	SNS+PP	No	No	SNS+PP	SNS+PP	No	No
Sequential port-symmetric	SNS	SNS	SNS+SS	No	No	No	No	No	No
Port-symmetric	SNS	SNS	No	No	No	No	No	No	No
Address-symmetric	SNS	No	No	No	No	No	No	No	No

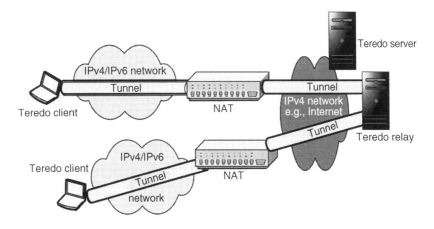

Figure 3-15. Two Teredo clients communicating via the IPv4 Internet [39].

As we've seen, the Teredo IPv6 address is formatted with the client and its server Teredo server IPv4 addresses. The Teredo IPv6 address has the format shown in Figure 3-16.

The Teredo prefix is a pre-defined IPv6 prefix: 2001::/32. The Teredo server IPv4 address comprises the next 32 bits. RFC 5991 [44] redefined the Flags field from its original RFC 4380 definition to incorporate a random string and to deprecate the cone bit, though it is still interpreted in some scenarios. The Flags field has the following format as shown in Figure 3-17:

- C = cone bit
- z = reserved (set to 0)
- Random1 = random bits
- U = universal/local bit (set to 0)
- G = individual/global bit (set to 0)
- Random2 = random bits.

The U and G bits are set to zero to indicate a locally administered unicast address and the random bits discourage Teredo IPv6 address scanning even if a mapped IPv4 address is known (12 random bits provide 4096 combinations of Teredo addresses for a given mapped IPv4 address). The client port and client IPv4

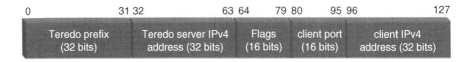

Figure 3-16. Teredo IPv6 address format [39].

Figure 3-17. Teredo Flags field.

address fields represent obfuscated values of these respective values by reversing each bit value (Figure 3-18).

3.2.3 Tunneling Scenario for IPv4 Packets Over IPv6 Networks

During an IPv6 implementation, some IPv6 clients on IPv6 networks may still need to communicate with IPv4 applications or hosts on IPv4 networks, such as the Internet. Tunneling of IPv4 packets over the IPv6 network provides a means to preserve this communications path.

3.2.3.1 Dual Stack Transition Mechanism DSTM is a tunnel broker approach that provides a means to tunnel IPv4 packets over IPv6 networks, ultimately to the destination IPv4 network and host. The host on the IPv6 network intending to communicate with the IPv4 host would require a dual stack, as well as a DSTM client. Upon resolving the host name of the intended destination host using DNS to only an IPv4 address, the client would initiate the DSTM process, which is very

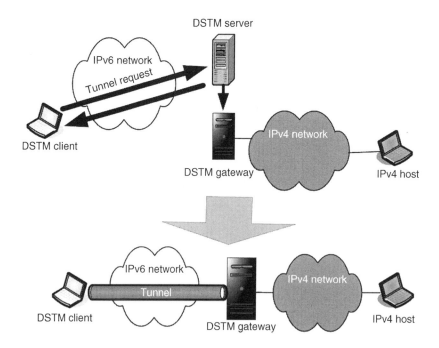

Figure 3-18. DSTM tunnel setup [45].

similar to the tunnel broker approach. The process begins with the DSTM client contacting a DSTM server to obtain an IPv4 address preferably via the DHCPv6 protocol[5], as well as the IPv6 address of the DSTM gateway. The IPv4 address is used as the source address in the data packet to be transmitted. This packet is encapsulated with an IPv6 header using the DSTM client's source IPv6 address and the DSTM gateway's IPv6 address as the destination. The next header field in the IPv6 header indicates an encapsulated IPv4 packet with this "4over6" tunneling approach.

A variant of DSTM supports VPN-based access from a DSTM client outside of the native network, for example, a home-based worker. In this scenario, assuming the DSTM client obtains an IPv6 address but no IPv4 address, it can connect to the DSTM server to obtain an IPv4 address. This access should require authentication to establish a VPN between the DSTM client and DSTM gateway.

3.2.4 Tunneling Summary

Table 3-3 summarizes the applicability of tunneling based on the source host capabilities/network type and the destination address resolution and network type.

The cells with entries in italic font (in upper left and lower right) in the table indicate use of a native IP version from end-to-end. Any intervening networks of the opposite protocol must be either tunneled through via a router-to-router tunnel or translated at each boundary using a translation technology, discussed in the following section.

The cells with entries in roman font indicate a tunneling scenario. The "→" symbol represents a transition point or tunneling endpoint within the network that converts the corresponding native protocol to a tunneled protocol or vice-versa.

The cells with "N/A" indicate an invalid connection option via tunneling. However, translation technologies could be employed to bridge these gaps as we'll discuss next.

3.3 TRANSLATION APPROACHES

Translation techniques perform IPv4-to-IPv6 translation (and vice-versa) at a particular layer of the protocol stack, typically network, transport, or application. Unlike tunneling, which does not alter the tunneled data packet but merely appends a header or two, translation mechanisms do modify, that is, translate IP packets commutatively between IPv4 and IPv6. Translation approaches are generally recommended in an environment with IPv6-only nodes communicating with IPv4-only nodes; that is, for the cells with "NA" scenarios in Table 3-3. In dual stack environments, native or tunneling mechanisms are preferable.

IPv4/IPv6 translation methods developed early on in the specification stages of IPv6 have proven inconsistent and in many scenarios insecure. Leveraging early "lessons learned," a new series of RFCs were published to define IPv4/IPv6

---

[5] While the DSTM RFC drafts [45] denote DHCPv6 as the preferable method to obtain an IPv4 address, DHCPv6 does not currently define assignment of IPv4 addresses natively or via an option setting.

TABLE 3-3. Tunneling Summary

To→ ↓ From	IPv4 destination on IPv4 network	Dual stack destination on IPv4 network resolved to IPv4 address	Dual stack destination on IPv4 network resolved to IPv6 address	Dual stack destination on IPv6 network resolved as IPv4 address	Dual stack destination on IPv6 network resolved as IPv6 address	IPv6 destination on IPv6 network
IPv4 client on IPv4 network	*Native IPv4*	*Native IPv4*	N/A	Native IPv4 → IPv4-compatible	N/A	N/A
Dual stack client on IPv4 network	*Native IPv4*	*Native IPv4*	Host-to-host IPv6 over IPv4*	Native IPv4 → IPv4-compatible	Host-to-router IPv6 over IPv4*	Host-to-router IPv6 over IPv4*
Dual stack client on IPv6 network	DSTM → Native IPv4	DSTM → *Native IPv4*	Native IPv6→ Router-to-host IPv6 over IPv4*	DSTM	*Native IPv6*	*Native IPv6*
IPv6 client on IPv6 network	N/A	N/A	Native IPv6 → IPv6 over IPv4*	N/A	*Native IPv6*	*Native IPv6*

*Resolution to an IPv6 address could be a native IPv6 address, or a 6to4 address, ISATAP, Teredo, 6over4 or IPv4-compatible address. The host must select the destination address based on its support of the corresponding technology.

TABLE 3-4. Viable Translation Approaches [46]

Scenario	Source network	Destination network	Applicability
1	IPv6 network	IPv4 Internet	Stateless translation approach is viable with DNS64
2	IPv4 Internet	IPv6 network	Stateless translation approach is viable with network-specific prefix
3	IPv6 Internet	IPv4 network	Stateful translation approach is viable with network-specific prefix and IPv4 translatable addresses published in DNS (AAAA records)
4	IPv4 network	IPv6 Internet	Translation NOT viable
5	IPv6 network	IPv4 network	Like scenario 1, viable
6	IPv4 network	IPv6 network	Like scenario 2, viable
7	IPv6 Internet	IPv4 Internet	Translation NOT viable
8	IPv4 Internet	IPv6 Internet	Translation NOT viable

translation methods, addressing and consistent approaches. RFC 6144 [46] defines the framework for IPv4/IPv6 translation and defines internetworking scenarios for which such translation applies. These scenarios are instructive as they scope the applicability of translation approaches as summarized in Table 3-4. Each scenario portrays the initiation of communications from a host on a private network or the global Internet of one protocol attempting to connect with a host on a network or the global Internet of the other protocol.

Scenarios 4 and 8 are not viable given the inability to uniquely translate an IPv6 address within the scope of the entire Internet into an IPv4 address representation. Unlike scenario 3 which is viable given the ability to constrain an IPv4 network's addresses within a single IPv4-translatable IPv6 address prefix, scenario 7 is not constrainable in such a way across the entire Internet address space.

3.3.1 IP/ICMP Translation

Now that we've introduced the scenarios under which IPv4/IPv6 translation is viable, let's explore the mechanics of translation. The algorithm for translating between IPv4 and IPv6 packets is the IP/ICMP Translation algorithm specified in RFC 6145 [47], which is implemented on a host or gateway to convert outgoing IPv6 packet headers into IPv4 headers, and incoming IPv4 headers into IPv6 or vice versa. While the translation algorithm may be implemented on hosts (i.e., "Bump in the Host" approach described later), we'll consider the case of a network translation gateway performing this function to simplify our discussion. The translation process involves consideration of address translation, packet fragmentation, ICMP mapping and translation of IP header fields.

3.3.1.1 Address Translation Address translation is defined in RFC 6052 [48] and applies to any entity needing to translate IPv4 and IPv6 addresses including not only translation gateways but DNS64 services for example. Semantically, an

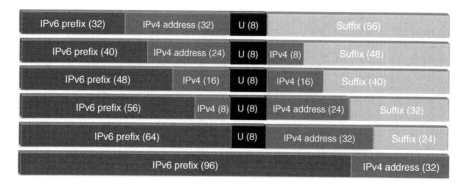

Figure 3-19. IPv4-translatable and IPv4-converted IPv6 address format.

IPv4-converted IPv6 address is an IPv6 address used to represent an IPv4 node, while an *IPv4-translatable* IPv6 address is an IPv6 address assigned to an IPv6 node for use with stateless address translation. The former is essentially the output of a translation process while the latter represents a pre-mapped IPv6 address with an embedded IPv4 address.

Both have exactly the same format, which consists of an IPv6 prefix concatenated with the 32- bit IPv4 address, followed in most cases by a suffix. The only twist is that bits 64-71 (the first eight bits of the IID) are set to zero in all cases for compatibility with the IPv6 addressing architecture which specifies bit 70 as the universal/local ("u") bit and bit 71 is the individual/group ("g") bit, where zeroes in these bits indicate a locally administered unicast address. Depending on the length of the IPv6 prefix, the IPv4 address is inserted after the prefix and around this "U" byte as shown in Figure 3-19.

IPv6 prefix lengths must be defined as in Figure 3-19: 32, 40, 48, 56, 64, or 96 bits in length. A well-known 96-bit prefix has been assigned as 64:ff9b::/96, though this can only be used to represent unique public IPv4 addresses and generally only applies to organizations operating a translation service. Use of the 96-bit prefix must also assure zero bit values in the U field. For example, one could assign a /64 prefix and append 32 zeroes to derive a compliant 96-bit prefix. But the concept is that an organization would allocate a prefix dedicated for use to represent IPv4-translatable addresses from their assigned address space, generally 8 bits longer than the total allocation (1/256 of allocated space, e.g., use a /56 if allocated a /48), and advertise this prefix if not already rolled up in an aggregated advertisement. The translation gateway would need to be configured to recognize this IPv4-translatable prefix and translate the IPv6 packet to IPv4, using the embedded IPv4 address as the destination address.

As an example, consider representing a host's IPv4 address of 198.51.100.49 as reachable through a translation gateway with configured IPv4-translatable IPv6 prefix 2001:db8:3a01:4f00::/56 prefix. Mapping the IPv4 address to hex, c633:6431, and appending it to the prefix while retaining the U zero bits, we arrive at 2001: db8:3a01:4fc6:33:6431:: as the IPv6-translatable address. In Figure 3-20, this is the

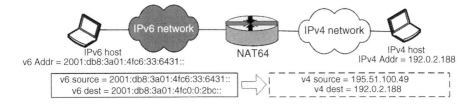

Figure 3-20. IP/ICMP translation example.

host on the left, with only its IPv6 address represented. Its reachability in DNS could be published with a A record for 195.51.100.49 and a AAAA record for 2001: db8:3a01:4fc6:33:6431::. Likewise the host on the right has IPv4 address 192.0.2.188 which can be represented as an IPv4-converted IPv6 address of 2001: db8:3a01:4fc0:0:2bc:: with corresponding A and AAAA records (or DNS64-generated AAAA records as we'll discuss later). Resolving this information for the IPv4 host, the host on the left sends a packet as shown in the figure destined for 2001: db8:3a01:4fc0:0:2bc::. Packets destined for 2001:db8:3a01:4f00::/56 are routed to the NAT64 gateway, which performs the IP/ICMP translation function described in this chapter, including mapping IPv6 addresses to corresponding IPv4 addresses as shown in the figure. If the host on the right was dual stacked and reachable directly via IPv6, the translation function would have been bypassed; it is only applied when no native protocol routes exist.

3.3.1.2 *Packet Fragmentation* Packet fragmentation enables a large packet to be subdivided into two or more smaller packets to enable traversal of intermediate networks between the source and destination that have a smaller maximum transmission unit (MTU) than the original packet size. With IPv4, routers along the path of a packet could fragment a packet if needed; in IPv6, fragmentation is performed solely by endpoints, not by routers. IPv6 hosts engage in MTU path discovery to ascertain the minimum path MTU to properly size packets prior to transmission. Hosts transmit packets to the intended destination initially assuming the path MTU is equal to that of the local link MTU; if an intermediate hop's MTU is less than the packet size, an ICMPv6 *packet too big* error message is returned to the host indicating the MTU of the offending link. The host may then begin retransmission adjusting the packet size to the indicated MTU size; this process may repeat if smaller MTUs further along the path are discovered. IPv4 nodes may also perform MTU path discovery by sending a packet of the desired MTU to the destination, but because routers may automatically fragment large packets in IPv4, the host sets the Don't Fragment (DF) bit in the IPv4 header to disable intermediate fragmentation. Analogous to the IPv6 case, if the packet size exceeds the MTU along the way, an ICMP *fragmentation needed* error message is returned by the corresponding router detecting the issue.

When a translator receives an IPv4 packet with the DF bit set and the MTU of the next (or subsequent IPv6 hops upon receipt of an ICMPv6 *packet too big* message) is less than the IPv4 packet size +20 (to account for the IPv6 header

TABLE 3-5. ICMP(v4) to ICMPv6 Translation

ICMPv4 message type	Translated ICMPv6 message type
Echo (8) and Echo Reply (0)	Echo Request (128) and Echo reply (129), respectively
ICMP Router Advertisement/Solicitation (9, 10)	Obsoleted in ICMPv6, silently drop
Timestamp and Timestamp Reply (13, 14)	Obsoleted in ICMPv6, silently drop
Information Request/Reply (15, 16)	Obsoleted in ICMPv6, silently drop
Address Mask Request/Reply (17, 18)	Obsoleted in ICMPv6, silently drop
IGMP messages	Generally link-local focused, silently drop
Destination Unreachable (3)	
Code 0, 1 (net, host unreachable)	Destination Unreachable (1), Code = 0 (no route to destination)
Code 2 (protocol unreachable)	ICMPv6 Parameter Problem (4) Code = 1 (unrecognized next header type)
Code 3 (port unreachable)	Destination Unreachable (1), Code = 4 (port unreachable)
Code 4 (fragmentation needed and DF was set)	Packet too big (2), Code = 0, MTU field to be adjusted to account for translated header differences
Code 5 (source route failed)	Destination Unreachable (1), Code = 0 (no route to destination)
Codes 6, 7, 8 (destination network unknown, destination host unknown, source host isolate)	Destination Unreachable (1), Code = 0 (no route to destination)
Codes 9, 10 (communication with destination network/host is administratively prohibited)	Destination Unreachable (1), Code = 1 (communnication with destination administratively prohibited)
Codes 11, 12 (Destination network/host unreachable for type of service)	Destination Unreachable (1), Code = 0 (no route to destination)
Code 13 (communication administratively prohibited)	Destination Unreachable (1), Code = 1 (communnication with destination administratively prohibited)
Code 14 (host precedence violation)	Silently drop
Code 15 (precedence cutoff in effect)	Destination Unreachable (1), Code = 1 (communnication with destination administratively prohibited)
Source quench (4)	Obsoleted in ICMPv6, silently drop
Redirect (5)	Link-local focused, silently drop
Alternative host address (6)	Silently drop
Time exceeded (11)	Time exceeded (3), with same code value
Parameter problem (12)	Parameter problem (4)
Code 0 (pointer indicates the error)	Code = 0 (erroneous header field encountered) and update the pointer value or silently drop as per Table 3-6
Code 1 (missing a required option)	Silently drop
Code 2 (bad length)	Code = 0 (erroneous header field encountered) and update the pointer value or silently drop as per Table 3-6
Other code values or unknown ICMPv4 types	Silently drop

incremental size), then an ICMP *fragmentation needed* message is sent back to the source IPv4 address. If the DF bit is not set and the packet's size likewise exceeds the next and subsequent hops' MTU, the translator should fragment the packet. If the packet is smaller than the MTU, the translator may also be configured to add a fragment header merely to indicate fragmentation is permissible. The fragmentation header should never be included if DF was set despite ample MTU sizing for the packet.

When a translator translates an incoming IPv6 packet to IPv4, it sets the DF flag by default. If it then receives an ICMP *fragmentation needed* in reply, this in turn is translated to an ICMPv6 *packet too big* message and sent back to the originating IPv6 host. The originating host is not required to use a packet size smaller than the minimum IPv6 MTU of 1280 octets, but it will retransmit the packet with a fragment header from which the translator will map the IPv4 identification header value for each derived fragment transmitted to the IPv4 destination. In this scenario, the DF flag is not set indicating that subsequent IPv4 fragmentation is permissible.

3.3.1.3 ICMP Translation

Within the IP header translation process described next, the IPv6 next header value for ICMPv6 (58) is mapped to the IPv4 protocol value for ICMP (1). The actual ICMP header values must also be mapped in accordance with the intended recipient's protocol version. Table 3-5 summarizes ICMP[v4] to ICMPv6 translation.

For parameter problem error messages, header pointer values are translated as shown in Table 3-6.

ICMPv6 checksums must be calculated based on the completed translation. ICMP error payloads may cause interpretation problems especially if an IP address of the opposite protocol is included. Translation gateways will generally attempt to translate "attached" IP header values accordingly if this too is part of the returned error message.

Table 3-7 summarizes ICMPv6 to ICMP translation.

For parameter problem error messages, header pointer values are translated as shown in Table 3-8.

TABLE 3-6. ICMP(v4) to ICMPv6 Parameter Problem Translation

ICMPv4 pointer value	Translated ICMPv6 pointer value
Version/IP Header Length (0)	Version/Traffic Class (0)
Type of Service (1)	Traffic Class/Flow Label (1)
Total Length (2, 3)	Payload Length (4)
Identification (4, 5), Flags/Fragment Offset (6, 7), Header Checksum (10, 11)	Silently drop
Time to Live (8)	Hop Limit (7)
Protocol (9)	Next Header (6)
Source Address (12–15)	Source Address (8)
Destination Address (16–19)	Destination Address (24)

TABLE 3-7. ICMPv6 to ICMP(v4) Translation

ICMPv6 message type	Translated ICMPv4 message type
Echo Request (128) and Echo reply (129)	Echo (8) and Echo Reply (0) respectively
Multicast Listener Discovery Query, Report, Done (130, 131, 132)	Generally link-local focused, silently drop
Neighbor Discovery messages (133–137)	Generally link-local focused, silently drop
Destination Unreachable (1)	Destination Unreachable (3)
Code 0 (no route to destination)	Code = 1 (host unreachable)
Code 1 (communication with destination administratively prohibited)	Code = 10 (communication with destination network/host is administratively prohibited)
Code 2 (beyond scope of source address)	Code = 1 (host unreachable)
Code 3 (address unreachable)	Code = 1 (host unreachable)
Code 4 (port unreachable)	Code = 3 (port unreachable)
Packet too big (2)	Destination Unreachable (3), Code = 4 (fragmentation needed, DF set)
Time exceeded (3)	Time exceeded (11), with same code value
Parameter problem (4)	
Code 0 (erroneous header field encountered)	Parameter problem (12) Code = 0 (erroneous header field encountered) and update the pointer value or silently drop as per Table 3-8
Code 1 (unrecognized next header type encountered)	Destination Unreachable (3), Code = 2 (protocol unreachable)
Code 2 (unrecognized IPv6 option encountered)	Silently drop
Other code values or unknown ICMPv6 types	Silently drop

ICMPv4 checksums must be calculated based on the completed translation. ICMP error payloads may cause interpretation problems especially if an IP address of the opposite protocol is included. Translation gateways will generally attempt to translate "attached" IP header values accordingly if this too is part of the returned error message, though this may be unrealizable if the IPv6 address falls outside of the allocated IPv4-translatable space.

TABLE 3-8. ICMPv6 to ICMP(v4) Parameter Problem Translation

ICMPv6 pointer value	Translated ICMPv4 pointer value
Version/Traffic Class (0)	Version/IP Header Length (0)
Traffic Class/Flow Label (1)	Type of Service (1)
Flow Label (2, 3)	Silently drop
Payload Length (4, 5)	Total Length (2)
Next Header (6)	Protocol (9)
Hop Limit (7)	Time to Live (8)
Source Address (8–23)	Source Address (12)
Destination Address (24–39)	Destination Address (16)

3.3.1.4 IP Header Translation The IP header translation process applies the following field mapping on each packet. The field mapping is summarized below for both translation directions:

IPv4 -> IPv6 header translation	IPv6 -> IPv4 header translation
Version = 6	**Version** = 4
	Header Length = 5 (no IPv4 options)
Traffic Class = IPv4 header TOS bits or translator-configured value	**Type of Service** = IPv6 header Traffic Class field or translator-configured value
Flow Label = 0	
Payload Length = IPv4 header Total Length value – (IPv4 header length + IPv4 options length)	**Total Length** = IPv6 header payload length field + IPv4 header length
	Identification = 0
Next Header = IPv4 header Protocol field value (change ICMP (1) to ICMPv6 (58))	**Flags** = Don't Fragment = 1, More Fragments = 0 (unless the IPv6 packet had a fragment header indicating fragmentation is permissible)
	Fragment Offset = 0
Hop Limit = IPv4 TTL field value – 1	**TTL** = IPv6 Hop Limit field value – 1
	Protocol = IPv6 Next Header field; ICMPv6 (58) is changed to ICMP (1) and IPv6 headers IPv6 hop-by-hop (0), IPv6-Route (43), IPv6-Frag, and IPv6-Opts (60) are skipped over as not applicable to IPv4
	Header Checksum = Computed over the newly formed IPv4 header
Source IP Address = IPv4-translatable IPv6 address based on the associated IPv6 prefix and IPv4 source address	**Source IP Address** = IPv4 address derived from the IPv4-translatable IPv6 address that falls within the IPv6 translatable prefix; or a mapped IPv6 address based on the translator's stateful address maps (binding information base) for the source IPv6 address
Destination IP Address = IPv4-translatable IPv6 address derived from the destination IPv4 address (stateless) or a mapped IPv6 address based on the translator's stateful address maps (binding information base)	**Destination IP Address** = IPv4 portion of the IPv4-converted IPv6 destination address
	Options = None

Now let's look at some techniques that employ the IP/ICMP translation algorithm to translate IPv4 and IPv6 packets.

3.3.2 Bump in the Host (BIH)

Bump in the host (BIH) is a host-based IPv4/IPv6 translation technique that enables a host running IPv4 applications to communicate with IPv6-only hosts. The concept is to shield IPv4 applications from any knowledge of the underlying IPv6 communications. The class of IPv4 applications for which BIH applies include those that use DNS for address resolution and that do not use IP address literals in application protocol payloads. Defined in RFC 6535 [49], BIH is not recommended for use in conjunction with NAT64, which would introduce double protocol translation, and is recommended only when native dual stack or tunneling cannot be used.

BIH is a successor combination of bump in the stack (BIS [50]) and bump in the API (BIA [51]) technologies. As such it incorporates a choice of either of these techniques where BIS translates IP packets in the IP stack (network) layer while BIA translates at the application programming interface (API) or socket layer.

The API (socket) layer strategy, the recommended alternative among the two architectures, translates between IPv4 and IPv6 APIs and is implemented between the application and TCP/UDP layer of the stack on the host. The architecture of this approach comprises an API Translator, Address Mapper, Extension Name Resolver, and Function Mapper as depicted in Figure 3-21.

When the IPv4 application sends a DNS query to determine the IP address of a destination host, the Extension Name Resolver intercepts the query and creates an additional query requesting AAAA records. An affirmative DNS reply to the A record query will provide the answer to the API query with the given IPv4 address. Resolution of only a AAAA record stimulates the extension name resolver to request an IPv4 address from the Address Mapper to map to the returned IPv6 address. The Name Resolver utilizes the mapped IPv4 address to create an A record response to the application via the API. The Address Mapper maintains this mapping of IPv6 addresses to those IPv4 adddresses assigned from an internal address pool consisting of the private (RFC 1918) IPv4 address space. The Function Mapper intercepts API function calls and maps IPv4 API calls to IPv6 socket calls and returns results as in response to the IPv4 API call.

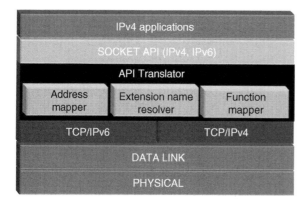

Figure 3-21. BIH socket-based architecture.

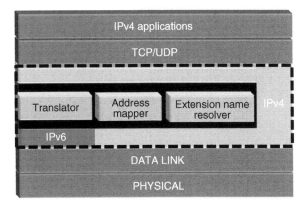

Figure 3-22. BIH network layer architecture.

The network layer approach snoops data flowing between the TCP/IPv4 module and link layer devices (e.g., network interface cards) and translates the IPv4 packet into IPv6. The components of the network layer approach are shown in Figure 3-22.

The Translator component translates the IPv4 header into an IPv6 header according to the IP/ICMP translation algorithm described in the prior section. The Extension Name Resolver snoops DNS queries for A record types; upon detecting such a query, the Extension Name Resolver component creates an additional query for the AAAA record type for the same host domain name (Qname) and class (Qclass). If no affirmative answer is received from the AAAA query, the communications ensues using IPv4; if the AAAA query is successfully resolved, the Extension Name Resolver instructs the Address Mapper component to associate the returned IPv4 address (A record) with the returned IPv6 address (AAAA record). If only a AAAA response is received, the Address Mapper assigns an IPv4 address from an internally configured pool of private IPv4 addresses.

The IPv4 address is needed in order to provide a response up the stack to the application requesting resolution to the A query. Thus, the Address Mapper maintains the association of the real or self-assigned IPv4 address with the IPv6 address of the destination. Any data packets destined to that IPv4 address are then translated by the Translator into IPv6 packets for transmission via IPv6 networks.

Requests for PTR records that map a given IP address to a host domain name are handled by either form of BIH. The PTR call/query is intercepted and if the corresponding IP address has been mapped by the Address Mapper, a PTR query for the corresponding IPv6 address will be issued and the host domain name results mapped to the original request.

DNSSEC validation of DNS queries is natively supported in the socket version of BIH as socket calls simply request resolution and validation is handled at the resolver/network level. Support for the network layer approach requires configuration of the Extension Name Resolver with trusted keys to assure it can validate DNSSEC responses.

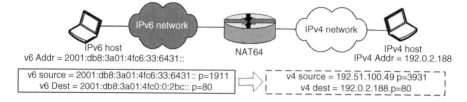

Figure 3-23. NAT64 protocol and address translation.

In the case of the BIH host receiving an IPv6 packet initiated from an external host that is not already mapped, the Address Mapper will assign an IPv4 address from its internal pool and translate the IPv6 header into IPv4 for communication up the stack.

3.3.3 Network Address Translation for IPv6/IPv4 (NAT64)

NAT64 is defined in RFC 6146 [52] and defines the functions of stateful operation. NAT64 enables IPv6 hosts to initiate connections to IPv4 hosts but not the reverse, barring an existing configuration of IPv4/IPv6 address mappings in the NAT64 gateway. NAT64 uses a network address and port translation (NAPT) approach to conserve IPv4 addresses. This approach enables a single IPv4 address to map to multiple IPv6 addresses by virtue of differentiating the TCP/UDP source port number. For example a host initiating a UDP/IP packet with source IPv6 address 2001:db8::1 and port 4040 might by mapped outbound from the NAT64 gateway as having source IPv4 address 192.0.2.31 and port 1024, while another IPv6 host using 2001:db8::2 port 3701 might be mapped to 192.0.2.31 port 1025. This protocol mapping information is stored in a binding information base (BIB), of which three are dynamically maintained: one for TCP, one for UDP and one for ICMP (ICMP identifiers are associated with addresses instead of port numbers). Likewise three session tables, one for each of these upper layer protocols is maintained to track each session in terms of source and destination addresses and ports for the IPv4 leg and the IPv6 leg. In the example in Figure 3-23, a slightly modified reproduction of Figure 3-20, we've added port numbers, signified by the p=<port> notation shown within each data packet. If this was a TCP session, the TCP BIB would contain:

$$(2001 : db8 : 3a01 : 4fc6 : 33 : 6431 ::, 1911) \Leftrightarrow (195.51.100.49, 3931)$$

And the TCP session base would track the entry:

$$(2001 : db8 : 3a01 : 4fc6 : 33 : 6431 ::, 1911), (2001 : db8 : 3a01 : 4fc0 : 0 : 2bc ::, 80) \Leftrightarrow$$
$$(195.51.100.49, 3931), (192.0.2.188, 80)$$

Thus at a basic level, the NAT64 performs two main functions: IP/ICMP protocol translation in accordance with the discussion in the prior section and address translation to map inbound and outbound addresses. Address translation requires the NAT64 gateway to maintain two address pools: an IPv6 address pool to represent IPv4 addresses within the IPv6 network and an IPv4 address pool to represent IPv6

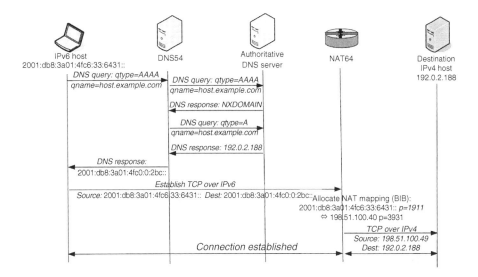

Figure 3-24. DNS64 resolution process.

addresses in the IPv4 network. The IPv6 address pool consists of the prefix allocated for the purpose of IP/ICMP translation we discussed earlier, for example, 2001: db8:3a01:4f00::/56 per our prior example. The IPv4 address pool is an allocation of public IPv4 addresses for use in initiating IPv4 communications on behalf of IPv6 originating hosts, which in our preceding example was 195.51.100.0/24. We'll discuss the relationship between NAT64 and DNS64 next.

3.3.3.1 NAT64 and DNS64 As we just discussed, NAT64 translates IPv6 packets into IPv4 packets using the IP/ICMP translation process described earlier in this chapter, with the optional addition of a stateful component, featuring an IPv4/IPv6 address mapping process independent of the IPv4 address being translated. Using either stateless or stateful translation enables an IPv6 host to communicate with IPv4 destinations.

Key to this strategy is the DNS64 component, which is a special recursive DNS server in that it processes queries for AAAA records normally and passes through valid responses for IPv6 addresses, but it additionally issues A record queries for failed AAAA responses in an attempt to identify an IPv4 destination address in the absence of an IPv6 address. If a valid A resource record set is received by the DNS64 server, it formulates a response to the resolver for the initial AAAA query comprised of the IPv4-converted IPv6 address in accordance with the IP/ICMP translation algorithm previously described. This process is illustrated in Figure 3-24 for the connection example just discussed.

3.3.4 Other Translation Techniques

Other translation techniques utilizing network gateways are summarized here for completeness and in some cases for historical trivia.

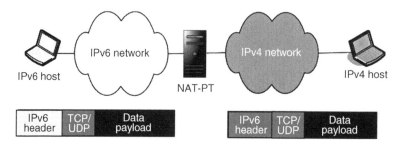

Figure 3-25. NAT-PT deployment (deprecated) [53].

3.3.4.1 Network Address Translation with Port Translation (NAT-PT) As the name implies, the NAT-PT [53] process entails translating IPv4 addresses into IPv6 addresses like a familiar IPv4 NAT, but also performs protocol header translation as described earlier[6]. A NAT-PT device serves as a gateway between an IPv6 network and an IPv4 network and enables native IPv6 devices to communicate with hosts on the IPv4 Internet for example. The NAT-PT device maintains an IPv4 address pool, and associates a given IPv4 address with an IPv6 address while the communications ensues. Figure 3-25 illustrates the architecture of a NAT-PT deployment. For numerous reasons enumerated in RFC 4966 [54], NAT-PT has been deprecated and should not be deployed.

3.3.4.2 Network Address Port Translation with Protocol Translation (NAPT-PT) NAPT-PT enables IPv6 nodes to communicate with IPv4 nodes using a single IPv4 address. Thus, in Figure 3-25, instead of maintaining a one-to-one association of an IPv6 address and a unique IPv4 address as in NAT-PT, NAPT-PT maps each IPv6 address to a common IPv4 address with a unique TCP or UDP port value set in the corresponding IPv4 packet. The use of a single shared IPv4 address minimizes the possibility of IPv4 address pool depletion under the NAT-PT scenario and is a technique used for NAT64 as described earlier.

3.3.4.3 SOCKS IPv6/IPv4 Gateway SOCKS, defined in RFC 1928 [55], provides transport relay for applications traversing firewalls, effectively providing application proxy services. RFC 3089 [56] applies the SOCKS protocol for translating IPv4 and IPv6 communications. And like the other translation technologies already discussed, this approach includes special DNS treatment, termed *DNS name resolving delegation*, which delegates name resolution from the resolver client to the SOCKS IPv6/IPv4 gateway. An IPv4 or IPv6 application can be "socksified" to communicate with the SOCKS gateway proxy for ultimate connection to a host supporting the opposite protocol. Figure 3-26 illustrates the case of an IPv6 host configured with a SOCKS client connecting to an IPv4 host. A socksified IPv4

---

[6] With the exception of the source and destination IP address fields which are governed by associations within the NAT-PT gateway.

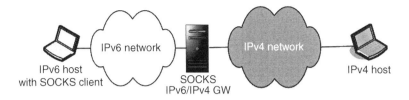

Figure 3-26. Basic SOCKS gateway configuration [56].

host could just as well communicate via the SOCKS gateway to an IPv6 host, from right-to-left.

3.3.4.4 Transport Relay Translator (TRT)   Much like the SOCKS configuration, TRT [57] features a stateful gateway device that interlinks two "independent" connections over different networks. The TCP/UDP connection from a host terminates on the TRT, and the TRT creates a separate connection to the destination host and relays between the two connections. TRT requires a DNS-Application Layer Gateway, DNS-ALG[7], which acts as a DNS proxy. TRT is specified to enable IPv6 hosts to communicate with IPv4 destinations. As such, the primary function of the DNS-ALG is to perform a AAAA resource record query as requested by IPv6 resolvers; if a AAAA record is returned, the reply is passed on to the resolver and the data connection may ensue as an IPv6 connection. If no AAAA records are returned, the DNS-ALG performs an A record query, and if an answer is received, the DNS-ALG formulates an IPv6 address using the IPv4 address contained in the returned A record. RFC 3142, which defines TRT as an informational RFC, specifies use of the prefix C6::/64 followed by 32 zeroes plus the 32-bit IPv4 address. However, IANA has not allocated the C6::/64 prefix. Thus a locally configured prefix is required instead (Figure 3-27).

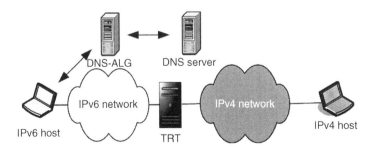

Figure 3-27.   TRT configuration with DNS-ALG [57].

---

[7] Sometimes referred to as "trick or treat DNS-ALG" or totd.

3.3.4.5 Application Layer Gateway (ALG) ALGs perform protocol translation at the application layer and perform application proxy functions, similar to HTTP proxies. A client's application would typically need to be configured with the IP address of the proxy server, to which a connection would be made upon opening the application, for example, web browser for the HTTP proxy case. An ALG may be useful for web or other application-specific access to the IPv4 Internet by hosts on an IPv6-only network.

3.4 APPLICATION SUPPORT OF IPv6

The de facto application programming interface (API) for TCP/IP applications is the *sockets* interface originally implemented on BSD UNIX. The sockets interface defines program calls to enable applications to interface with TCP/IP layers to communicate over IP networks. Microsoft's Winsock API is also based on the sockets interface. Both sockets and Winsock interfaces have been modified to support IPv6's longer address size and additional features. In fact, most major operating system have implemented support for sockets or Winsock including Microsoft (XP SP1, Vista, 7, Server 2003 & 2008), Solaris (8+), Linux (kernel 2.4+), Mac OS (X.10.2), AIX (4.3+), and HP-UX (11i with upgrade).

The updated sockets interface supports both IPv4 and IPv6 and provides the ability for IPv6 applications to interoperate with IPv4 applications by use of IPv4-mapped IPv6 addresses. Check with your applications vendors for IPv6 compatibility and requirements. If your applications use the older non-updated sockets calls such as *gethostbyname( )*, for example, this portion of the application will require updating, which may not be trivial. As an example, please refer to [58] for more details on one application developer's experience.

3.5 SERVICE PROVIDER IPv4/IPv6 CO-EXISTENCE[8]

Service providers, residential broadband service providers in particular, can implement IPv6 within their networks and ultimately deploy IPv6 addresses to customers. However, their network is generally more complex than an enterprise, which can be roughly broken down into an internal enterprise network domain and an external Internet-facing public domain. Remaining at the same high and perhaps over-simplified network view, a service provider adds to the two domain model a third domain, the customer access network. The addition of this third domain requires an IPv6 deployment approach that utilizes one or several of the techniques discussed so far in this chapter.

The customer premises equipment (CPE), typically a router, cable modem, fiber termination unit, or wireless router device, terminates the service provider access link and is referred to as a customer-edge (CE) router. The CE router forwards all outbound customer-initiated IP packets to the service provider network via the

---

[8] Portions of the section are based on [59].

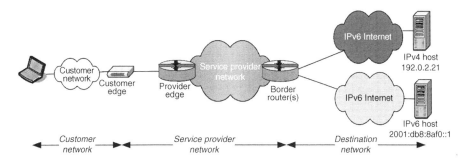

Figure 3-28. Basic three layer architecture: customer/service provider/destination.

provider-edge (PE) router to which its connection to the service provider network terminates. The PE router then routes the packets to other customer-facing PE routers or the Internet either directly or via service provider core or backbone routers (also known as *provider* or *P* routers).

Conversely, the PE router routes inbound traffic to the customer site from the service provider network originating from the Internet or other customer sites for business network applications. The service provider "core" network consists of P routers which route packets among themselves and PE routers. The service provider generally provisions the service-provider facing network interface of the CE device with an IP address. For business applications, the CE router is the interface to several networks within the corresponding customer site, whereas for residential applications, the CE device sometimes serves as a DHCP server to provision addresses to a relatively small number of hosts for IP services.

3.5.1 Reference Architecture

Within the service provider network, IP packets can be routed over a variety of underlying services such as multi-protocol label switching (MPLS) ultimately to the intended destination. For destinations accessible via the public Internet, the destination host may be accessible via an IPv4 address (via "IPv4 Internet"), IPv6 address (via "IPv6 Internet") or both. Physically, this is one Internet, though we illustrate it as logically separate to distinguish IP routing by version. Connectivity to one or both of these "Internets" depends on service provider capabilities and route advertisements in terms of supporting routing via IPv4, IPv6, or both (Figure 3-28).

We'll consider the deployment of IPv6 along each of the three tiers of this basic architecture:

- *Customer Network.* Depends on whether the service provider supports IPv4, IPv6, or both versions for customers.
- *Service Provider Network.* The PEs and "core" of the service provider's network interconnecting customers and the Internet.
- *Destination Network.* Depending on the capabilities of the destination web site, email server, and so on, reachability may require one or either IP version.

3.5.2 Deployment Approaches Overview

The service provider generally controls their network and in most cases, the IP address assigned to the service provider-facing interface of the CE device. The customer may independently implement either protocol version, though their ability to connect via a particular version of IP will depend in part on the version supported by the intended destination and on the transport supported by the service provider. Table 3-9 summarizes the connectivity options available across this simple three-tier architecture for differing IP versions at each tier.

The first four rows of the table illustrate connectivity options for a service provider maintaining an IPv4 network, at least for the time being. For example, the first row of the table highlights an end-to-end IPv4 connection, which reflects today's dominant transport scenario. To support any other scenario in the following three rows, implementation of some form of IPv6 compatibility is required. In the second and third rows, support of IPv4 customers communicating with IPv6 destinations and vice-versa, requires deployment of dual stack. The fourth row interconnects IPv6 endpoints via the service provider IPv4 network. Various approaches are available to address this scenario including dual stack, end-to-end configured tunnels (e.g., VPNs), 6rd, or if using MPLS, 6PE, or 6VPE.

The four rows at the bottom of the table illustrate a service provider implementation of IPv6 and its ability or requirements to support various connection types. Of course service providers may implement multiple technologies at once during a phased IPv6 deployment; for example, phased in by market or geography.

As is clear from the table, the dual stack option offers support of all combinations, though it requires a comprehensive IPv4/IPv6 address plan and implementation of dual stack on PE or all service provider routers. To state the obvious, note that when configuring dual stack or other approaches serving both versions facing the Internet, border routers must be configured to advertise both IPv4 and IPv6 routes.

3.5.3 Routing Infrastructure Deployment Approaches

This section provides an overview of each of these implementation strategies. We won't address the configured tunnels option as this implies a pre-arranged VPN or tunnel between the customer and destination network hosts to tunnel over the service provider's network, without direct involvement by the service provider. Automated tunnels or "softwires" are tunnels created on the fly and are core components of several deployment approaches as we'll see.

3.5.3.1 NAT444 The NAT444 [60] strategy is technically not an IPv6 implementation strategy. But the NAT444 approach serves as a means of "buying time" in prolonging the lifecycle of IPv4 in order to deploy supplemental address space in the form of IPv6. NAT444 features a large scale ("carrier grade") IPv4-IPv4 network address translation (LSN NAT44) gateway which allows multiple subscribers to share a common IPv4 address. NAT44 provides the benefit of not requiring replacement of existing IPv4 CPE though at the cost of limiting the number of customer sessions often required by applications such as AJAX and RSS feeds as well as loss of CPE geolocation information (E911) and more [61] (Figure 3-29).

TABLE 3-9. Basic Deployment Options Based on Protocol Versions Supported

Customer network	Service provider network	Destination network	IPv6 deployment approach								
			NAT444	Dual stack	6PE/6VPE	Config. tunnels	6rd	4over6	Dual stack lite	NAT64 with DNS64	Full IPv6
IPv4	IPv4	IPv4	•								
IPv4	IPv4	IPv6		•							
IPv6	IPv4	IPv4		•							
IPv6	IPv4	IPv6		•	•	•	•				
IPv4	IPv6	IPv4		•		•		•			
IPv4	IPv6	IPv6		•					•		
IPv6	IPv6	IPv4		•		•			•	•	
IPv6	IPv6	IPv6		•							•

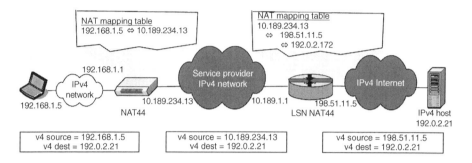

Figure 3-29.   NAT444 architecture.

This architecture shows the use of two NATs in the data path, one within the CPE, translating the home network IPv4 space to service provider-supplied private address space. A second NAT, the LSN NAT44, translates the subscriber's CPE address to a public IPv4 address. Port numbers differentiate different sessions among the same and multiple end customers. The term "NAT444" is illustrative of the dual concatenated IPv4-IPv4 NATs and the resultant use of IP addresses from three IPv4 address spaces (customer private, service provider access, and public Internet).

3.5.3.2 Dual Stack   As described earlier, the dual stack implementation requires the configuration of both an IPv4 address and an IPv6 address on each infrastructure (or at least routing) device, and possibly device interface. A dual stack CPE can function effectively regardless of the version(s) supported by the corresponding service provider; connecting end-to-end however does require protocol continuity between the service provider network and the corresponding destination network.

Support of dual stack within the service provider network may be deployed throughout or on the "edge(s)." For example, PE routers facing customers can implement dual stack to enable support of IPv4 and IPv6 customers, while PE routers facing the Internet enable connectivity using the protocol version of the destination (Figure 3-30). However, without full dual stack deployment also on core routers interconnecting PEs, tunnels between PEs would be required to transport traffic of the version not implemented. This implementation is illustrated in the next section on IPv6 over MPLS deployments.

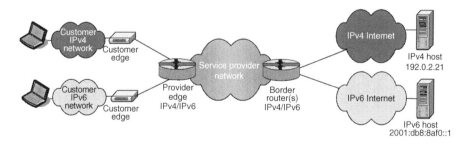

Figure 3-30.   Dual stack architecture.

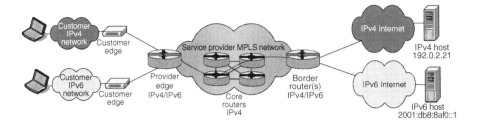

Figure 3-31. 6PE architecture.

3.5.3.3 IPv6 over MPLS There are several approaches for implementing IPv6 over MPLS including support of native IPv6, but the most common interim approaches include IPv6 PE (6PE) over MPLS or IPv6 VPN PE (6VPE) over MPLS (Figure 3-31). The 6PE architecture [62] features dual stack PE routers with IPv4-only core routers; this approach could serve as an intermediate step to full dual stack or IPv6 deployment.

The dual stack PE routers communicate IPv6 network reachability via their respective core-facing IPv4 address(es) via multi-protocol border gateway protocol (MP-BGP) over IPv4. This enables the ingress 6PE router to identify the IPv4 address of the appropriate egress 6PE router and to identify a label switch path (LSP) and associated IPv4 label to enable label switching through the core IPv4 routers to the egress 6PE router. This technique requires use of both an IPv6 label and an outer IPv4 label but obviates the need to pre-define IPv6 over IPv4 tunnels.

The 6VPE [63] architecture is similar at a high level though IPv6 over IPv4 "VPN tunnels" are utilized to traverse the core, which provides improved privacy over 6PE and support of overlapping address space. A given customer's VPN is associated (provisioned) with one or more VPN Routing and Forwarding (VRF) table entry(ies) in corresponding PE devices. The PE router associates the customer's physical circuit into the network (and possibly layer 2 header information) with the appropriate VPN identified within the VRF table.

Each CE device advertises routes (reachable networks at the corresponding site) to its connected PE router(s). An MPLS label is assigned to the VPN (whether by VPN, CE device, or route), and the label is communicated with the corresponding route during MP-BGP route distribution within the service provider's network among other PE routers serving the customer's network (VPN). IPv6 routes are carried over MP-BGP in the VPNv6 address family configurations with next hop reachability information as an IPv4-*mapped* IPv6 address [::ffff:<ipv4_address>]. Since the backbone is IPv4-only, the next hops will be IPv4 addresses to get around the BGP requirement of the next hop being in the same address family. As IPv4 packets arrive on a PE interface from a CE router, the PE router determines the VPN from the VRF table, then applies the corresponding label for use in switching the packets to the appropriate PE and ultimately the destination.

3.5.3.4 6rd (IPv6 Rapid Deployment) RFC 5569 [64] defines "IPv6 Rapid Deployment on IPv4 Infrastructures (6rd)" as a technique to enable a service provider to provision IPv6 addresses to end customers for IPv6 connectivity while maintaining an IPv4 infrastructure. RFC 5969 [65] specifies the 6rd protocol. This method calls for softwire tunneling of customer IPv6 traffic from the customer premises to an IPv6 destination via a modified 6to4 technique. The modification entails use of the service provider's IPv6 prefix (/32) in lieu of the 6to4 prefix, 2002::/16 to provide better round-trip control as opposed to relying on loosely maintained 6to4 anycast relays.

Like 6to4, the next 32 bits of the 6rd IPv6 prefix consists of the IPv4 address of the 6to4 gateway, in this case the customer premises broadband router. Hence a 6to4 prefix is defined as 2002:{32-bit IPv4 address}::/48, while the 6rd prefix is {32-bit service provider IPv6 prefix}:{32-bit IPv4 address}::/64.

This enables the service provider to provision a /64 to each customer, which comprises a single IPv6 subnet. Thus, a service provider with an RIR-allocated IPv6 block 2001:db8::/32 would provision a customer gateway device with IPv4 address 192.0.2.130 with a 6rd subnet address of 2001:db8:c000:282::/64 as shown in Figure 3-32.

A device within the residence requiring an IPv6 address would assign an address from this subnet. For example, in Figure 3-32, a PC is assigned IPv6 address 2001:db8: c000:282::9a. The 6rd customer gateway tunnels native IPv6 packets over IPv4 to a 6rd gateway (relay router). The other address-related change between 6rd and 6to4 is that the 6to4 anycast address is fixed (192.88.99.1), while the 6rd anycast address is defined by the service provider themselves from its own address space. Each customer router must be provisioned with the 6rd relay agent or anycast address(es).

The 6rd relay router terminates the IPv4 tunnel, then routes the IPv6 packet natively to its destination. The use of the service provider's prefix enables 6rd-reachable destinations to be advertised along with the service provider's native IPv6 traffic.

3.5.3.5 4over6 The 4over6 approach, specified in RFC 5747 [67], is an automated tunneling (i.e., softwire) approach for interconnecting IPv4 subscribers to IPv4 destinations via an IPv6 network. As a converse to the 6PE approach, 4over6

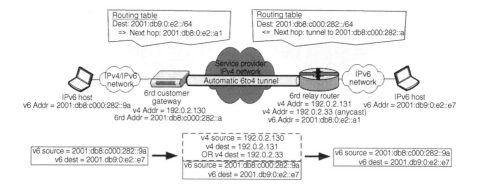

Figure 3-32. 6rd deployment example [66].

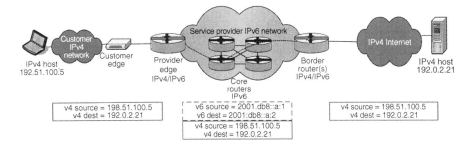

Figure 3-33. 4over6 example.

features an IPv6 core of P routers which route native IPv6 packets and IPv4 packets tunneled over IPv6 among the PE routers. A subscriber with IPv4 address space can communicate with an IPv4 destination using this technique.

Each CE router provides routing updates to its connected PE router. The PE routers use MP-BGP to communicate 4over6 routes and PE routers route traffic accordingly. Considering Figure 3-33, the subscriber CE on the left side of the diagram advertises reachability to the 198.51.100.0/24 network while the destination CE (not shown in the figure explicitly) advertises reachability to 192.0.2.0/24. The respective PE routers use MP-BGP to communicate this reachability. When a packet arrives at the PE router on the left of the diagram, the route to the destination is identified and the packet is encapsulated with an IPv6 header for routing via the IPv6 core (P) routers. Upon receipt of the IPv6 packet at the egress PE router, the PE router decapsulates the packet (removes the IPv6 header) and routes the original IPv4 packet to its destination via the serving CE router.

The current 4over6 architecture supports only a single autonomous system (AS) number, so support of multiple customer private networks is limited, though support of multiple AS numbers is an area of future study.

3.5.3.6 *Dual-Stack Lite* Dual-stack lite [68] is a technology that enables a service provider to deploy IPv6 within their network, while facilitating long-term support and efficient utilization of IPv4 addresses assigned to customer network devices. Service providers typically assign an IP address to a customer router or gateway which interfaces directly to the broadband access network. The customer gateway performs DHCP server functions in assigning IP addresses to IP devices in the home network. The assumption is that such home network devices will support only IPv4 for quite some time.

The components comprising a dual-stack lite implementation include the following:

- *Basic Bridging BroadBand (B4) Element*. Bridges the IPv4 home network with an IPv6 network; the B4 function may reside on the customer gateway device or within the service provider network.
- *Softwire IPv4-in-IPv6 Tunnel*. Tunnels IPv4 traffic between the B4 and the AFTR over IPv6.

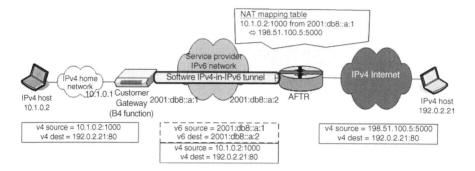

Figure 3-34. Dual-stack lite architecture [68].

- *Address Family Translation Router* (AFTR). Terminates the IPv4-in-IPv6 softwire tunnel with the B4 element and also performs IPv4-IPv4 NAT functionality.

Figure 3-34 illustrates the inter-relationship of these three components within an end-to-end IP connection. Starting on the left of the figure, the IPv4 host obtains an IPv4 address, 10.1.0.2, from the DHCP server function of the customer gateway. Let's say this IPv4 host desires to connect to a website, which has been resolved to IP address 192.0.2.21. The IPv4 host formulates an IP packet with source address 10.1.0.2 and source port of 1000 for example, and destination address 192.0.2.21 port 80. The host transmits this packet to its default route, the customer edge gateway.

The customer gateway in this example includes the B4 element, which sets up the softwire IPv4-in-IPv6 tunnel if it is not already established. The customer gateway has been assigned an IPv6 address on its WAN port (facing the service provider network) and it is over this connection that the tunnel is established. The customer gateway has also been configured with the AFTR IPv6 address manually or via DHCPv6. As shown in Figure 3-34, the B4 element encapsulates the original IPv4 packet with an IPv6 header and transmits it to the AFTR.

The AFTR terminates the tunnel and removes the IPv6 header. The AFTR then performs an IPv4-IPv4 NAT function. This is required to translate the original packet's private (RFC 1918) IPv4 source address into a public IPv4 address. Thus, the service provider must provision a pool of public IPv4 addresses which can be used as source IP addresses on packets destined for an IPv4 destination as in this case. This pooling enables the service provider to more efficiently utilize the increasingly scare public IPv4 address space. The AFTR also generally performs port translation as well and must track this mapping for each NAT operation in order to properly map IPv4 addresses and port numbers bi-directionally.

In Figure 3-34, the AFTR has mapped the customer's source IPv4 address and port, 10.1.0.2:1000 to 198.51.100.5:5000. Since customers generally utilize private address space where overlaps may occur, the NAT mapping table also tracks the tunnel over which the packet originated. The packet ultimately transmitted to

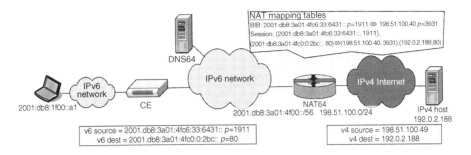

Figure 3-35. NAT64/DNS64 service provider architecture.

the destination host includes this mapped IPv4 address and port, 198.51.100.5:5000. Return packets destined for this address/port are mapped to [destination] address 10.1.0.2:1000 and tunneled to 2001:db8::a:1.

Customers deploying native IPv6 or dual stack hosts can have respective IPv6 addresses provided by DHCPv6 functionality implemented in the customer gateway or via autoconfiguration. IPv6 packets transmitted over the home network to the customer gateway would not utilize the softwire tunnel, but instead be routed natively over the service provider IPv6 access network.

3.5.3.7 NAT64/DNS64   As we discussed in detail earlier in this chapter, the NAT64/DNS64 solution facilitates communications from IPv6 hosts to IPv4 destinations. For service providers, this approach is applicable when CPE are deployed that support IPv6 only as it enables subscribers to communicate with the IPv4 Internet, which will be around for quite some time. The basic architecture from a service provider perspective is illustrated in Figure 3-35. An IPv6 host desiring to initiate a web session may initiate a DNS resolution for the corresponding IP address. Having deployed DNS64 functionality on their recursive name servers, the service provider is able to automatically translate the requested host address (in this case IPv4 only) into an IPv6 address to enable http session establishment via the NAT64 gateway.

Whether a service provider implements IPv6 for subscribers immediately or at some point in the future, DNS64/NAT64 deployment could enable these subscribers to reach what will eventually become legacy IPv4 websites.

3.5.4   Comparison of Deployment Approaches

Table 3-10 summarizes the relative characteristics of each deployment approach.

3.6   ADDRESSING AND DNS CONSIDERATIONS

Whichever strategy(ies) you choose, appropriate IPv6 address allocation and DNS configuration is crucial to the success of IPv6 deployment. Unless you're planning a greenfield deployment, IPv6 address space will need to be managed and allocated in

TABLE 3-10. High Level Comparison of Deployment Approaches

Basic criteria	IPv6 deployment approach								
	NAT444	Dual stack	6PE/6VPE	Config. tunnels	6rd	4over6	Dual stack lite	NAT64 with DNS64	Full IPv6
Business or residential	Both	Both	Bus	Bus	Res	Bus	Res	Both	Both
Provides IPv6 support	No	Yes	Yes	Yes	Yes	Yes	Yes	Yes	Yes
IPv4/IPv6 co-existence	No	Yes	Yes	Yes	Yes	Yes	Yes	Yes	No
Implementation complexity	High	High	Mod	Mod	Low	Low	Mod	High	Mod
Requires CPE changes	No	No	No	No	Yes	No	Yes	No	Yes
Requires new SP equipment	Yes	No	Yes	No	Yes	No	Yes	Yes	No
Incremental operations & troubleshooting complexity	Mod	Mod	Mod	Low	Mod	Mod	Mod	Mod	Mod
Supports overlapping IPv4	Yes	No	6VPE	No	N/A	No	Yes	No	N/A

conjunction with the current and future deployed IPv4 address space. For example, with a dual stack deployment, tracking of IPv4 and IPv6 addresses not only at the subnet level but down to the dual-stacked device interface is critical for accurate IP address inventory and management.

Allocating IPv6 assigned from your RIR requires careful planning. As a general guideline, the difference in prefix length from that of the block you received from your RIR and the address space size you intend to allocate to your customers will dictate what you have to work with in terms of address hierarchy. For example, if you received a /32 from your RIR and plan to allocate /64s to subscribers, you'll have 32 bits with which the address space can be allocated hierarchically, for example, by region (e.g., /36s), city (e.g., /44s), service node (e.g., /52s), and PE (e.g., /56s). This example allocation hierarchy allows up to 16 region allocations from which 256 city allocations may be made respectively, from each of which 256 service node allocations may be made, from which 16 PE allocations may be made, each of which can support 256 /64s (customers). Of course this is just one example and you may have more or fewer levels of differing sizes.

If you are allocating larger blocks to customers, you will have fewer bits to work with. If you are allocating non-uniform address blocks to customers (e.g., /48s to businesses, /64s to SOHO customers), a more sophisticated allocation and tracking mechanism should be considered in terms of allocating space in a sparse, best-fit or a random manner, as we'll describe in Chapter 5.

DNS configuration will drive end user traffic to IPv4 or IPv6 addressable destinations within your network (name space). Resolution of destination addresses is under the scope of the respective domain name administrator. Return of responses for IPv6 addresses (AAAA query types) and not IPv4 (A query type) will indicate to the querying host that this destination is reachable only via IPv6, in which case IPv6 service support will enable connectivity.

Some IPv4/IPv6 transition technologies have direct requirements from DNS, such as NAT64/DNS64. If you allocate reverse zones to customers along with address space, provisioning of the correct (accurate!) ip6.arpa zone and corresponding NS/glue records in your DNS servers is required. This should follow a process similar to that for IPv4 allocations, but with obvious syntactical differences with hexadecimal versus decimal domain labels.

CHAPTER 4

IPv6 READINESS ASSESSMENT

IPv4 is the prevalent protocol used today as the worldwide communications vehicle for the Internet, and serves as the work horse for commercial and residential access. IPv6 has, until now, been used in a limited capacity. However this is already changing and will likely accelerate as IPv6 usage will grow to overtake the role of its older brother. The question of why it has taken so long for IPv6 to be adopted was the topic of many discussions over the last 15 years. The answer is that there was no compelling event such as we saw with Y2K that forced the technology upon us with a deadline. And while IPv4 address space has been running out for some time, the creation of technologies such as NAT helped to lengthen IPv4's lifetime, stalling the adoption of IPv6.

Although some organizations including the U.S. government have identified target dates for their IPv6 deployments, IPv4/IPv6 transition technologies are in place to support a long coexistence and transition time frame. But what will be the IPv6 Internet density trigger that will push IPv6 into the prominent role and when will it happen? Will the adoption of mobile devices drive IPv6's density growth, the depletion of available IPv4 address space, cloud computing, or the explosion of virtualization within the data center? What is the tipping point that will finally move IPv6 into a more prominent role? The answer is "all the above."

Widespread adoption of the IPv6 protocol will materialize in a logical progression that starts with the networking equipment providers, into the service providers, into the application/content providers, and then move its way down into enterprise and residential use. This is a progression that is well under way and happening today with most equipment providers and service providers already having implemented IPv6.

In June 2012, service providers and content providers such as Google (www.google.com), Facebook (www.facebook.com), Bing (www.bing.com), and Yahoo (www.yahoo.com) permanently enabled IPv6 on their main websites. This "World IPv6 Launch" was a major milestone, and marked the beginning of real adoption of IPv6 on the Internet. As a result of World IPv6 Launch, the Internet Society reported that "thousands of companies and millions of websites" now support IPv6 [69]. Leading companies across several industries have made significant investments into supporting IPv6, proving that the protocol is moving from the laboratory and into commercial production environments.

IPv6 Deployment and Management, First Edition. By Michael Dooley and Timothy Rooney.
© 2013 by The Institute of Electrical and Electronics Engineers, Inc. Published 2013 by John Wiley & Sons, Inc.

4.1 PUTTING A PLAN IN PLACE

Given that the deployment of IPv6 is not a question of "if" it will happen but one of "when," how do we prepare? Simply put, by planning. The intent of this book is to help you in the planning process. Having a solid well-thought-out plan in place will streamline the process and reduce surprises during deployment. The planning process to deploy IPv6 should be started now.

No two networks are exactly alike, and specific requirements and infrastructure elements of your network must be addressed when deploying IPv6. As such, the deployment of IPv6 within your organization will not likely be a trivial task. On the other hand, if you've kept your network infrastructure reasonably updated with recent vintage router, switch and operating system versions, you may already be well on your way. Because of the pervasive nature of TCP/IP within your network, the IP fabric weaves through the foundation of the very core of the network, and all impacted groups within the business must be involved. The plan must encompass all the major IT groups including the infrastructure, networking, security, and applications. Any IT partners involved in managing, monitoring, or sourcing IT services such as web hosting, external DNS, and so on, also need to be involved when these organizations' functions fall within the desired scope of IPv6 deployment.

Some key points that need to be considered as part of the plan are as follows:

- Develop a business case that outlines the benefits of IPv6. What it is, why it's needed, and what are the risks associated with the transition. Use this to present to senior management and make sure they have a firm understanding and buy-in to the project. It may make sense to focus initially on a particular scope or subset of your network in order to "pilot" the deployment and to garner a successful deployment to leverage for further deployment. This process was described in Chapter 1.

- Establish a dedicated project work team within your organization that is responsible for IPv6. Require membership from all areas of the IT organization as well as other impacted divisions within your overall organization.

- Understand your current environment. As we'll discuss in this chapter, perform network discovery or use your current IP address management (IPAM) solution to map out your existing IP address space. Take inventory of your existing infrastructure and applications. After all, you need to know where you are now with IPv4, before you can begin your journey to coexisting IPv4/IPv6.

- Leverage external resources if needed. Consider using consultant services to help with network discovery, IPv6 planning, project management, and training if needed.

- Leverage key refresh intervals within the IT organization. The normal hardware and software refresh planned for in most organizations can be used to your advantage to align IPv6 "refreshes" with existing IT refresh plans.

- Develop addressing, security and network management plans and roadmaps specifically related to IPv6. Start this early in the process as this is time consuming and must support existing security architectures within your organization. We dedicate the next three chapters to each of these areas respectively.

4.2 IP NETWORK INVENTORY

4.2.1 IPv6 Readiness

We use the concept of *IPv6 readiness* to represent the compatibility of a piece of networking equipment, operating system, end user device, application or network provider. Be aware that the concept is applicable not only to hardware and software but also encompasses the entire IT function including software, processes, and operational knowledge.

Your organization should create an IPv6 readiness program that is specific to your network. It should include the following:

- A review of your current IP address inventory and utilization.
- An assessment of your network and computing infrastructure with respect to compatibility with IPv6. This should include hardware and software including network services.
- A review of your business applications to make sure they are IPv6 ready and can operate correctly on an IPv6 network.
- An assessment of your organization's technical competency with IPv6 in all roles within your IT organization including engineering, operations, and support.
- A review of current IT processes to make sure they include IPv6.
- Analysis of security policies, architecture, and practices.
- Determination of IPv6 readiness of customer, partner, and supplier systems that your business interacts with over a network.

For each assessment category described above, you should identify and track detailed criteria and categorize each in one of three ways:

- Already IPv6 capable
- Capable with an upgrade
- Not IPv6 capable or upgradable.

To assist with these assessment areas for your network, we have created an IPv6 readiness boilerplate. You can use this boilerplate to identify and categorize IPv6 readiness. Boilerplate sections are described in the sections that follow and the full boilerplate is provided in the appendix; an electronic version is also available at www.ipamworldwide.com.

4.2.2 Discovery

The first step is to identify every component of your network. If you already have a detailed network and computing inventory repository, you are to be congratulated! If you don't or you'd like to verify this inventory information, the goal of the network discovery process is to gather system details directly from each device. Discovery of your network devices in preparation of IPv6 readiness is fairly straightforward using one or more of the many available network element/device discovery tools that are available today, such as the following:

- Netformx Discovery™ [70]
- HP DDMI (Discovery and Dependency Mapping Inventory) [71]
- OPNET NetMapper® [72]

These tools and others like them will provide you with key pieces of information about each element of your network including the vendor, hardware version, and the version of operating system/IOS that is running on the network equipment.

4.2.3 IPv6 Assessment

The next task requires comparing your network inventory with itemized model/version of your network and computing equipment, software, and applications with the published IPv6 capabilities of each. There are very few, if any, tools that can automate this manual and tedious process of comparing devices and software with vendors' datasheets and IPv6 readiness statements.

As you work through the assessment phase analyzing your current network hardware, software, and applications, there are several resources that you can leverage that will help you to identify and evaluate the IPv6 capabilities of your equipment and applications. These resources include vendor information, interoperability testing laboratory results, and general IPv6 readiness informational sites. Here are some resources that may be able to assist you:

- *IPv6 Application Compatibility List—University of Wisconsin-Madison* (*http://kb.wisc.edu/helpdesk//page.php?id=11691*). A collection of IPv6 software application compatibility version information and vendor statements.

- *Comparison of IPv6 Application Support—Wikipedia* (*http://en.wikipedia. org/wiki/Comparison_of_IPv6_application_support*). A listing of IPv6 software application compatibility version information. The information is a bit dated, but does have links to the application developer's sites that should have more current information.

- *IPv6 to Standard—The IETF IPv6 and IPv6 Maintenance Groups* (*http:// www.ipv6-to-standard.org/*). A database maintained by the IETF containing a list of IPv6-enabled products that have achieved successful operational experience with IPv6.

- *IPv6 Forum—IPv6 Ready Logo Program* (*www.ipv6ready.org*). Provides an IPv6 Ready Logo Program Approved List of software and hardware devices. This is a list of software and hardware that have passed the logo specification testing and have achieved IPv6 Ready Status.

- *Equipment and Software Vendors.* Most major equipment and software vendors have updated their websites with IPv6 readiness and IPv6-related compliancy statements. Work closely with vendors to ensure you understand their IPv6 roadmaps if they are not yet fully IPv6 compliant. Demand true

IPv6 support, and be careful to understand the full meaning of partial compliance.

Various vendors do offer IPv6 assessment services to offload this task if you prefer. An IPv6 deployment assessment does not just cover the hardware and software that is capable of running IPv6. An assessment must cover all aspects of your IT fabric including the following:

- IP addressing.
- Critical network services.
- Network infrastructure equipment.
- Software applications including off the shelf and custom built business applications, operational support system (OSS) applications, monitoring systems, provisioning systems, and other support systems.
- Technical skills and knowledge.
- IT-related processes including network management.
- Security policies, architecture, and practices.
- Customer, partner, and supplier systems that your business interacts with over a network.

4.2.3.1 IP Addressing Assessment The first step in the IPv6 assessment process entails identifying currently assigned IP addresses. You must understand completely what IPv4 space you have deployed, how and where it is allocated, and the current utilization. If you are using a free or commercially available IPAM tool to manage your IP address space, then you should have a head start on collecting this data. If not, you need to perform IP address discovery and collect this data. The assessment of your IP address infrastructure must include the following:

- *Allocations of Root Blocks.* Collect a list of all the allocations (IPv4 and IPv6 if any) that your organization currently has and place that information into a repository. This includes public space that you are "leasing" from a Regional Internet Registry (RIR) as well as private address space, that is, RFC 1918 space. An IPAM tool is the perfect repository for this information, but even a simple spreadsheet will work. Include the technical and business contacts assigned to each of these blocks for future reference.
- *An IP Address Plan Itemizing Allocations from Each of Your Root Blocks.* This plan consists of a detailed list or diagram of how the IP address space is allocated within your network. Typically, IP address space is allocated by application and by location and in large networks may be allocated hierarchically in multiple layers. Having these designators of "use" and hierarchy on each IP address allocation is desirable, as well as technical and administrative contact information.
- *IP Utilization Information for All Your IP Address Allocations.* Having the utilization information of each IP address allocation available will save a tremendous amount of time during the design phase. Collect this information

by using network scanning tools (to capture the static address assignments), and by collecting DHCP lease information from your existing DHCP servers. There are several tools and services available on the market today that will assist you in this collection.

- *Establish IP Addressing Policies.* If you don't already have standardized policies that you use within you organization, now is a great time to put those in place. Consider using a template or cookie cutter approach to IP address allocations and assignments, and defining a standardized methodology for allocating space moving forward. Hierarchical allocation is critical to maintaining efficient routing. We'll discuss the logic behind this statement and help guide you in defining IP addressing policies in the next chapter.

The sample IP addressing assessment boilerplate shown in Figure 4-1 enables you to enumerate the root address blocks from each RIR. List each block in CIDR notation in the Block Address column and enter the renewal or end date for each block regarding its status with respective RIRs. Many RIRs have address return policies, so you may be able to take advantage of this over time as you consolidate IPv4 traffic or move completely to IPv6 (though this ultimate end state may take years to reach). If you've already obtained some IPv6 address space or if you're experimenting with the private address equivalent unique local address (ULA) space, denote this from the root and allocation levels as well.

The "Next Steps" column enables you to place a check mark for an item that will require some action when moving forward with IPv6. For example, if you have not yet obtained IPv6 address space, denote the need to do this in the Next Steps column for the IPv6 address space section. An example root block assessment is illustrated in Figure 4-2. In this example, we've denoted a pair of public IPv4 blocks, one fictitiously allocated from ARIN and the other from APNIC. We've denoted the current utilization of these blocks as well as their respective renewal dates and some next steps. We've also noted our private IPv4 space, a single 10.0.0.0/8 block and a pair of 192.168.0.0/16 blocks that resulted from a company acquisition. For each of these, we've also noted the utilization and assessment notes. A 2001:db8:4af0::/48

Functional area	Item	Block address	Usage/ utilization	Assessment	Next Steps
IPv4 address space					
	ARIN root block allocation				
	RIPE root block allocation				
	APNIC root block allocation				
	LACNIC root block allocation				
	AfriNIC root block allocation				
	RFC 1918 root block allocation				
IPv6 address space					
	ARIN root block allocation				
	RIPE root block allocation				
	APNIC root block allocation				
	LACNIC root block allocation				
	AfriNIC root block allocation				
	ULA root block allocation				

Figure 4-1. Sample IP addressing readiness boilerplate.

Functional area	Item	Block address	Usage/ utilization	Assessment	Next Steps
IPv4 address space					
	ARIN root block allocation	192.0.2.0/24	62%	Expires 3/17/2014	Retain for IPv4 Internet
	RIPE root block allocation				
	APNIC root block allocation	198.51.100.0/24	99%	Expires 10/22/2013	Need to supplement with IPv6 allocation
	LACNIC root block allocation				
	AfriNIC root block allocation				
	RFC 1918 root block allocation	10.0.0.0/8	87%	Fully integrated	
		192.168.0.0/16 (Main)	72%	Separated network	
		192.168.0.0/16 (Acquired)	69%	Acquired company network	
IPv6 address space					
	ARIN root block allocation				
	RIPE root block allocation				
	APNIC root block allocation	2001:db8:4af0::/48	1%	Initial allocation	Block to be used for IPv6 deployment
	LACNIC root block allocation				
	AfriNIC root block allocation				
	ULA root block allocation				

Figure 4-2. IP addressing assessment example.

IPv6 block has also been allocated to this organization from the APNIC for our IPv6 deployment efforts.

To supplement your IP address assessment, further document your current IP address plan in the form of a map, list, or spreadsheet that depicts how each public and private root block has been allocated and assigned within your organization, similar to the example below for our 10.0.0.0/8 root block. To the extent possible, model your address space in conjunction with your routing topology. For example, if you implement the common three-tier core-distribution-access topology, denote address allocations at each level, which should roll up hierarchically as shown in Figure 4-3 via indentations for respective address blocks, with a top-level global

Core Site	Region	Sites	IPv4 Networks
Global Allocation			10.0.0.0/8
North America			10.0.0.0/12
	East		10.0.0.0/16
		Philadelphia	10.0.0.0/24
		Montreal	10.0.1.0/24
		Washington	10.0.2.0/24
	Central		10.1.0.0/16
		Ottawa	10.1.0.0/24
		Houston	10.1.0.1/24
		Denver	10.1.0.2/24
	West		10.2.0.0/16
		San Francisco	10.2.0.0/24
		Seattle	10.2.0.1/24
		San Diego	10.2.0.2/24
Europe Allocation			10.16.0.0/12
	East		10.16.0.0/16
		Berlin	10.16.0.0/24
		Kiev	10.16.1.0/24
	West		10.17.0.0/16
		London	10.17.0.0/24
		Paris	10.17.1.0/24
		Rome	10.17.2.0/24

Figure 4-3. Example IP addressing hierarchical allocations.

allocation (/8), a continental core-level allocation (/12), followed by respective regional allocations (/16) and then access/subnet allocations (/24).

4.2.3.2 *Network Infrastructure Boilerplate* The network infrastructure boilerplate provides a convenient tracking sheet for documenting and denoting IPv6 readiness for your core network services, routing and switching infrastructure, end user devices, software applications, and customer or partner connections. We'll discuss each of these areas in turn. Figure 4-4 illustrates a consolidated boilerplate, which enables identification of each network component by identity (IP address, application name, serial number, MAC address, or however you prefer to track your devices and applications). For each component, you should denote the vendor who supplied the component and the current version of the hardware, operating system, and the "function" itself; for example, denote the version of DNS that is installed on a server, which has its own hardware and OS version.

The assessment entails defining the IPv6 capability of each "subcomponent" to determine if the function or item is fully IPv6 capable as is, with an upgrade or not at all. Indicate this by checking one of the corresponding columns on the boilerplate under *Assessment*. The boilerplate also provides sections for denoting any IPv6 limitations or caveats, the need to procure additional units for replacement or testing, and next steps toward IPv6 capability. Let's now explore each of these areas in more detail.

4.2.3.3 *Network Services* Your critical network services must also be assessed early in the process. These services include DNS, DHCP, Radius, and other services needed for basic networking. These foundational services must be upgraded to support IPv6 if they do not already. It is important to note that as you research the capabilities of each of these services, some of them may require configuration and management via IPv4, while providing IPv6 services to network users. In other words, some may be dual stack from a functional aspect. In general, deploying IPv6 cannot be viewed as a replacement for IPv4 and supporting IPv4 and IPv6 together for a long period of time should be expected. The assessment must include the following for each network service within your network:

- Collect the current vendor of the network service that is implemented. This is a good time to document your network services architecture if it does not already exist as part of your overall network plan or map.

- Collect the current version of each network service that is implemented. Denote if each is open source or a commercial network service, and make sure you understand the specific version of the network service.

- Itemize the current hardware platform and operating system of each network service platform. This is important to understand and document, because though the network service may support IPv6 fully, if the underlying hardware and operating system do not, you will not be able to take advantage of these IPv6 capabilities.

Functional area	Item	Item ID	Current vendor	Current version	Current hardware & OS	OS IPv6 capable?	Function IPv6 capable?	Assessment: check one			IPv6 specific limitations	Additional units required	Next steps to IPv6 capability
								Item fully IPv6 capable	Item IPv6 capable with upgrade	Item NOT IPv6 capable			
Network services													
	DHCP												
	DNS												
	NTP/SNTP												
	Radius/Diameter												
	FTP												
	TFTP												
	Rsync												
	SMTP/POP/IMAP												
	HTTP												
	Other												
Network infrastructure													
	Routers												
	Core switches												
	Distribution/edge switches												
	Load balancers												
	Application servers												
	Firewalls												
	SAN/NAS storage systems												
	Wireless access points												
	IP telephony servers												
	Other												
End user/end point systems													
	Desktop/laptop/workstation												
	Tablet/PDA												
	Smart phone												
	Other hand held device												
	Printer												
	Point of sale device												
	CPE device												
	Other												
Software applications													
	Business application 1												
	Network mgmt application 1												
	OSS application 1												
Customer/partner systems/links													
	Partner system 1												
	Partner system 2												

Figure 4-4. Network assessment boilerplate.

99

- Document the current versions' IPv6 capabilities and limitations for each network service. Working with each network service vendor, or by collecting information about open source network services, document the current version's IPv6 capabilities and limitations. Vendors should be able to provide you with an IPv6 readiness statement if requested.

The network services section of the readiness boilerplate provides fields for entry of this information with some network services specific questions and points to consider. Make sure to note IPv6 capability with respect to IPv6 transport as well as supporting IPv6 addresses at the "application" layer as appropriate. You can replicate rows in the boilerplate provide opportunities to review served constituencies for each network service to assist with determining potential capacity issues.

You can have multiple rows for a given network service if needed if you use multiple vendors or you may have one per server if you'd like to track to that granularity. The assessment column should be used to denote whether each network service is able to support both IPv4 and IPv6 requests as is, with a software upgrade, with a hardware upgrade, with upgrades of both hardware and software or not supportable.

You can check one *Assessment* column and then denote such stipulations in the *Next Steps* column and if appropriate with an entry in the "shopping list" or *Additional units required* column. Figure 4-5 illustrates an example assessment within a network comprising a set of ISC and Microsoft DHCP servers. Here, we've "zoomed in" on the worksheet and noted the relevant information for each server, respective IPv6 capability and assessment, and next steps.

In some cases, you may want to add a network service to the shopping list even if your current network service can support both IPv4 and IPv6. This strategy seeks to minimize the risk of modifying a working IPv4 configuration to support the unproven configuration of both IPv4 and IPv6. Your assessment should indicate this, whether a new network service is required for functional reasons, or required/desired for risk mitigation. Isolating IPv6 network services traffic can help soak in IPv6 operation without impacting IPv4 operation until a comfort level is attained with IPv6. In addition, you may desire to procure one or more network services servers for your test laboratory if you don't have servers available for the testing phase of deployment. In any case, if a particular network service requires an upgrade of any kind, replacement, supplementation, or laboratory installation, note this in the *Next Steps* column.

4.2.3.4   *Network Infrastructure Equipment*   While many hardware and application vendors support IPv6 in various capacities, hardware or software upgrades may be needed. Most recent vintage network infrastructure equipment and software already supports IPv6 at least to some degree. Make sure you identify particular IPv6 features you intend to use, that is, Mobile IPv6 or address autoconfiguration, and verify feature support per vendor.

	Item	Item ID	Current vendor	Current version	Current hardware & OS	OS IPv6 capable?	Function IPv6 capable?	Assessment: check one			IPv6 specific limitations	Additional units required	Next steps to IPv6 capability
								Item fully IPv6 capable	Item IPv6 capable with upgrade	Item NOT IPv6 capable			
services													
	DHCP	10.200.0.11	ISC	3.2	RHEL v5	Yes	No		✓				Upgrade to ISC 4.2
		10.16.35.98	ISC	4.1	RHEL v5	Yes	Yes	✓			DHCPv4 or v6 not both	1	
		172.19.23.55	Microsoft	2003	Win 2003	Yes	No		✓				Upgrade to 2008R2
		10.104.39.213	Microsoft	2008R2	Win 2008R2	Yes	Yes	✓				2	

Figure 4-5. Example DHCP assessment entries.

Vendors should be able to provide you with all the detail that you need on the IPv6 readiness and capabilities of their equipment. There are also a number of resources available on the Internet, specifically IPv6 interoperability laboratories that have documented IPv6 testing and interoperability test results. To complete your assessment, perform the following:

- Itemize the current vendor and model of the network equipment that is implemented. This may be a good time to implement a network equipment asset system if your organization does not already have one in place.

- Enumerate the current version of the operating system or software that is running on the network equipment. This may be a good time to standardize on operating system code levels if your organization hasn't already.

- Identify current equipment IPv6 capabilities and limitations. Working with the vendor, or by collecting information about open source network services, document the current version's IPv6 capabilities and limitations. Vendors should be able to provide you with an IPv6 readiness statement if requested.

As with the network services section of the boilerplate, you may want to replicate rows for each network infrastructure implementation in your network to track each device and application individually, or you may simply summarize by type and version. Indicate IPv6 capability at the transport level and the processing level. For those elements requiring a software and/or hardware upgrade or replacement, denote the specifics in the Next Steps column. Also denote any desired procurements for sparing or laboratory installations in the *Additional Units Required* column.

4.2.3.5   *End User/End Point Equipment*   The bulk of the devices within most organizations consists of end user and end point devices. End user equipment also often comprises the widest diversity of device types, especially with the explosion of "BYOD" (Bring your own device) onto today's corporate networks. This volume and diversity is growing as well. From a service provider perspective, end point equipment likely consists of customer premises equipment (CPE) such as customer edge routers, or wireless, fiber, DSL or cable modems.

As with all of the other hardware and software that connects to your network, all end user and end point devices should be assessed as well to the extent possible. Unlike network equipment, upon which most organizations have standardized preferred vendors and models, the end point devices may be quite varied and the sheer volume of different device types may require a bit of work for proper IPv6 readiness assessment. We recommend focusing on the critical devices first, such as laptops, desktops, printers, VoIP phones, point of sale, and handheld devices that are critical to the business.

To complete your assessment, perform the following:

- Itemize the current vendor and model of the end user/point equipment that is being used on your network. If you provide laptops and desktops to your employees, you most likely have an asset database that you can query.
- Enumerate the current version of the operating system or software that is running on these devices. Focus on the most critical systems first.
- Identify current equipment IPv6 capabilities and limitations. Working with the vendor, or by collecting information about open source network services, document the current version's IPv6 capabilities and limitations. Vendors should be able to provide you with an IPv6 readiness statement if requested.

Assess each version of end user device type by replicating item rows, and completing the assessment for each. Test each device type's IPv4 and IPv6 stack as well as support for planned tunneling technology support. If you plan to use translation, your predeployment test plan will need to include testing on common end user devices to assure proper communications as discussed in Chapter 8.

Test common or corporate applications as appropriate for each device type to identify any issues with IPv6 address representation or DNS processing. Consult corresponding vendor information regarding any questions or issues identified. For any detected shortcomings, record these in the corresponding *IPv6 specific limitations* column and mitigation paths in the *Next Steps* column. In addition, you may want to procure a quantity for device types that pass your IPv6 readiness assessment but require predeployment testing as a reminder.

4.2.3.6 Software Applications

As most of us know all too well, upgrading a critical business application, management software, or a custom-coded system to a new version can become a major project on its own. It is extremely important to get an accurate and complete inventory of your software applications early in the process. The lead time needed to upgrade software can be lengthy waiting for vendors to complete a release, test it internally, and then facilitate a project for deployment. Fortunately, IPv6 has been on the radar for a very long time, and most vendors have added or are in the process of adding IPv6 support.

The assessment must include the following:

- Itemize the current vendor of the software that is implemented. This may be a good time to implement a software asset system if your organization does not already have one in place.
- Denote the current version of the software that each is running.
- Note any component dependencies such as database vendors and versions and assess IPv6 readiness of each component.
- List the purpose of each application.

- Identify and document the current software's IPv6 capabilities and limitations, working with the vendor or software developers. Vendors should be able to provide you with an IPv6 readiness statement if requested.

As with network services and network infrastructure, replicate row sets for each business, network management, and OSS application in use in your network. For each, identify its IPv6 capability and limitations and determine actions required to achieve IPv6 support. Make sure to test the "client" side of the application from common end user devices as mentioned in the prior section. Don't forget to update the *Next Steps* column for applications requiring an upgrade, supplementation, or replacement.

4.2.3.7   Customer, Partner, and Supplier Systems   Any customer, partner, and supplier systems that your business interacts with over a network will need to be reviewed for compatibility. In many cases, you will need to work on a plan with your partners and suppliers to allow IPv6 traffic. Identify specific upgrades and/or configuration parameter changes required to bring partner and supplier systems into IPv6 compliance and document this in the *Next Steps* column for those requiring action.

4.2.3.8   Processes, Practices, and Staff Readiness   The third major assessment area beyond IP addressing and network infrastructure entails assessing existing management and security practices and processes, as well as overall staff readiness for IPv6. An example boilerplate for these key areas is illustrated in Figure 4-6.

Itemize each process and staff member in respective rows. For each process, determine if IPv6 has been considered. IPv6 will need to be added in some form to most security and management processes and practices. Staff members will need to be well versed if not expert in IPv6, depending on respective roles.

Functional Area	Item	IPv6 ready or certified?	Next steps to incorporate IPv6
IT management processes			
	Process 1		
	Process 2		
Security processes			
	Process 1		
	Process 2		
Staff readiness			
	Network architect 1		
	Network engineer/analyst 1		
	Network technician 1		
	IT help desk staff 1		

Figure 4-6.   Process and staff readiness assessment.

4.2.3.9   Technical Skills and Knowledge   Training your engineers is a vital part of your IPv6 deployment. Although there are a number of available resources for IPv6 technical training, the IPv6 Forum launched an IPv6 Education Certification program in order to facilitate consistent training programs for IPv6. The program was designed to help encourage and accelerate the education on IPv6 and promote faster adoption of the protocol. There are several vendors that offer IPv6 courses. Look for the vendors that are certified IPv6 trainers and courses that have achieved IPv6 certified logos. The IPv6 forum offers a database that contains the list of IPv6 certified instructors. Some organizations worth noting are

- IPv6college—A business unit of Tonex
- Nephos6
- 6Deploy

For each position type, list each staff member and his or her current level of IPv6 expertise and corresponding training required to attain the desired level. You can leave the *Next Steps* column empty for any staff members who are already at the IPv6 expertise level required of their position, but for others indicate recommended IPv6 training courses in this column.

4.2.3.10   IT-Related Processes   Every IT organization has IT-related processes; some are more formal than others. If you employ ITIL® processes to manage your IT network, you can enumerate each process area and assess its IPv6 readiness. Be sure to include these processes in your planning phase and revise to include IPv6-related support. Define your next steps for each process requiring updated documentation and communication to impacted teams.

4.2.3.11   Security Policies, Architecture, and Practices   Even though IPv6 was developed with security in mind, the introduction of IPv6 within a network will challenge the existing security of the network. Your organization's security architecture will need to be reviewed and modified to include IPv6. We'll discuss security in detail in Chapter 6 in terms of security system configurations. At this point, verify the ability to process IPv6 packets. As you review Chapter 6, you may find that particular filtering features are required that may drive further refinement of your assessment to upgrade or replace security hardware and/or software. Review and evaluate the following:

- IPv4 Deployment Architecture Issues. Review the specific vulnerabilities associated with your type of deployment. This will serve as an important security baseline.
- IPv6 intrusion detection systems
- IPv6 capability on firewalls
- Software/hardware patches required specifically for IPv6 security

A brief sample of a partially completed process and staffing assessment is illustrated in Figure 4-7.

Functional Area	Item	IPv6 ready or certified?	Next steps to incorporate IPv6
IT management processes			
	Release management	Yes	Process documentation updated; requires lab verification
	Configuration maangement	No	IPv6 configuration aspects need to be added to this process and tested
Security processes			
	Monitor firewall logs	Policies updated for IPv6	Need to run test cases to verify firewall logging and documented methods and procedures
	Lockdown process	Policies updated for IPv6	Testing required in lab prior to deployment
Staff readiness			
	Steve Jones	Yes	Certified in 2010 - could use a refresher class
	Mary Thompson	Yes	Certified in 2012
	Julia Starkly	No	Schedule training - overview, network engineering
	Greg Libar	No	Schedule training - overview, network engineering
	Mark Alexander	No	Schedule training - overview, help desk

Figure 4-7. Example assessment for processes and staff.

4.3 IPv6 TO DO LIST

Once you have completed the assessment phase, you should have a consolidated itemization of all hardware, software, application, and end user devices on your network. The *Next Steps* column in each completed assessment boilerplate now provides a quick summary of all items requiring action across the various disciplines assessed. Based on this assessment of each of these items, you can create an IPv6 remediation or "To Do" list for each item that requires upgrading, replacement, supplementation, or laboratory procurement to bring into IPv6 compliance and/or to support IPv6 deployment testing. Process updates and training next steps are also key parts of the To Do list.

For those To Do items requiring procurement, you can generate a shopping list, which then needs to be priced out, at least at a high level to ascertain potential capital costs. This information should be fed back to the business case to refine it as more detail is gathered. You may decide to forgo certain noncritical systems due to high cost or lack of benefits. Such "non-IPv6 compliant elements" should be denoted in your network repository. You may also need to scale back on desired laboratory purchases to remain within a budget. Ideally you should prioritize the shopping list by necessity to help determine the range of capital required from best case to absolute minimum as necessary. The sum total for your shopping list can be presented to the key stakeholders within your organization for approval. Don't forget to leverage computing refresh intervals within your IT organization. The normal IT refresh that occurs in most organizations can be used to your advantage and will fall in line with existing overall IT plans.

4.4 IPv6 READINESS ASSESSMENT SUMMARY

Figure 4-8 summarizes in flowchart form the assessment process. Taking stock of every aspect of your IP network and support structure including processes and people is critical to define your starting point and action items for deploying IPv6 within your network and/or within your chosen network scope.

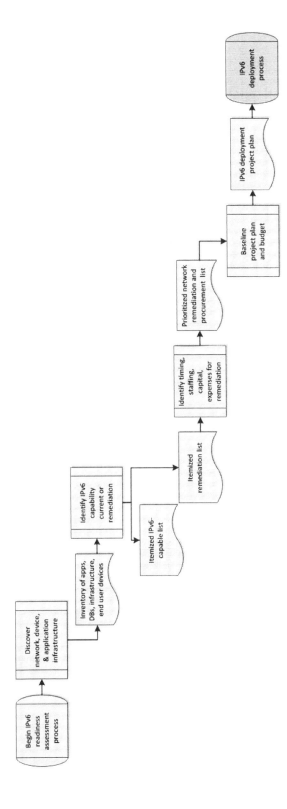

Figure 4-8. Basic IPv6 readiness assessment process.

CHAPTER **5**

IPv6 ADDRESS PLANNING

One output of the IPv6 readiness assessment stage is a complete network inventory listing all infrastructure and user devices along with an inventory of IPv4 and IPv6 address allocations. This IP address inventory should be mapped topologically to the IP network in terms of address roll-ups (aggregation), subnets, and DHCP pools. Many IP address management (IPAM) solutions integrate this functionality, so the discovery process merely validates the IPAM database. If you are not already utilizing an IPAM solution or your IPAM solution does not cover the full IP address life cycle from block to subnet to pool or individual assignment, this mapping will need to be performed manually. If block and subnet allocations have been recorded in spreadsheets or another repository, this information would be helpful input to this process.

A top-to-bottom IP address plan is required to baseline your IPv4 "plan" first to provide a solid foundation on which to overlay your IPv6 addresses. The extent of your IPv6 overlay will depend on your chosen scope of deployment. If you plan to operate a fully dual-stack network, you'll need to allocate IPv6 space wherever you have IPv4 today. If you plan to support IPv6 initially only on Internet-facing infrastructure, your allocation will be limited to this subset of your network. Support of partner links also requires allocation consideration, as well as possible support for tunneling or translation technologies discussed in Chapter 3. In any case, your IPv6 overlay will start with the block you receive from your Regional Internet Registry (RIR) or Internet Service Provider (ISP). Let's take a closer look at this IPv6 addressing hierarchy.

5.1 INTERNET REGISTRIES

IP addresses must be unique on a given network for proper routing and communication[1]. How is this uniqueness assured across the global Internet? The Internet Assigned Numbers Authority (IANA) is responsible for global allocation of IP address space for both IPv4 and IPv6, as well as other parameters used within the TCP/IP protocol, such as application port numbers. In fact, you can view these top-level allocations by browsing to the www.iana.org website and selecting "Internet Protocol v4 Address Space" or "IPv6 Address Space" under Number Resources [73].

---

[1] An exception to this statement is that anycast addresses are typically assigned to multiple hosts, and multicast addresses likewise are shared. This statement applies to unicast addresses.

IPv6 Deployment and Management, First Edition. By Michael Dooley and Timothy Rooney.
© 2013 by The Institute of Electrical and Electronics Engineers, Inc. Published 2013 by John Wiley & Sons, Inc.

IANA is, in essence, the top-level address registry, and it allocates address space to RIRs. The RIRs, as introduced in Chapter 1 and listed below for convenience, are organizations responsible for allocation of address space within their respective global regions from their corresponding space allotments from IANA.

- *AfriNIC (African Network Information Centre).* Africa Region [74]
- *APNIC (Asia Pacific Network Information Centre).* Asia/Pacific Region [75]
- *ARIN (American Registry for Internet Numbers).* North America Region including Puerto Rico and some Caribbean Islands [76]
- *LACNIC (Regional Latin American and Caribbean IP Address Registry).* Latin America and some Caribbean Islands [77]
- *RIPE NCC (Réseaux IP Européens Network Coordination Centre).* Europe, the Middle East, and Central Asia [78]

The goals of the RIR system are as follows:

- *Uniqueness.* Each IP address must be unique worldwide for global Internet routing.
- *Registration.* A publicly accessible registry of IP address assignments eliminates ambiguity and can help when troubleshooting. This registry is called the *whois* database. Today, there are many whois databases, operated not only by RIRs but also by LIR(ISPs as well for their respective address spaces.
- *Aggregation.* Hierarchical allocation of address space assures proper routing of IP traffic on the Internet. Without aggregation, routing tables become fragmented that could ultimately create tremendous bottlenecks within the Internet. This is considered the most important goal for IPv6 allocations.
- *Conservation.* With IPv4 in particular but also for IPv6 space, address space needs to be distributed according to actual usage requirements.
- *Fairness.* Unbiased address allocation based on true address needs and not long-term "plans."
- *Minimized Overhead.* Streamline the process for requesting and receiving initial and subsequent allocations.

Organizations would do well to bear these goals in mind for their own networks, particularly uniqueness, registration (tracking), aggregation and conservation. As such, the allocation methods we'll discuss in this chapter are similar to those employed to allocate address blocks to RIRs, and by RIRs to allocate to National or Local Internet Registries, and in turn to service providers and end users. Allocation guidelines for RIRs are documented in RFC 2050 [4]. The general address allocation hierarchy is depicted in Figure 5-1. National Internet Registries are akin to Local Internet Registries, but are organized at a national level.

Back in the 1980s and early 1990s, many corporations (end users per Figure 5-1) obtained address space directly from RIRs. However, the additional LIR/ISP layer was

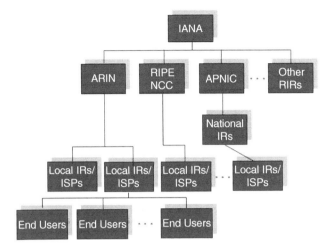

Figure 5-1.   IP address allocation from the top down [4].

inserted during the transition to CIDR addressing to provide further delegation of address allocation responsibility. Today, most organizations obtain address space from LIRs or ISPs. The process for obtaining such address space is generally dictated by the LIR/ISP with whom you conduct business, though RIRs recommend use of consistent policies to maximize efficiency.

As space is allocated to an ISP, the ISP may then advertise the address space on the Internet. Thus, this insertion of the LIR/ISP layer helps aggregate route advertisements on the Internet. Multiple customers served by the ISP can be summarized in one route on the Internet. If business is good and the LIR/ISP requires more address space, the LIR/ISP can request additional space from their RIR. Each RIR generally has its own defined process for fulfilling address requests, so please consult the RIR in your region for details.

5.1.1 RIR Address Allocation Policies

From an RIR perspective, RIRs *allocate* space to LIR/ISPs, and LIR/ISPs *assign* address space to their customers. The term *allocate* technically refers to the provision of an IP address block to serve as a "pool" of address space that can be drawn from for *assignment* to customers. Customers can then use the assigned address space, allocating blocks, and subnets from it, then assigning IP addresses from allocated subnets to individual hosts. The mechanics of this allocation and assignment are based on the procedures we will describe later in this chapter in accordance with hierarchical allocation procedures. However, RIRs differentiate allocations from assignments because assignments comprise addresses in use, while allocations are pools for assignment that begin as unused but in theory grow in utilization with a number of assignments from the allocation over time. Technically, RIRs count both allocations and assignments as in-use, but leave open the ability to audit allocated space for actual address utilization as needed to process additional allocation requests from each LIR/ISP.

5.1.2 Address Allocation Efficiency

During the development of IPv6, much thought went into deriving the 128-bit address size. While IPv4 provides a 32-bit address field that provides a theoretical maximum of 2^{32} addresses or over 4.2 billion addresses, in reality the theoretical maximum is much less than 4.2 billion. This is due to the hierarchical allocation of address space for multiple layers of networks, then subnets and finally hosts. RFC 1715 [79] provides an analysis of address assignment efficiency, in which a logarithmic scale was proposed as a measure of allocation efficiency, which was defined as the H ratio:

$$H = \frac{\log_{10}(\text{number of objects})}{\text{number of available bits}}$$

With about 2.4 billion users on the Internet today according to Internet World Stats [1], today's H ratio is 0.293. The H ratio for 100% utilization of 4.2 billion IP addresses is 0.301, so today's H ratio is relatively high.

Assignment efficiency measurements for IPv6, with its massive amount of address space, are calculated based on the HD ratio [80]:

$$\text{HD} = \frac{\log_{10}(\text{number of allocated objects})}{\log_{10}(\text{maximum number of allocatable objects})}$$

The "objects" measured in the HD ratio for IPv6 are the assigned IPv6 block addresses (/48s) assigned from an IPv6 prefix of a given size. The /48 address blocks are those expected to be assigned to each end user by the LIR/ISP. So, an LIR/ISP with a /32 allocation that has allocated 100 /48s would have an HD ratio of log(100)/log(65,536) = 0.415.

5.2 IPv6 ADDRESS PLANNING

Consider the fundamental purpose of IP address allocation within an organization, which is to provide IP addresses to end nodes on your network in order to enable such nodes to communicate with other nodes on your network (or not) and Internet nodes (or not) using a variety of media (data, voice, video, etc.). In addition to considering end user addressing needs, your address allocation scheme must consider network operations to facilitate network management and security as implied with permitting communications internally or with Internet nodes.

Examining the needs of the second constituency first, the network operations team, consider how the address plan impacts router and firewall settings and policies. The network is easier to manage if one can ascertain information about a device being managed simply from its IP address. In the IPv4 world, most address planners assign address ".1" on each subnet for a router, for example. Network, routing, and security policies are also easier to manage with fewer address-based entries defining policies such as those related to access control lists (ACLs) or routing treatment (e.g., voice vs. data packet handling). For example, some organizations define various address "types" to reflect address space allocated for application-based packet treatment. IP address space is easier to manage if through sufficient planning and perhaps some luck, the address hierarchy remains intact through the years without requiring renumbering, which can be painful.

The user constituency will primarily drive allocation sizings across your network topology for each type of address space required within end offices or "leaf nodes" of your network. The address planner must allocate sufficient space to meet capacity requirements for each address type while adhering to the overarching primary goals of uniqueness, aggregation, and conservation. As we shall see in our allocation example, trade-offs must be considered in terms of your address allocation plan and hierarchy. But first let us consider the various methods of IPv6 address allocation.

An important step in deploying IPv6 is to request an IPv6 address block from your RIR or ISP. Though IPv6 addresses are represented differently than IPv4 addresses, the allocation process within your network works essentially the same way. The main difference is in converting hexadecimal to binary and back instead of decimal to binary and back. The process of optimal assignment of the smallest available free block commonly used for IPv4 allocation is an example of the best-fit allocation algorithm. Due to the vast difference in available address space, IPv6 supports not only an analogous best-fit algorithm but also a sparse allocation method. We'll discuss this sparse method as well as a random allocation method that can be used in lieu of simple subnet numbering starting from 1 and counting up. We'll talk first about these allocation methods, then come back to where and how you may want to apply these methods from a practical standpoint to your IPv6 address plan.

5.3 IPv6 ADDRESS ALLOCATION METHODS[2]

The process for IPv6 and IPv4 allocation works essentially the same way, and we'll discuss some shortcuts later. The *optimal* address block allocation method entails allocation of the smallest available free block. This method is known as the *best-fit* allocation algorithm. Due to the vastness of available IPv6 address space, applying the rigor of the best-fit algorithm may prove unwarranted.

The IETF has also defined a *sparse* address allocation method for IPv6 to allocate equal-sized blocks, though with room for growth and a random allocation method can be used in lieu of simple subnet numbering starting from 1 and counting up.

We'll illustrate each of these algorithms using the example IPv6 network 2001: db8::/32. Realistically, a /32 (or any) sized global unicast allocation requires pre-qualification with a Regional Internet Registry, and it's unlikely that a modestly sized enterprise organization would receive such an allocation. However, we'll initially use this in our example to keep the number of bits from running off the page! Later we'll use a more practical /48 example allocation. The algorithm will be equivalent whether starting with a /32 or a /48, there'll just be more intermediate prefix bits with the/48 network.

---

[2] This discussion of IPv6 allocations is based on Ref. [81].

5.3.1 Best-Fit Method

The best-fit approach seeks to allocate the required block size using the smallest available address block. If you are using equal-sized block allocations (which as we'll see later is recommended for simplicity), this method is trivial. However, to optimally allocate address space, a block no larger than the size required should be allocated. Hence, one could allocate a /56 block during one allocation, then a /61 on another. This approach is commonly used for IPv4 block allocations today given the necessity of conserving address space. This requirement is not as stringent with IPv6 given the vast address space, but we will illustrate the process nonetheless.

The best-fit method entails selecting a free "parent" block within your addressing hierarchy that exactly meets the size needed or is the smallest block of greater size. Unless you can perform hexadecimal calculations in your head, this approach generally requires allocation in the binary domain. This is due to the need to track variably sized block allocations from blocks of equal or greater size. The latter case will result in the desired block for allocation, along with additional free blocks that themselves may be further allocated or carved up later. Let's take a closer look at how this occurs by considering our example network 2001:0db8::/32, expanded [partially] below in binary format.

0010 0000 0000 0001 0000 1101 1011 1000 0000 0000 0000 0000 0000 . . .

Now let's say we need to allocate three /40 networks from this /32 space. If we think of our /32 available address space as a pie from which allocations can be made, we can slice it up accordingly. Cutting our pie in half yields two /33 blocks, 2001:db8::/33, listed first, and 2001:db8:8000::/33, listed second.

*0010 0000 0000 0001 0000 1101 1011 1000 0*000 0000 0000 0000 0000 . . .
*0010 0000 0000 0001 0000 1101 1011 1000 1*000 0000 0000 0000 0000 . . .

Let's leave the second half, 2001:db8:8000::/33 intact, in order to provide the largest possible block available for subsequent allocation requests. Meanwhile, we split our 2001:db8::/33 slice into two /34s: 2001:db8::/34 and 2001:db8:4000::/34, respectively.

*0010 0000 0000 0001 0000 1101 1011 1000 00*00 0000 0000 0000 0000 . . .
*0010 0000 0000 0001 0000 1101 1011 1000 01*00 0000 0000 0000 0000 . . .

Now leaving the 2001:db8:4000::/34 block intact, we split the 2001:db8::/34 block again into two /35s, and so on until we reach a pair of /40s as shown below:

*0010 0000 0000 0001 0000 1101 1011 1000 1*000 0000 0000 0000 0000 . . .
*0010 0000 0000 0001 0000 1101 1011 1000 01*00 0000 0000 0000 0000 . . .
*0010 0000 0000 0001 0000 1101 1011 1000 001*0 0000 0000 0000 0000 . . .
0010 0000 0000 0001 0000 1101 1011 1000 0001 0000 0000 0000 0000 . . .
*0010 0000 0000 0001 0000 1101 1011 1000 0000 1*000 0000 0000 0000 . . .
*0010 0000 0000 0001 0000 1101 1011 1000 0000 01*00 0000 0000 0000 . . .

*0010 0000 0000 0001 0000 1101 1011 1000 0000 001*0 0000 0000 0000 . . .
0010 0000 0000 0001 0000 1101 1011 1000 0000 0001 0000 0000 0000 . . .
0010 0000 0000 0001 0000 1101 1011 1000 0000 0000 0000 0000 0000 . . .

Thus, the best-fit method successively halves the address space down to the desired size. In our example, we now have two /40 networks available (shaded above). Translating these back into hex we have: 2001:db8:100::/40 and 2001:db8::/40. To allocate the requested third /40 using the best-fit approach, we can then take the next smallest available network, in this case 2001:db8:200::/39 and split it into two /40s:

0010 0000 0000 0001 0000 1101 1011 1000 0000 0010 0000 0000 0000 . . .
0010 0000 0000 0001 0000 1101 1011 1000 0000 0011 0000 0000 0000 . . .

We split this in half by assigning the next bit, yielding two /40s. We can choose one for allocation and the other will be free for future assignment. So our three /40s for allocation are 2001:db8::/40, 2001:db8:100::/40, and 2001:db8:200::/40. The other /40, that is 2001:db8:300::/40, is available for future assignment. Figure 5-2 illustrates this successive halving in a pie chart form.

When a subsequent allocation request arises for a /40, /38, /37, /36, /35, /34, or /33 sized block, we have blocks readily available for allocation without having to allocate multiple possibly noncontiguous blocks to supply the requested address capacity. For a request for another block size, a /44 block, for example, we can follow the allocation process above starting with our smallest free block, 2001:db8:300::/40.

The best-fit approach retains larger blocks when variable block sizes are allocated by policy. This approach is the most arithmetically intensive, but makes

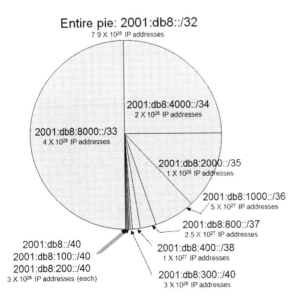

Figure 5-2. Allocation results from carving three /40 networks from a /32 network.

best use of available address capacity. Thus is may make sense for service providers to help maximize address utilization, but most enterprises may find other methods we'll describe simpler to manage.

5.3.2 Sparse Allocation Method

You'll notice from the prior algorithm that by allocating a /40 from a /32, we incrementally extended the network length to the 40th bit. We then assigned the network by assigning a 0 or 1 to the 40th bit as our first two /40 networks. In essence, we process each bit along the way, considering "1" the free block and "0" the allocated block. However, if we step back and consider the eight subnet ID bits that extend the /32 to a /40 as a whole, instead of incrementally halving the network, we observe that we've actually allocated our subnets by simply numbering or counting within the subnet ID field as denoted by the shaded bold italic bits below:

0010 0000 0000 0001 0000 1101 1011 1000 0000 0000 0000 0000 0000 . . . 2001:db8::/40

0010 0000 0000 0001 0000 1101 1011 1000 0000 0001 0000 0000 0000 . . . 2001:db8:100::/40

0010 0000 0000 0001 0000 1101 1011 1000 0000 0010 0000 0000 0000 . . . 2001:db8:200::/40

Thus, if you knew in advance that the original /32 network would be carved uniformly into only /40-sized blocks, a simpler allocation method would be to simply increment the subnet ID bits. The next allocation of /40s would use subnet ID values of 0000 0011, 0000 0100, 0000 0101, and so on.

In some networks where address allocation efficiency is of utmost importance, this uniformity policy of allocating same-sized blocks may not apply, so the best-fit method of successive halving may be more appropriate. On the other hand, the sparse allocation method provides a simpler approach and yields similar though nonoptimal benefits. The sparse allocation method seeks to spread out allocations to provide room for growth by allocating with the maximum space *between* allocations. The sparse algorithm also features halving of the available address space, but instead of continuing this process down to the smallest size, it calls for allocating the next block on the edge of the new half. This results in allocations being spread out and not optimally allocated. Again, the philosophy is that this provides room for growth of allocated networks by leaving ample space between allocations in the plentiful IPv6 space. Considering an example, our allocation of three /40's from our 2001:db8::/32 space would look like

0010 0000 0000 0001 0000 1101 1011 1000 0000 0000 0000 0000 0000 . . . 2001:db8::/40

0010 0000 0000 0001 0000 1101 1011 1000 1000 0000 0000 0000 0000 . . . 2001:db8:8000::/40

0010 0000 0000 0001 0000 1101 1011 1000 0100 0000 0000 0000 0000 . . . 2001:db8:4000::/40

These translate as 2001:db8::/40, 2001:db8:8000::/40, and 2001:db8:4000::/40, respectively. This allocation enables spreading out of address space as illustrated graphically in Figure 5-3. Should the recipient of the 2001:

Entire pie: 2001:db8::/32

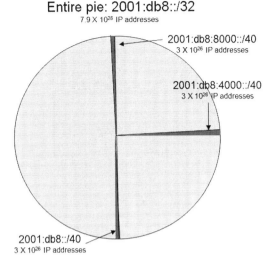

Figure 5-3. Sparse allocation example.

db8:8000::/40 network require an additional allocation, we could allocate a contiguous or adjacent block, 2001:db8:8100::/40. This block will be among the last to be allocated under the sparse method, so there's a good chance it will be available. In such a case, the recipient of our two contiguous blocks could identify (and advertise) their address space as 2001:db8:8000::/39. Note that our subnet ID bits are effectively counted from left-to-right, instead of the conventional right-to-left method used for "normal" counting.

RFC 3531 [82] describes the sparse allocation methodology. Because network allocations are expected to follow a multilayered allocation hierarchy, several sets of successive network bits can be used by different entities for successive allocation. For example, an Internet Registry may allocate the first block to a regional registry, who in turn will allocate from that space to a service provider, who may in turn allocate from that subspace to customers, who can further allocate across their networks. RFC 3531 recommends the higher level allocations, for example, from the registries, utilize the left most counting or sparse allocation, the lowest level allocations use the rightmost or best-fit allocation, and others in the middle use either, or even a center-most allocation scheme. For an enterprise organization, we can use the sparse method to allocate our intercontinental or core networks, leaving room for future growth at the top level without overcommitting address space up front.

5.3.3 Random Allocation

The random allocation method selects a random number within the sizing of the subnetwork bits to allocate subnetworks. Using our /40 allocations from a /32, a random number would be generated between 0 and $2^8 - 1$ or 255 and allocated assuming it's still available. This method provides a means for randomly spreading allocations across allocated entities and generally works best for "same size" allocations. Randomization provides a level of "privacy" in not ordering blocks and subnets consecutively starting with "1." Be aware that random allocation may render the identification of larger contiguous blocks more difficult as well as the freeing up contiguous space for renumbering purposes. Thus, while it makes sense to allocate sparsely at the top layer of allocation, the random or best-fit methods are more appropriate at the bottom or subnet allocation level.

5.3.4 DHCPv6 Prefix Delegation

DHCPv6 can be used not only to assign individual IP addresses and/or associated IP configuration information to hosts, but can also to delegate entire networks to requesting router devices. This form of delegation via DHCPv6 is called *prefix delegation*. This original motivation for prefix delegation arose from broadband service providers seeking to automate the process of delegating IPv6 subnets (e.g., /48 to /64 networks) to broadband subscribers in a hierarchical manner. A requesting router device at the edge of the service provider network, facing subscribers, would issue a request for address space via the DHCPv6 protocol to a delegating router.

The prefix delegation process utilizes the same basic DHCPv6 message flow used by a device to obtain an individual IPv6 address. Additional information within the corresponding DHCPv6 messages is used to determine an appropriate network for delegation. Like IPv6 addresses, prefixes have preferred and valid lifetimes. The requesting router can request a lifetime extension via the DHCPv6 Renew and Rebind messages. Please refer to [11] for more details about DHCPv6.

5.3.5 Unique Local Address Space

While IPv6 does not have designated "private" address space, the concept of unique local address (ULA) space is essentially equivalent. By using the fc00::/7 prefix, setting the L bit to "1" (i.e., fd00::/8) indicating local assignment, and assigning a random 40 bit Global ID, one can derive a/48 prefix for internal use. Like RFC 1918 IPv4 space, ULA-addressed packets cannot be routed outside an organization, that is, on the Internet. So should you allocate ULA address space? Yes for your laboratory implementation, but not generally for devices requiring Internet access. These devices will require public IPv6 address assignments and the usage of network prefix translation (NPT), while specified as an experimental solution [83] may impede performance.

5.4 DEFINING YOUR IPv6 ADDRESS PLAN

Now that we've defined the various allocation methods, let's discuss where you might use each. We'll discuss allocation assuming a hierarchical routing topology with a top-level core network, from which campus or access networks feed, and from each of which local subnets are allocated. This simple three-layer hierarchy can be extended in our examples to any number of layers based on your network size and complexity. The first consideration is whether you prefer to map an IPv6 block or subnet for every IPv4 block or subnet in your network. Given the vast size of a single /64 IPv6 subnet with over 18×10^{18} addresses, one could conceivably address one's entire IP network with a single /64! This of course would defeat the benefits and efficiencies of network routing and associated features. But some form of network consolidation may make sense. This does not imply a complete network redesign that would introduce an additional layer of complexity in the IPv6 deployment process in terms of debugging and troubleshooting routing and data flow issues. If your network is performing poorly, you may want to consider redesigning and optimizing your IPv4 network first, then deploying IPv6.

Assuming your IPv4 network is performing adequately if not optimally, your IPv4 addressing will serve as a solid basis for your IPv6 plan, which is why baselining your IPv4 plan is so important. Generally your top-level IPv6 allocations will likely mimic those of IPv4, with an aggregate address block allocated for each core router. Core routers may thus advertise fewer routes as each corresponding block will be further allocated and assigned downstream at access and local levels. Before allocating their ISP allocation to core routers, some network administrators first carve up their space on an application basis, for example, for VoIP versus data versus wireless, and so on. This facilitates configuration of routing policies or ACLs across the network for application-specific traffic using such macroallocations. For example, one may allocate an ISP-provided /48 into 16 /52s to define per-application space. Then each allocated /52 may be further allocated, say into 16 blocks each, yielding 16 /56s per-application allocation. Such allocation of IPv6 space at the top level(s) of your network may utilize the sparse algorithm to facilitate capacity growth without routing table growth.

Let's illustrate this process using this example ISP allocation, 2001: db8:4af0::/48. We'll apply sparse allocation iteratively at the application allocation layer then the core regional level. At the application level, we sparsely allocate the 13th nibble or bits 49–52 as follows.

Core allocation	Bits 49–52	Public space allocation
Data	0 0 0 0	2001:db8:4af0::/52
VoIP	1 0 0 0	2001:db8:4af0:**8**000::/52
Wireless	0 1 0 0	2001:db8:4af0:**4**000::/52
Management	1 1 0 0	2001:db8:4af0:**c**000::/52

Notice that one can essentially define a uniform per-application policy statement across the entire network. For example, "apply VoIP packet handling if the source address falls within 2001:db8:4af0:8000::/52." And thanks to the sparse algorithm, at such time when I need to allocate more "VoIP" address space, I can simply allocate 2001:db8:4af0:9000::/52 (bits 49–52 = 1 0 0 1), which is contiguous to 2001:db8:4af0:8000::/52. Then I can simply update my routes, policies, and ACLs from 2001:db8:4af0:8000::/52 to 2001:db8:4af0:8000::/51. Next, in order to allocate this VoIP space across my core routers, I simply allocate the next (14th) nibble, or bits 53–56, to my continental allocations:

Subcore allocation	Bits 53–56	Public space allocation
North America	0 0 0 0	2001:db8:4af0:**8**000::/56
Europe	1 0 0 0	2001:db8:4af0:**8**800::/56
Asia	0 1 0 0	2001:db8:4af0:**8**400::/56
South America	1 1 0 0	2001:db8:4af0:**8**c00::/56
Africa	0 0 1 0	2001:db8:4af0:**8**200::/56
Australia	1 0 1 0	2001:db8:4af0:**8**a00::/56

Notice that this approach provides a visual mapping of the network address to the corresponding application and region. This is a key advantage to using nibble-incremented allocations as we have in our example. After a while, you'll be able to recall that a host from the 2001:db8:4af0:**8**400:: address allocation is a VoIP device located in the Asia region as the 13th nibble value of 8 indicates VoIP and the 14th nibble value of 4 indicates Asia.

With a /48 allocation, you really only have four nibbles to work with between /48 and /64, so plan accordingly. You can stray from nibble boundaries but the hex mapping becomes more challenging and you sacrifice the visual mapping. In our case, with two remaining nibbles, we can allocate one each for our access networks and local networks, respectively. At these lower allocation levels, it may make sense to allocate sequentially or randomly depending on your security concerns. But in continuing a structured allocation, you facilitate the visual mapping of addresses to types and locations. The ISP prefix is the same for all of your public addresses, so homing in on the subnet ID portion, such mapping is simplified.

Table 5-1 illustrates a sample mapping down to /64 subnets for the 2001: db8:4af0::/48 IPv6 allocation example we've been discussing. In this example, we've architected our IPv6 addressing plan based on the IPv4 addressing assessment results as depicted in Figure 4-3. Notice how we've used various shading to illustrate each hierarchy layer starting from the global /48 allocation to an application-level allocation to /52 (horizontally by column), down to core /56 allocations, then /60 regional and finally /64 sites/subnets. Notice that I may identify the address 2001:db8:4af0:**c812**::/64 as a management subnet in Rome within the Western Europe region with sedectet "c812" mapping to management (c), Europe (8), Western Europe (1), and Rome (2) per the entry in the bottom right corner of Table 5-1.

Following up on an earlier point regarding subnet consolidation, in our example allocation, we have 16 subnets allocatable in Western Europe, with subnet 2 being Rome. If I had three IPv4 subnets in my Rome office, I could possibly consolidate these into one IPv6 subnet. Again, consider routing implications and if possible the initial reasons for multisubnet allocation. It may be necessary to retain multiple subnets for security or other reasons.

DNS is another consideration in IPv6 allocation. If DNS administration is delegated to different groups within your organization, delegation of reverse zones accordingly can be simplified with some forethought. In our example above, if your VoIP team manages all VoIP DNS, you can delegate to them the 8.0.f.a.4.8.b. d.0.1.0.0.2.ip6.arpa zone. However, if the Europe team runs DNS across applications, you may have to delegate up to 16 reverse zones using our allocation strategy

TABLE 5-1. IPv6 Hierarchical Block Allocation Example

Core Site	Region	Sites	IPv4 Nets	Data Nets	VoIP Nets	Wireless Nets	Management Nets
		Global allocation	10.0.0.0/8	2001:db8:4af0::/52	2001:db8:4af0:8000::/52	2001:db8:4af0:4000::/52	2001:db8:4af0:c000::/52
North America	East		**10.0.0.0/12**	**2001:db8:4af0::/56**	**2001:db8:4af0:8000::/56**	**2001:db8:4af0:4000::/56**	**2001:db8:4af0:c000::/56**
		Philadelphia	10.0.0.0/16	2001:db8:4af0::/60	2001:db8:4af0:8000::/60	2001:db8:4af0:4000::/60	2001:db8:4af0:c000::/60
		Montreal	10.0.0.0/24	2001:db8:4af0::/64	2001:db8:4af0:8000::/64	2001:db8:4af0:4000::/64	2001:db8:4af0:c000::/64
		Washington	10.0.0.1/24	2001:db8:4af0:1::/64	2001:db8:4af0:8001::/64	2001:db8:4af0:4001::/64	2001:db8:4af0:c001::/64
			10.0.0.2/24	2001:db8:4af0:2::/64	2001:db8:4af0:8002::/64	2001:db8:4af0:4002::/64	2001:db8:4af0:c002::/64
	Central		10.1.0.0/16	2001:db8:4af0:10::/60	2001:db8:4af0:8010::/60	2001:db8:4af0:4010::/60	2001:db8:4af0:c010::/60
		Ottawa	10.1.0.0/24	2001:db8:4af0:10::/64	2001:db8:4af0:8010::/64	2001:db8:4af0:4010::/64	2001:db8:4af0:c010::/64
		Houston	10.1.1/24	2001:db8:4af0:11::/64	2001:db8:4af0:8011::/64	2001:db8:4af0:4011::/64	2001:db8:4af0:c011::/64
		Denver	10.1.2.0/24	2001:db8:4af0:12::/64	2001:db8:4af0:8012::/64	2001:db8:4af0:4012::/64	2001:db8:4af0:c012::/64
	West		10.2.0.0/16	2001:db8:4af0:20::/60	2001:db8:4af0:8020::/60	2001:db8:4af0:4020::/60	2001:db8:4af0:c020::/60
		San Fran.	10.2.0.0/24	2001:db8:4af0:20::/64	2001:db8:4af0:8020::/64	2001:db8:4af0:4020::/64	2001:db8:4af0:c020::/64
		Seattle	10.2.1/24	2001:db8:4af0:21::/64	2001:db8:4af0:8021::/64	2001:db8:4af0:4021::/64	2001:db8:4af0:c021::/64
		San Diego	10.2.2.0/24	2001:db8:4af0:22::/64	2001:db8:4af0:8022::/64	2001:db8:4af0:4022::/64	2001:db8:4af0:c022::/64
Europe allocation	East		**10.16.0.0/12**	**2001:db8:4af0:800::/56**	**2001:db8:4af0:8800::/56**	**2001:db8:4af0:4800::/56**	**2001:db8:4af0:c800::/56**
		Berlin	10.16.0.0/16	2001:db8:4af0:800::/60	2001:db8:4af0:8800::/60	2001:db8:4af0:4800::/60	2001:db8:4af0:c800::/60
		Kiev	10.16.0.0/24	2001:db8:4af0:800::/64	2001:db8:4af0::8800::/64	2001:db8:4af0::4800::/64	2001:db8:4af0::c800::/64
			10.16.1.0/24	2001:db8:4af0:801::/64	2001:db8:4af0:8801::/64	2001:db8:4af0:4801::/64	2001:db8:4af0:c801::/64
	West		10.17.0.0/16	2001:db8:4af0:810::/60	2001:db8:4af0:8810::/60	2001:db8:4af0:4810::/60	2001:db8:4af0:c810::/60
		London	10.17.0.0/24	2001:db8:4af0:810::/64	2001:db8:4af0:8810::/64	2001:db8:4af0:4810::/64	2001:db8:4af0:c810::/64
		Paris	10.17.1.0/24	2001:db8:4af0:811::/64	2001:db8:4af0:8811::/64	2001:db8:4af0:4811::/64	2001:db8:4af0:c811::/64
		Rome	10.17.2.0/24	2001:db8:4af0:812::/64	2001:db8:4af0:8812::/64	2001:db8:4af0:4812::/64	2001:db8:4af0:c812::/64

above, namely, 8.*x*.0.f.a.4.8.b.d.0.1.0.0.2.ip6.arpa zones where $x = \{0 - f\}$. Generally data routing and policies override reverse zone considerations, but this is something to bear in mind and helps illustrate the trade-offs with allocation strategy and its implication on network operations.

5.5 MULTIHOMING AND IP ADDRESS SPACE

The term *multihoming* refers to an enterprise provisioning multiple (>1) connections to the Internet. A simple architecture is depicted in Figure 5-4. A multihoming strategy provides several benefits [84], [85]:

- Link redundancy, providing continued Internet connectivity availability in the event of a connection outage.

- ISP redundancy if multiple ISPs are used to limit exposure in the event of an ISP outage.

- Load sharing of Internet traffic over multiple connections.

- Policy and performance benefits achieved through routing of traffic based on congestion or on requirements to route traffic of differing applications to differing links or ISPs.

Multihoming offers several attractive benefits though it does require care in configuring routers interfacing to each ISP. As we show in Figure 5-4, the enterprise border routers interfacing directly to their respective ISP edge routers participate in an exterior routing protocol (e.g., BGP) to advertise reachability to the respective address blocks (by address prefix). Thus, the enterprise router connected to ISP X will advertise reachability to the address space provided to the enterprise by ISP X. Similarly, the enterprise router connected to ISP Y will advertise reachability to the address space provided by ISP Y.

These two enterprise routers also communicate with each other using an interior routing protocol via the enterprise IP network. In this manner, loss of connectivity to an ISP may be detected, though this is where things get interesting. To

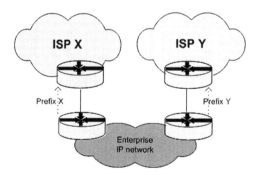

Figure 5-4. Multihoming architecture.

illustrate this without going into all of the routing details, the following summarizes the most common multihoming deployment options, outage impacts, and implications on IP address space:

- *Case 1.* Two or more diverse physical links to the same ISP. This "multiattached" architecture provides link redundancy but not ISP redundancy. Referring to Figure 5-4, the two ISP clouds would be collapsed into a single cloud but still with two (or more) links from the enterprise. With one ISP, Prefix X = Prefix Y, so this public address space allocated from the ISP may be advertised uniformly on all connections.

- *Case 2.* Two or more connections to one or more ISPs using provider independent (PI) address space. PI space is allocated to an organization directly and independently of ISP associations. Referring to Figure 5-4, the advertised prefix is again the same on both connections, though we could denote it as Prefix Z as being independent of the ISP address space. As in Case 1, the PI space may be advertised to all ISPs and allocated across the organization as needed.

- *Case 3.* Two or more connections to two or more ISPs using Provider Aggregate (PA) address space from each ISP. In this case, each ISP allocates address space as part of its service. Figure 5-4 reflects this scenario as is. With two independent address blocks, X and Y, if the link to ISP X fails, the enterprise router connected to ISP Y will detect this by virtue of the interior routing protocol update from the enterprise router connected to ISP X. Thus, the enterprise router connected to ISP Y could now advertise reachability to Prefix X. Depending on ISP Y's policies it may or may not propagate the route because it does not fall within ISP Y's address space but ISP X's.

Another approach is to perform an indirect BGP peer update from the ISP Y-facing enterprise router to an ISP X router peer. In this manner, ISP X routers may be notified of an alternate route to reach the enterprise's address space via ISP Y. These two alternative approaches are shown in Figure 5-5 with the former shown with Prefix X being advertised to ISP Y's router and the latter with Prefix X being advertised to ISP X's router [86].

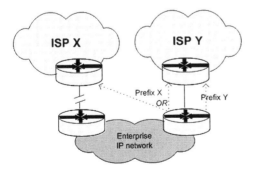

Figure 5-5. Multihoming link outage recovery.

124

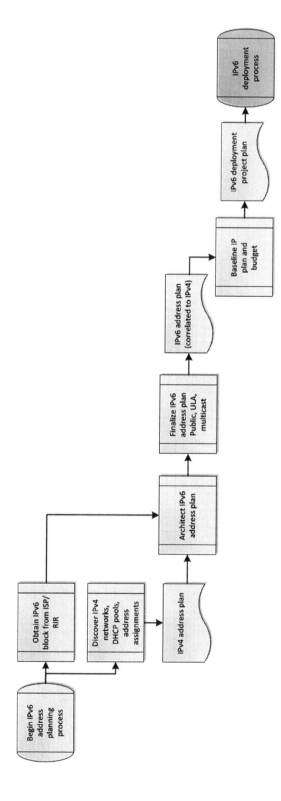

Figure 5-6. IPv6 address planning.

Another approach is to deploy shim6 [87], which is a "shim" in the protocol stack right above the IPv6 layer to map a destination address with a corresponding best next hop. End devices initiating IPv6 traffic would require a shim6 within their IP stacks to enable such optimal routing, which would also reroute around failed ISP connections.

NAT gateways at each ISP connection enable address pooling, translating a given packet's internal private address into a public address based on the ISP connection proximity, for example, from Prefix X or Y. Barring the use of NAT gateways, enterprise border router policies should be implemented to minimize or prevent routing of traffic among internally addressed hosts from routing via the ISP(s).

5.6 IP ADDRESS PLANNING SUMMARY

In this chapter, we've discussed the mechanics and techniques for deriving your IPv6 addressing plan. The basic process is summarized in Figure 5-6. As part of your initial overall discovery and assessment within your chosen scope of deployment, one output should be an IPv4 address inventory as discussed in Chapter 4. This inventory should be modeled hierarchically in accordance with your network topology, reflecting topology levels, associated allocations, down to the subnet and individual IP address assignment levels. The inventory must also enumerate DHCP address pools, as well as pool associations for failover, split scopes or shared subnets.

The end product of this assessment effort, the IPv4 address plan, provides the foundation for IPv6 address planning as we have seen in this chapter. This assumes that you plan to retain the basic data flow and routing currently in place to improve the probability of deploying an IPv6 overlay without disrupting traffic flows. Coupled with the IPv4 address plan, your ISP-allocated IPv6 prefix may be applied and allocated accordingly. Based on your network topology applications, management and policy needs, and administrative delegation requirements, devise an IPv6 allocation hierarchy and allocate sparsely, optimally, and/or randomly at successive levels.

Mapping the IPv6 address plan alongside the IPv4 plan is helpful in assuring complete allocation coverage and to assure allocation hierarchy compliance with network hierarchy. Plans should also include consideration of ULA space as well as multicast addressing requirements if applicable. Once defined, the IPv6 plan is referenced during deployment to direct and assure proper router and individual device IPv6 subnet/address provisioning. Provision for DHCPv6 must also be accounted for in terms of host address allocations and possibly in terms of infrastructure investment. Additional infrastructure investment related to IP addressing is likely minimal unless you require an IPAM system for managing your IPv4 and IPv6 space together.

CHAPTER **6**

IPv6 SECURITY PLANNING

Plans to introduce a new network layer protocol into your network will certainly gain the attention of the security team. The fact is, you probably already have IPv6-addressed devices on your network that may even be attempting to connect to your web resources. It's critical to update your security policies as an integral component of your plan to introduce IPv6 into your network. This chapter examines the differences between IPv4 and IPv6 from a security perspective and highlights key considerations for updating your security policy.

6.1 THE GOOD NEWS: IP IS IP

Like IPv4, IPv6 is a network layer protocol within the OSI seven-layer protocol stack [88]. The addition of IPv6 into a network running IPv4 will have no inherent security impacts on layers above and below the network layer. IPv6 is not more or less inherently secure than IPv4, but it is different and must be accounted for from a security perspective. Thus, no new application, transport, link, or physical layer vulnerabilities should be introduced though none will be eliminated either. The following attack types should continue to be included within your security policies in general:

- Physical security and access.
- Unauthorized network admission via layer 2 (e.g., Extensible Authentication Protocol (EAP), Radius/Diameter) or layer 3 (DHCP or spoofing).
- Application, transport, link, or physical layer attacks.
- Man in the middle style attacks.
- Operating system vulnerabilities and attacks.
- Traffic sniffing.
- Denial of service (DOS) and distributed denial of service (DDOS) attacks.

Nevertheless, a dual-stack device running IPv4 and IPv6 is susceptible to these vulnerabilities from two network addresses instead of one. Given the relative industry inexperience in securing IPv6 versus IPv4, an upper layer attack directed at the IPv6 address could be more effective than a similar attack directed at the IPv4 address. Employing strategies discussed in this chapter to secure IPv6 should help reduce this risk.

IPv6 Deployment and Management, First Edition. By Michael Dooley and Timothy Rooney.
© 2013 by The Institute of Electrical and Electronics Engineers, Inc. Published 2013 by John Wiley & Sons, Inc.

127

The introduction of IPv6 is not expected to change traffic flows on a network, other than perhaps increase the flow to and from IPv6-only hosts. Ultimately end user devices are generating IP traffic based on end user behavior. If a user brings in an IPv6 device, new IPv6 traffic will certainly be generated but at the expense of IPv4 traffic the user otherwise may have generated using a legacy device. So unless you're planning a major network redesign coincidentally with IPv6 deployment, which is not recommended, overall IP traffic patterns should remain the same for the most part.

6.2 THE BAD NEWS: IPv6 IS NOT IPv4

While it's positive that vulnerabilities introduced with IPv6 will be largely constrained to the network layer, the "bad news" is that IPv6 is not the same as IPv4 and has unique characteristics that must be monitored and certain settings scrutinized if not blocked. First and foremost, while IPv6 is not new technology, deployment of IPv6 on a wide scale has not yet been achieved. This means that given the relatively low level of IPv6 deployment as yet, the "notoriety" of an attack may be less than one using high visibility IPv4 targets. Actual experience in identifying and dealing with such attacks is limited. As with IPv4 Internet attacks to date, as experience is gained on attack vectors, remediation implementations and processes may be enacted.

Security policies around IPv4 can be adapted to IPv6, though IPv6 does certain things differently and introduces unique characteristics that must be accounted for. For example, consider the following:

- While IPv4 uses address resolution protocol (ARP) to identify link layer addresses associated with IP addresses, IPv6 uses neighbor discovery protocol (NDP), which is required for address autoconfiguration and duplicate address detection. Mitigations for ARP attacks must be adapted for NDP.
- IPv4 supports broadcast while IPv6 does not but uses well-known multicast addresses instead, for example, for DHCP.
- Router resources can be sapped when requiring hop-by-hop router processing, for example, using IPv6 router alert options in hop-by-hop extension headers.
- Fragmentation is performed by routers in IPv4 and hosts in IPv6.
- Mobile IPv6 is similar but also quite different than Mobile IPv4 as we shall discuss in this chapter.
- Brute force pinging to identify hosts on a subnet is generally more difficult in IPv6 given the sheer size of IPv6 subnets. Of course if you address hosts starting with 1 and counting upward, this makes the discovery process much simpler.
- ICMP can generally be blocked in IPv4 but is a required protocol in IPv6 and cannot be entirely blocked.
- IPv6 extension headers keep the base IPv6 header small but can lead to header-related attacks.

- IPv6 stack software immaturity may lead to bugs that could be exploited by attackers.
- IPv4/IPv6 coexistence technologies, described in Chapter 3, often involve multiple interacting components and complex operations, vulnerabilities within which could be exposed and attacked.

Let's talk about these now in more detail in the context of an IPv6 security policy. You should update your network layer security policy document to incorporate IPv6 policies. Like your current security policy, IPv6 mitigations should be clearly documented, publicized, sanctioned by management and understood by network users. The following sections highlight suggested security policies in the context of potential vulnerabilities each seeks to mitigate.

6.3 UPDATE YOUR SECURITY POLICY

It's important that you think through the security implications of IPv6 deployment, many of which are pointed out in this chapter, then update your current network security policy document to account for these. Once you have updated and approved your revised security policy document, consideration of policy support in your firewalls, routers, servers, and other infrastructure and end user devices enables identification of shortcomings that can either be addressed through upgrades or replacements, or documented with identified mitigation. Such upgrade plans and policy implementation should be rolled into your overall IPv6 implementation plan in accordance with your overall scope and deployment phasing. The remainder of this chapter discusses potential attack types and mitigation methods organized by basic network security categories.

6.4 NETWORK PERIMETER MONITORING AND INTRUSION PREVENTION

The perimeter of your network is the first line of defense against attacks originating from the Internet. The traditional Internet-facing architecture featuring an Internet router, demilitarized zone (DMZ) containing externally reachable resources and firewall applies equally well to IPv6 as to IPv4. Enabling IPv6 reachability for your Internet-facing resources will require allowing IPv6 traffic at least into the DMZ. Enabling internal clients to communicate to IPv6 Internet destinations necessitates allowing IPv6 traffic into the internal network.

History has provided several examples of attack vectors originating from the Internet in attempts to infiltrate, deny service to, hijack, hinder performance of, and generally disrupt communications with organizations' IPv4 network infrastructure and services. Similar attacks will likely be attempted against IPv6 resources as well. Given the relative lack of operational experience with IPv6, well-known IPv4-style attacks may be launched against IPv6 nodes. In fact attackers may consider IPv6 the "back door" to a given attack target as well as mentioned previously. So care must be taken to monitor for attacks and to mitigate vulnerabilities. At the same time, it's a good idea to apply filters with the ability to log dropped packets; review of dropped packets will not only help identify potential attacks but also possible "good" traffic that should be allowed, thereby possibly requiring an update to filtering configurations.

6.4.1 IPv6 Address Filtering

Analogous to IPv4 address filtering, the following policies should be considered:

- Drop incoming packets from unallocated IPv6 address space to prevent spoofing through the use of illegal addresses. Depending on how granular you desire to filter, you can simply filter at the broad allocation level and by referring to http://www.iana.org/assignments/ipv6-address-space/ipv6-address-space.xml [89] or down to explicit IANA-allocated IPv6 blocks per http://www.iana.org/assignments/ipv6-unicast-address-assignments/ipv6-unicast-address-assignments.xml [90].

- Deny packets with source and destination addressing as defined below.

Most firewalls enable specification of policies on a "first match" basis so if you want to allow all-IANA allocated space for example, you could append to the above "deny" list with a "2000::/3 allow" statement, optionally "allow 64:ff9b::/96" if you're planning to support this well-known IP/ICMP IPv4/IPv6 translation prefix as discussed in Chapter 3, then "deny all." If you prefer RIR-level granularity you can explicitly allow at the more granular block level in place of the global unicast 2000::/3 allow entry.

Consider the following additional security policies:

- Drop inbound packets with destination addresses and outbound packets with source addresses outside the scope of your allocated and advertised public IPv6 address space.

- Configure unicast reverse path forwarding (uRPF) filtering that configures routers to drop packets with a source address that cannot be reached or is not reachable via the best route on the incoming interface. This helps detect packets with spoofed source addresses from a device likely of malicious intent.

- If possible, employ deep-packet inspection to analyze all IPv6 extension headers for consistency as discussed in Section 6.5.

- Consider your support of IPv4 protocol value of "41" that refers to a tunneled IPv6 packet. See the IPv4/IPv6 coexistence section later in this chapter for discussion of security implications of supporting various transition technologies.

- Drop inbound packets with destination port numbers corresponding to services or applications not supported externally, for example, ports 546-7 for DHCPv6.

- Secure routing protocols using authentication features.

- Publish DNS records in external DNS servers only for Internet-reachable hosts (e.g., web server and email server) and consider signing using DNSSEC.

- Review logs periodically to develop a baseline from which anomalies can be identified. Of course as more users in your organization or outside ramp up with IPv6, traffic patterns may take some time to converge.

6.4.2 ICMPv6 Messages

ICMPv6 is a core component of the IPv6 protocol. However, it may also be used for attacks. As such, you should consider filtering ICMPv6 packets (IPv6 next header value = 58) prudently at the perimeter and disallow entry to error message types and only those message types that you require certain ICMPv6 packets. RFC 4890 [91] defines ICMPv6 filtering recommendations. Among error messages, the following must be permitted to traverse:

- *Type 1*. Destination unreachable.
- *Type 2*. Packet too big.
- *Type 3*. Time exceeded.
- *Type 4*. Parameter problem Codes 1 and 2 (unrecognized next header type encountered, unrecognized IPv6 option encountered, respectively).

The RFC also discourages dropping of types 128 (echo request) and 129 (echo reply) that support the ping6 utility. Many security policies intentionally prohibit inbound echo requests for IPv4 to prevent detection of valid IP addresses on a given network. With 2^{64} IPv6 addresses within a /64 subnet, detecting hosts on a subnet is much more difficult, assuming one does not manually assign IPv6 addresses starting with ::1, ::2, ::3, and so on. Discovering the presence of a host at a given IP address is a possible first step in identifying attack targets or as potential "agents" from which attacks can be launched.

ICMPv6 error messages that normally should not be dropped include the following:

- *Type 3*. Time exceeded Code 1 (fragmentation reassembly time exceeded).
- *Type 4*. Parameter problem Code 0 (erroneous header field encountered).

Certain ICMPv6 error messages have been defined for Mobile IPv6 operations. If you explicitly do not support Mobile IPv6 on your network, the following ICMPv6 types should be filtered; otherwise, the following types normally should not be dropped:

- *Types 144, 145*. Home Agent Discovery Request/Reply.
- *Types 146, 147*. Mobile Prefix Solicitation/Advertisement.
- *Type 154*. Mobile IPv6 Proxy Router Solicitation/Advertisement.

RFC 4890 advises that the following link-local traffic will be dropped anyway and no special attention is needed, though you may want to explicitly define these types as filterable in your security policy, and verify such operation on your firewall:

- *Types 133, 134.* Router Solicitation/Advertisement.
- *Types 135, 136.* Neighbor Solicitation/Advertisement.
- *Type 137.* Redirect.
- *Types 141, 142.* Inverse Neighbor Solicitation/Advertisement.
- *Types 130, 131, 132, 143.* Multicast Listener Discovery Listener Query, Report, Done, Report (v2).
- *Types 148, 149.* Secure Neighbor Discovery (SEND) Certificate Path Solicitation/Advertisement.
- *Types 151, 152, 153.* Multicast Router Advertisement (RA), Solicitation, Termination.

As for ICMPv6 types that also should be dropped barring special circumstances requiring their use, consider carefully the following types:

- *Types 139, 140.* Node Information Query, Response.
- *Type 138.* Router renumbering.
- *Types 100, 101, 200, 201.* Private experimentation.
- *Types 127, 255.* Reserved types for expansion.
- *Type 150.* Experimental.
- *Types 5–99, 102–126, 156–198 Inclusive.* Undefined (unallocated) message types.

And unless you operate a low power and lossy network (LLN), you may also want to drop ICMPv6 type 155 messages that support the IPv6 routing protocol for LLNs (also known as RPL).

6.5   EXTENSION HEADERS

Generally a router is only required to analyze the base IPv6 header and if present, the hop-by-hop options header, destination header if present before a routing header, the routing header and the shim6 header if the router is a border router supporting shim6. However, a firewall must go beyond the header processing required of routers and needs to parse up to the upper layer protocol header information to ascertain whether the packet should be dropped or permitted to pass. Each extension header should only appear once in a given packet, except for the destination options header, which may appear prior to the routing header for router processing and right before the upper layer protocol header. This should be enforced to reduce the risk of DOS style attacks due to chained extension headers. Valid header types should be verified as well.

Despite validity and single occurrence of extension headers, they may still be leveraged for attacks despite their seemingly innocent appearance. Use of hop-by-hop or destination header padding options can be used to create a covert control channel for example. The padding options are intended to fill out header options to integer octet boundaries and should not contain any "data" payload. The router alert hop-by-hop option could be used by an attacker to deny service or reduce performance of network routers, as each router along the path must more deeply examine the packet, which can consume router resources.

Packets with routing headers should be filtered unless you are using Mobile IPv6. Use of the type 0 routing header has been deprecated, type 1 was use for experimental purposes and type 2 supports mobility routing options. At minimum, only type 2 routing headers should be supported if any at all.

Fragmentation headers are used when a packet size exceeds the path MTU. Only end points may fragment packets in IPv6. One issue with filtering packet fragments is that the upper layer header information may not be contained within the first fragment, requiring "stateful" analysis of multiple fragments to ascertain the packet's fate. Attackers may attempt to send many small fragments in an attempt to avoid such processing or to avoid filtering altogether while sending malicious information or intending to deny service. Fragments in packets smaller than 1280 bytes should be suspect given this is the minimum IPv6 MTU.

Unknown extension header types should be dropped, unless an explicitly defined header is required within your network (for routing or for hosts). Newer hop-by-hop and destination option definitions are to be defined as additional options within these existing respective header types [92]. Filtering of upper layer protocols should mirror current filtering practices for IPv4, other than ICMPv6 as discussed above. Remember that [distributed] denial of service, buffer overflow attacks, cross-site scripting, SQL injection, and other upper layer attacks are equally possible in an IPv6 network as in an IPv4 network.

6.6   INTERNAL NETWORK PROTECTION

Many organizations protect their internal networks by having a strong perimeter and intrusion detection systems in place. But internal protections are also necessary to protect against internal attacks, intentional or accidental, and as a second line of defense should an external attacker gain access to an internal host.

6.6.1   Network Reconnaissance

If an attacker is seeking a host on which to install a worm or backdoor agent, the first step is typically reconnaissance to find potential victims. With IPv4, ping sweeps if permitted, provide a simple and quick means to detect active IP addresses on a subnet. Added TCP port opens (SYNs) on given hosts could also be sent to attempt to identify each host's operating system. In IPv6, a ping sweep of a /64 subnet could take 5 billion years according to RFC 5157, *IPv6 Implications for Network Scanning* [93]. However, as RFC 5157 also points out, this unpredictable sparseness of assigned IPv6 addresses within a subnet is not a "security solution," though it can help reduce the effectiveness of worms that rely on network scanning to propagate. On the other hand, if you manually assign IPv6 addresses on subnets beginning with ::1, ::2, and so on. this makes the job of a scanner much simpler!

If you are using stateless address autoconfiguration (SLAAC) without privacy extensions, an attacker may be able to vastly reduce the candidate list of IP addresses from 2^{64} if he/she may be able to determine the network card manufacturer(s) in common use on your network. Perhaps a former employee or associate knows the set of NIC manufacturers and can compute the first 5 of 8 bytes of the interface ID, reducing the scan range down to 2^{24} for each NIC manufacturer by Ethernet OUI (Organizational Unit Identifier). The first 3 bytes of a 6-byte MAC address contain the IEEE-assigned OUI. By flipping the seventh most significant bit as part of the modified EUI-64 process, then appending 0xfffe, the first 40 bits of the IID are derivable, yielding a discovery requirement of only the remaining 24 bits. Using the "one address scanned per second" rate referenced in RFC 5157, such a scan would take about 195 days or about 6.5 months; a still lengthy time interval but a far cry from 5 billion years!

You can use SLAAC privacy extensions [29] to avoid the deterministic nature of IID calculation to avert this attack vector. SLAAC privacy extensions hinder address guessing but they also make it more challenging for network managers; perhaps gone are the days of mentally associating a given IP address with a given host with IPv6 in any case, but privacy extensions increase the difficulty. Network management tools can be employed to track IPv6–MAC address associations by polling switches and routers periodically for use in forensics and troubleshooting.

6.6.2   Network Access

Beyond discovering existing hosts with assigned IPv6 addresses, another form of local network attack involves an attacker obtaining an IPv6 address of its own on a given subnet. This form of attack could stem from a malicious attempt to install a bot remotely onto a customer network, an innocuous network access attempt from a visitor's device attempting to connect from a conference room for example, or other forms of "accidental" network access issues. The discipline of network admission control (NAC) was a hot topic during the mid-2000's with several high profile vendors providing solutions to detecting IP network access and preventing or quarantining unknown or unauthenticated devices for limited network access or to facilitate device scanning for updated virus protection among other things.

Some of the same principles of designing IPv4 NAC can be applied to IPv6 NAC, but implementing NAC is not simple and generally requires coordinated functions among two or more network services. For example, a layer 2 NAC approach would involve detecting switch port connectivity ("link up") via capture of a corresponding SNMP trap from the switch, followed by an authentication challenge to the port from a Radius server using EAP. A layer 3 approach involves a DHCP server, a DNS server, an authentication server, and optionally a device scanning server. These approaches are outlined in detail in Chapter 8 of [66].

Of course IPv6 adds another form of address assignment not supported in IPv4, SLAAC. A device may autoconfigure its IPv6 address, perform duplicate address detection, then gain access to the network. If such a device poses as a router intentionally or accidentally, it may issue false router advertisements on the link and serve to deny service or intercept packets. This type of attack can be mitigated by implementing RA-guard techniques on your switches to block RAs incoming on ports not connected to routers as defined in RFC 6105 [94].

For devices on networks receiving "legitimate" router advertisements with the "M" bit set, such devices are supposed to use DHCPv6 for address assignment, but most attackers are not following any rules. The DHCP LeaseQuery functionality could be used to verify that a given address has been assigned by DHCP prior to processing of a packet from a particular source address. The way this works is that a router, upon receiving a packet from a device on one of its connected subnets, may issue a LeaseQuery request to serving DHCP servers to determine if the given device, identified by its MAC address (for DHCPv4) or by its IPv6 address (or DUID if known), has a valid lease. If not, the packet may be dropped or otherwise handled by router policy. This does certainly add some overhead to router packet processing functions but may be worthwhile in your environment. Another option is to use SEND to require authentication of devices using the neighbor discovery protocol on your network.

6.6.3 DHCPv6

DHCPv6 has generally the same set of vulnerabilities and its IPv4 cousin, except that an attacker with access to your network could more easily setup a rogue DHCPv6 server by listening on the All DHCPv6 [Agents and] Servers multicast address, ff02::1:2 (link local) or ff05::1:3 (site local), and process Solicit or Renew messages. Both DHCP and DHCPv6 support an authentication mechanism, though in practice, this has seen few implementations in the IPv4 world due to initial configuration complexity. If your DHCPv6 server supports the disabling of these multicast addresses, you could configure DHCPv6 server reachability the "old fashioned" way, by configuring your relay agents with the unicast IPv6 addresses of your DHCPv6 servers. It's also generally a good idea to take snapshots of who's on your network periodically by polling each router's neighbor table and comparing with prior snapshots for changes to detect new devices on the network, whether addresses were obtained via DHCPv6, SLAAC, or even manually configured.

6.6.4 DNS

DNS update security is another consideration if a network is not configured to use dynamic DNS (DDNS) updates from a trusted DHCPv6 server. When using DHCPv6, the set of DHCPv6 server IP addresses can be defined within an ACL as permitted to update DNS information, besides other administrative authorities such as an IPAM system. This simplifies ACL specification on the DNS server (allow-update) to a fixed set of nodes or addresses. When statically configuring IPv6 addresses or when using SLAAC, the scope of addresses from which DDNS updates may originate spans the entire network, which certainly makes the DNS server vulnerable to mischievous updates. The first question to ask is whether DNS entries are required for such hosts. Certainly for web servers, printers, application servers, and so on, where users connect by URL or name thanks to DNS resolution, entries in DNS are critical. Most organizations create DNS entries at least for forward domain lookups (host domain name-to-IP address lookup). Reverse lookups (IP address-to-name) are needed for certain applications requiring existence proofs as a basic security measure. You may choose to preseed DNS with placeholder resolution information or use wildcard subdomains (e.g., *.8.b.d.0.1.0.0.2.ip6.arpa) to minimally meet the existence requirement. Use of an IPAM system as we'll discuss in the next chapter, can automate creation and provisioning of forward and reverse resource records for manually configured IPv6 addresses via the IPAM system.

6.6.5 Anycast Addressing

If you are using anycast addressing, for example, using a common IPv6 address assigned to multiple servers, consider configuring the server to use its anycast address as the source address of a return packet in response to an inbound packet to the anycast address. This works well for query/response applications but may be less reliable in connection-oriented applications. As outlined in RFC 4942 [95], this approach shields the unicast address of the server from detection, especially if the query was directed to a critical network server like a DNS server.

6.6.6 Internal Network Filtering

In terms of other internal network vulnerabilities, it's recommended that the following filtering approaches discussed previously for securing the network perimeter be applied to internal routers.

- Drop packets incoming on interfaces that have source addresses outside the provisioned interface prefixes.
- Filter ULA address space not explicitly defined for use on your network. If desired, deny traffic from unallocated or illegal address space as defined in Table 6-1.
- Secure routing protocols using authentication features. Note that OSPFv3 offers two forms of authentication: IPSec only as originally specified or with authentication trailers [96].
- Drop packets with routing headers unless you're supporting Mobile IPv6, and then only accept packets with type 2 routing headers.
- Drop neighbor discovery, duplicate address detection, and SLAAC ICMPv6 packets that do not have a link local or unspecified (::/128) address nor a hop limit of 255. This will prevent processing of these messages if sent from a source other than the same local area network. Consider implementing SEND if supported by your network devices (unfortunately Microsoft OSs do not yet support SEND); otherwise, consider reducing the scale of exposure to local network attacks by creating a larger number of smaller subnets than a fewer number of larger ones.
- As for other ICMPv6 types that should be dropped barring special circumstances requiring their use, consider carefully the following types:
  - *Types 139, 140*. Node Information Query, Response.
  - *Type 138*. Router renumbering.

TABLE 6-1. Address Space Filtering Suggestions

Addresses to filter	Reason
::	Deny unspecified source or destination address
::1	Deny loopback source or destination address
::/96	Deny IPv4-compatible source or destination addresses
::ffff:0:0/96	Deny IPv4-mapped source or destination addresses
2002::/24, 2002:7f00::/24, 2002:ff00::/24, 2002:e000::/19, 2001:6440::/26, 2002:0a00::/24, 2002:ac10::/28, 2002: c0a8::/32, 2002:a9fe::/32, 2002: c000::/40, 2002:c000:200::/40, 2002: c612::/31, 2002:c633:6400::/40, 2002: cb00:7100::/40	Deny illegal 6to4 source or destination addresses (corresponding to IPv4: 0.0.0.0/8, 127.0.0.0/8, 255.0.0.0/8, 224.0.0.0/3 (224.0.0.0/4 & 240.0.0.0/4), 100.64.0.0/10, 10.0.0.0/8, 172.16.0.0/12, 192.168.0.0/16, 169.254.0.0/16, 192.0.0.0/24, 192.0.2.0/24, 198.18.0.0/15, 198.51.100.0/24, 203.0.113.0/24, respectively)
fe80::/10	Deny link local source or destination addresses from external and from traversing from internal
fec0::/10	Deny deprecated site local source or destination addresses
ff00::/8	Deny multicast as source address and deny outbound traversal for packets with destination multicast addresses of nonglobal scope
2001:db8::/32	Deny documentation source or destination address
3ffe::/16	Deny deprecated 6bone source or destination addresses
fc00::/7	Deny IPv6 "private" (unique local) source or destination addresses from traversing

- ○ *Types 100, 101, 200, 201.* Private experimentation.
- ○ *Types 127, 255.* Reserved types for expansion.
- ○ *Type 150.* Experimental.
- ○ *Types 5–99, 102–126, 156–198 Inclusive.* Undefined (unallocated) message types.
- ○ Other ICMPv6 types for services not provided in your network including multicast, Mobile IPv6, SEND, and RPL (IPv6 routing protocol for low power and lossy networks).
- • Review logs periodically to develop a baseline from which anomalies can be identified.

6.7 NETWORK DEVICE SECURITY CONSIDERATIONS

The last line of defense for network and end user devices is of course security measures for each device itself. Common host security measures used today in IPv4 networks apply as well to IPv6 including

- Physical security controls, for example, for network and application infrastructure.
- Securing access via a local console, SSH and other network protocols, and at the application level.
- Password management policies.
- End user device security policies and procedures.
- Host packet filtering and firewalling:
  - Allow packets for supported services only (protocol and port).
  - Deny packets with source address among illegal addresses per Table 6-1.
  - Allow ICMPv6 packets in/outbound appropriately based on defined types and for those services in use in your network as discussed in the internal network security section.
  - Deny packets with incorrect or unknown IPv6 headers inbound or outbound.
  - Permit or deny tunneling protocols based on those explicitly supported in your network, for example, 6to4 and ISATAP.

In addition, if host operating systems in use support the ability to filter ICMPv6 packets, checking ICMPv6 error messages that include all or a portion of an IPv6 packet should be checked to verify that the packet [portion] was indeed sent by the host, and if not to drop it. ICMPv6 attacks may spoof error messages in hopes of having the host process a forged enclosed packet to infiltrate the device.

6.8   MOBILE IPv6 SECURITY

In Chapter 2, we covered a basic introduction to the concepts of Mobile IPv6. To more fully understand the security implications of this protocol, let's take a closer look at how communication paths are established among the mobile node (MN), home agent (HA) and correspondent node (CN). Recall that the MN is the mobile IPv6 device, the HA is the router that serves the link to which the MN has its home address (HoA, the address published in DNS for the MN for example) and the CN is the host to which the MN desires to communicate or from which communications is desired with the MN.

When a MN is "home," on its home network, the CN sends packets to the HoA and the HA delivers them via its local link to the MN. When roaming, the MN obtains an IPv6 address from the network to which it is currently attached. This address is known as the care-of address (CoA), and the MN notifies the HA of its current CoA as it roams. In this way, as the CN sends packets to the HoA, the HA intercepts these packets and tunnels them to the MN using its CoA. Return packets follow the reverse path, through the HA. This indirect mode utilizes the HA in all communications to the MN. A more efficient direct mode enables the CN and the MN to communicate directly without requiring tunneling via the HA. Let's take a look at how these two modes of communication are created.

6.8.1 Mobility Extension Header

The mobility extension header supports the communication of binding information related to the current reachability address of the MN. The type field value of the mobility header (MH) defines the message type and associated parameters:

- *Binding Update (Mobility Header Type = 5).* Sent by a MN to a HA or CN to update its CoA binding.
- *Binding Acknowledgment (Mobility Header Type = 6).* Sent by a CN or HA to a MN to acknowledge a binding update or to report an error.
- *Binding Error (Mobility Header Type = 7).* Sent by a CN to the MN to indicate a mobility-related error, including an inappropriate use of the destination option header home address option without an existing binding.
- *Binding Refresh Request (Mobility Header Type = 0).* Sent by a CN to the MN to request an update on its current binding. As we'll discuss next, Mobile IPv6 supports a return routability procedure (RRP) that enables a CN to verify that the MN is addressable at both its HoA and CoA such that it may reliably accept binding update messages from the MN.

Binding updates are sent from the MN to the HA to register the MN's current CoA. These updates must be communicated using an IPsec security association. This process is illustrated in Figure 6-1, where the message types are defined by respective MH, destination options header (DOH), routing header (RH) and ICMPv6 type values as shown in the figure and described following. Other header parameters,

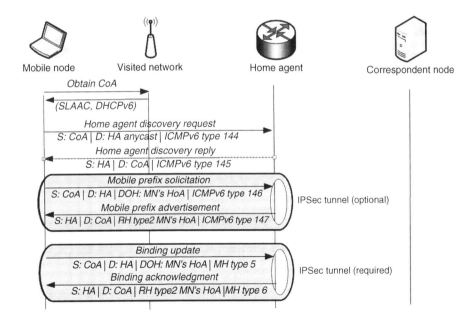

Figure 6-1. Home agent discovery and mobile node registration.

namely source IPv6 address, denoted as S and destination address, D, are indicated for each message.

Referring to Figure 6-1, after the mobile node obtains a CoA, it may need to perform a home agent address and prefix discovery task. HA address discovery allows an operator to use alternative HA addresses without hardcoding the HA address into each MN. Note that no security requirements are imposed on the HA address discovery process. The MN sends an HA address discovery message (ICMPv6 type 144) to the home agent anycast address ({home network IPv6 prefix}::7e). The HA responds with the active home agent address(es) using ICMPv6 message type 145. Once the HA has been identified, the MN may solicit a prefix advertisement from the home agent, which is analogous to a router advertisement for a fixed network. The prefix solicitation and advertisement messages can be sent using an IPsec security association, optionally using ESP (encapsulated security payload). The binding update process may then ensue, allowing the MN to register with the HA; the binding update process does require a security association.

The binding update and refresh processes for direct routing, that is, between the MN and CN without routing via the HA, is called the RRP. This procedure, illustrated in Figure 6-2, entails the MN initiating a Home Test and a Care-of Test by sending corresponding "init" messages, Home Test Init (HoTI) and Care-of Test Init (CoTI). The HoTI message uses the MN's HoA as the source address and the CN's address of the destination and is tunneled to the HA by appending an IPv6 header with source address of the CoA and destination address of the HA. The HA then strips the tunnel header and routes the HoTI message to the CN. The CN then replies back to the HA, which then tunnels the reply to the MN.

The CoTI message is sent directly from the MN to the CN with its CoA as the source address and the CN destination address. The CN replies directly to the MN. In addition to verifying routability, the RRP provides a level of assurance to the CN that the MN is addressable at both its HoA and CoA. The MN includes a cookie with each init message to the CN. The CN then responds with the corresponding cookie,

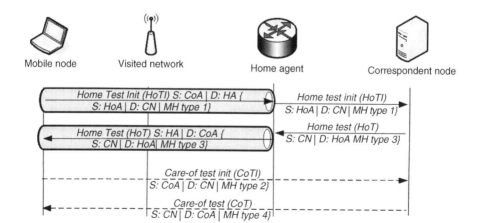

Figure 6-2. Mobile IPv6 return routability procedure.

a keygen token, and an index to a nonce stored on the CN. The home [address] keygen token is a hash produced using a secret key K_{CN} over the concatenation of the HoA, the nonce reference by the returned index and a single zero octet. Similarly, the care-of keygen token is a hash using the CN's secret key K_{CN} over the concatenation of the CoA, the nonce reference by the returned index and an octet of value 1, where the "|" character denotes concatenation:

```
home keygen token = hash(K_CN, (HoA | nonce | 0))
care-of keygen token = hash(K_CN, (CoA | nonce | 1))
```

The MN hashes a concatenation of the home keygen token and the care-of keygen token, to form a binding key K_{BM} to use with binding update messages to the CN for authentication[1]:

```
K_BM = hash(home keygen token | care-of keygen token)
```

The K_{BM} is then used to create a hash of a concatenation of the MN's CoA, CN address, and the binding update message. The HoA along with the home nonce index and care-of nonce indices are passed in the binding update message as well. Figure 6-2 illustrates the message exchange process; in general the MN sends the HoTI and CoTI messages at the same time, where the message types are defined by respective MH type values as shown in the figure and described following. Other header parameters, namely source IPv6 address, denoted as S and destination address, D, are indicated for each message; the curly brackets delimit inner (tunneled) packet parameters, which follow the outer packet values shown.

These four messages are also conveyed using the mobility header:

- *Home Test Init Message (Mobility Header Type = 1).* Sent from a MN to a CN via a tunnel to the HA to request a home test response from the CN.
- *Care-of Test Init Message (Mobility Header Type = 2).* Sent from a MN to a CN to request a care-of test response from the CN.
- *Home Test Message (Mobility Header Type = 3).* Sent from a CN to a MN via the HA in response to a HoTI from the MN.
- *Care-of Test Message (Mobility Header Type = 4).* Sent from a CN to a MN in response to a CoTI from the MN.

Other mobility header types have been defined for fast binding, active mobility handovers, heartbeats, and binding revocation. The current set of defined types is maintained by IANA at http://www.iana.org/assignments/mobility-parameters/mobility-parameters.xml.

6.8.1.1 *Routing Header Type 2*
The Routing header of type 2 supports routing of IPv6 packets directly from the CN to the MN's CoA. Routing headers must be

---

[1] To delete a prior binding, only the home keygen token is used for creation of the K_{BM} for authentication: $K_{BM} = $ hash(home keygen token).

analyzed by each router along the path of the packet. The type 2 routing header may contain only one IPv6 address, the home address of the MN. Thus, when the packet arrives at the MN as addressed to its CoA, its attempt to process the routing header will yield its HoA, its fixed address, meaning that the MN will terminate routing and process the packet (i.e., "interface local" forwarding within the MN).

6.8.1.2 Destination Options Header Mobile IPv6 leverages the standard IPv6 destination options extension header to enable a roaming MN to communicate its HoA to a recipient. The home address option within the destination options header is used to convey this information.

6.8.1.3 Mobile IPv6 Message Flow Summary Figure 6-3 illustrates the binding update/acknowledgment process and normal IPv6 communications following the return routability procedure.

6.8.1.4 ICMPv6 for Mobility As we discussed in Chapter 2, several ICMPv6 message types have been defined for Mobile IPv6. These are repeated here for convenience.

- *Home Agent Address Discovery Request (ICMPv6 Type = 144)*. Allows a MN to initiate dynamic HA discovery. Addressed to the home agents anycast address for the mobile's HoA prefix, this allows the mobile to identify a HA on its home network, for example, if a HA was reconfigured while it's been roaming.

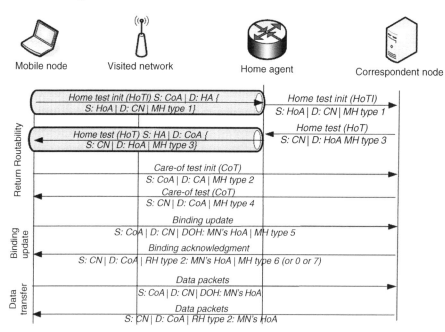

Figure 6-3. Mobile IPv6 message flow.

- *Home Agent Address Discovery Response (ICMPv6 Type = 145).* Reply from a HA in response to a home agent address discovery request to identify its unicast address in the capacity of the mobile's HA.

- *Mobile Prefix Solicitation (ICMPv6 Type = 146).* Enables a MN to gather prefix information about its home network, for example, in the event of a home network reconfiguration.

- *Mobile Prefix Advertisement (ICMPv6 Type = 147).* A HA can communicate current home network prefix information using this message.

- *Mobile IPv6 Fast Handover Messages (ICMPv6 Type = 154).* This type is used both by a MN to stimulate routers to send proxy router advertisements and for proxy routers to provide such advertisement for fast mobile handover.

6.8.2   Mobile IPv6 Vulnerabilities

Mobile IPv6 was designed with security in mind to be nearly equivalent to that of nonmobile connections. Nevertheless, vulnerabilities exist that can be exploited by attackers. First, if you do not support Mobile IPv6 services on your network, you should explicitly disable associated ICMPv6 messages as discussed above including:

- filter packets with the IPv6 routing header (all types, including type 2), IPv6 mobility header, or with the destination options header with home address option,

- filter ICMPv6 packets of types 144–147 and 154.

If you do need to support Mobile IPv6, the following vulnerabilities need to be considered:

- Man-in-the-middle attacks to intercept and redirect communications through impersonation of the home agent or correspondent node.

- Attacks directed to the mobile device operating system, software, and information.

- Communications security to prevent interception.

- Denial of service attacks.

- Visited network (while mobile) security policies.

6.8.2.1   Rogue Home Agent Attacks   Setting up a rogue HA would enable an attacker to intercept MN binding information to the home network as well as to disrupt the return routability procedure by dropping HoTI packets, thereby necessitating packet routing through the HA. To establish a rogue HA, the attacker would require an IPv6 address on the home network, which itself requires an internal network compromise.

6.8.2.2   Man-in-the-Middle Attacks   The rogue HA is one form of man-in-the-middle attack. A rogue MN or set of MNs could be utilized to deny service or at least impact performance of the HA by issuing DDOS attacks through multiple imposter MNs. MN registration with the HA requires an IPsec connection, which could prove difficult for an attacker. An imposter CN is an analogous scenario where the MN could be steered to a falsified website to phish for private information, though this is no different from a non-Mobile IPv6 connection.

6.8.2.3 Mobile Node Attacks Like end user devices on a fixed network, MNs are susceptible to attacks on the device's operating system, applications, and sensitive data stored on the MN. The vulnerability is exacerbated by the fact that the MN "owner" has no control of the visited network filtering policies if any. Mobile devices should be provisioned with some form of device firewalling to reduce the risk of device attacks.

6.8.2.4 Communications Confidentiality Presumably most Mobile IPv6 communications involve at least one wireless connection, so the opportunity for eavesdropping is greater than with fixed network communications. If wireless communications are not encrypted, authentication of the MN–HA communications (optionally with the use of ESP functionality) can provide data encryption services to mitigate this vulnerability.

6.8.2.5 Denial of Service Like any device, mobile devices may be the target of DOS attacks or they may be sought for installation of bot software for use in a coordinated DDOS attack utilizing several nodes simultaneously. These attacks feature transmission of a large number of packets to a given IP address, which may correspond to a mobile node. Alternatively, reflector or smurf attacks spoof the target's IP address as the source address of a set of packets that requests large data transfers such as FTP or even DNS queries. Rate-limiting nonmobile devices or serving network infrastructure could help deflect this attack though impact performance of the intended traffic flow in the process.

6.8.2.6 Visited Network Security When a MN is roaming it must obtain an IPv6 address from a foreign visited network. The MN registers this care-of address with its HA and with the CN if Mobile IPv6 compliant. The home network manager manages the MN, HA, and home network, but generally the visited network is under the control of another entity as is the CN. An attacker may attempt to impersonate any one of these entities in order to disrupt or divert communications similar to the man-in-the-middle style attacks. Adherence to use of IPsec requirements can help secure Mobile IPv6 control messages. Virtual private networks (VPNs) can also be utilized to secure data traffic over the visited network.

The bottom line is to turn off Mobile IPv6 control message types if you do not support Mobile IPv6. But if you do support it, apply appropriate filters and keep in mind that IPsec is a key technology in securing Mobile IPv6 communications. Check the level of IPsec support on your selected HA products as well as MNs.

6.9 IPv4/IPv6 COEXISTENCE MEASURES

As discussed in Chapter 3, several options are available for deploying IPv6 within an IPv4 network, though they fall within three main strategies: dual stack, tunneling, or translation. Dual stack in and of itself adds no new requirements beyond what we've discussed so far; communications security policies for both IPv4 and IPv6 traffic must be defined, documented, implemented, and managed. One additional management requirement would be to track a device by all of its IP addresses, IPv4 and IPv6. This is required for accountability, auditing, network access tracking, forensics analysis, and troubleshooting tasks.

6.9.1 Securing Tunneling Implementations

Tunneling has been used as an attack vehicle in IPv4 to wrap malicious packets within an innocent tunnel header. Filters that analyze only the exterior header are susceptible to this type of attack. Automatic tunneling technologies are also prone to attack given there is no *a priori* tunnel setup other than IP address formatting and tunneled packets will generally be accepted and processed assuming basic packet parameters are properly formatted. Most configured or manual tunnels can be prohibited by filtering IPv4 packets with the protocol field of 41, indicating an enclosed IPv6 packet.

6.9.1.1 6to4   6to4 provides IPv6 in IPv4 automatic tunneling featuring use of the 2002::/16 address space. If you desire to explicitly deny 6to4 traffic, you can drop packets with source or destination IPv6 address 2002::/16. 6to4 routers enable routing of 6to4 IPv4 packets to 6to4 relay routers, which serve as gateways between the 6to4 IPv4 domain and native IPv6. RFC 3964 [97] defines security considerations for 6to4 and recommends the following filtering for 6to4 routers:

- Table 6-1 indicated 6to4 addresses corresponding to private or illegal IPv4 address space that should be filtered.
- Filter packets with an outer source IPv4 address that does not correspond to the IPv4 address embedded into the source IPv6 address, 6to4 prefix.
- Filter packets where the destination IPv6 address is a link local or IPv4-mapped address.
- Configure relay routers to advertise 2002::/16 to utilize them only for relaying packets to/from the IPv6 domain, not for routing among 6to4 nodes (6to4 relay routers should always be a 6to4 tunnel end point). When so configured, filter 6to4 packets received from a relay router with a source address differing from the relay router's 6to4 address (mapping to the outer IPv4 source address).
- Filter out packets with destination 6to4 addresses falling outside your advertised 6to4 prefix(es).
- For relay routers, discard 6to4 packets where the destination address is not that of the relay router itself.

6.9.1.2 ISATAP   The ISATAP specification indicates that use of IPv6 IPSec is required. It also recommends IPv4 ingress filtering in general, particularly for packets with the IPv4 protocol header field set to 41 indicating a tunneled IPv6 packet to minimize vulnerability to packet injection within an ISATAP link. Filtering

TABLE 6-2. Teredo Vulnerabilities and Mitigation

Vulnerability	Mitigation
Hole in the firewall	• Restrict some services to link local • Implement a local (host) firewall • Use IPSec, which is supported within Teredo tunnels
Teredo server as man-in-the-middle by intercepting and spoofing router advertisements	• Nonce verification procedure between Teredo client and server. Attacker must be "on path" so attack is very difficult to mount with minimal attack value other than denying a client's service
Teredo relay spoofing	• Use of the Teredo direct IPv6 connectivity test procedure secured by a nonce
End-to-end confidentiality	• Use IPSec to prevent spoofing and eavesdropping
Denial of Teredo service	• Using host-local Teredo relays, requiring authentication, disabling local discovery, and deploying multiple Teredo servers can help mitigate the various denial of service attacks
Reflector attacks using Teredo server to deny service to a target host	• Reflected traffic can be identified given its observed regularity and semantics

configuration on ISATAP routers should also block native IPv6 packets between ISATAP routers to prevent ping-ponging, and block packets with source IPv4 address outside the scope of valid ISATAP users within the organization.

Manipulation of the preferred routers list (PRL), to which ISATAP clients tunnel IPv6 packets, enables attackers to redirect ISATAP traffic to an attacker's router. PRLs should be kept up to date and associated DNS entries for the hostname "isatap" should be reviewed often.

6.9.1.3 Teredo Teredo by design opens a hole in your firewall to enable tunneling of IPv6 packets through the firewall. RFC 4380, the Teredo specification, highlights several security vulnerabilities and suggested mitigations as outlined in Table 6-2.

6.9.2 Securing Translation Implementations

Translation gateways process all packets requiring translation, which may be all Internet-facing traffic depending on your deployment plan. Protections against DOS attacks and filtering of undesirable IP source and destination addresses should be implemented. Configuration of the IPv6 prefix(es) used for translation must be secured as well, given that an attacker having the ability to modify such prefixes can disrupt communications. In addition, RFC 6052 recommends supporting the same level of filtering of embedded IPv4 addresses within IPv6-translatable addresses as supported for these IPv4 addresses natively [48].

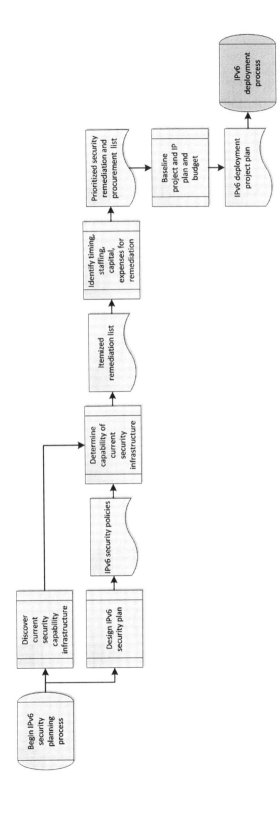

Figure 6-4. Security planning for IPv6 deployment.

Note that the IPSec authentication header cannot be used across an IPv4/IPv6 translator, though packets with tunnel mode ESP can be translated. Transport mode ESP may only be used successfully across IPv4–IPv4 translation if checksum-neutral addresses are used [47].

6.10   SUMMARY

As with infrastructure, IP addressing and network management, defining a security policy to support IPv6 implementation is an important planning step. Updates to your current IP security policy should account for IPv6 features you plan to support based on discussion from this chapter. These updated policies then need to be mapped to capabilities of current security infrastructure and systems. Gaps need to be identified then addressed in terms of mitigation by upgrades, purchases or replacements of hardware or software, or by acknowledging any shortcomings and documenting workarounds.

Figure 6-4 illustrates this process of discovery and comparison with required IPv6 security policies that have been outlined in this chapter. Any mitigations steps must be documented and potentially budgeted in terms of money and staff resourcing, and fed into the overall deployment project plan.

CHAPTER 7

IPv6 NETWORK MANAGEMENT PLANNING

Technically, this chapter should be entitled IPv4/IPv6 network management planning, since in all likelihood, you will be deploying IPv6 while retaining an IPv4 network. As we've seen, adding an additional network layer protocol in IPv6 to a network introduces numerous considerations around addressing, reachability, applications support, and security. Managing the IPv6 components of the network is an equally important component of the IPv6 implementation plan. After all, if IPv6 components are ready to be deployed but cannot be properly configured or monitored, there are few organizations that would proceed with the deployment. And rightly so, as network management provides a critical function in facilitating the operation of a network. Beyond a network of a handful of localized devices, which can be configured via brute force per-device interfaces, network management offers substantial value in providing a centralized perspective of a distributed network, and as a result, streamlined resource requirements and efficiencies in correlating and prioritizing detected network events.

7.1 MANAGEMENT MODEL

The most commonly applied network management framework is that of the FCAPS[1] model for network management. The Information Technology Infrastructure Library (ITIL®), has emerged as a popular set of guidelines for managing enterprise IT infrastructures. Developed by the UK Office of Government and Commerce (OGC), ITIL is a best practices framework with the perspective of the IT organization as a service provider to the enterprise and incorporates analogous FCAPS functionality though with more of a service orientation.

The FCAPS model covers the following key functions within the practice of network management:

- *F = Fault Management*. Involves monitoring and detection of network faults with the ability to diagnose, isolate, and resolve them. As network elements such as routers, servers, and switches are monitored to detect faults or outages,

---

[1] FCAPS is defined in ITU standard M.3400 as part of the Telecommunications Management Network (TMN) framework for managing data networks.

IPv6 Deployment and Management, First Edition. By Michael Dooley and Timothy Rooney.
© 2013 by The Institute of Electrical and Electronics Engineers, Inc. Published 2013 by John Wiley & Sons, Inc.

network services such as DHCPv6 and DNS should likewise be monitored. Appropriate workaround mechanisms such as providing for high availability services may also be implemented.

- *C = Configuration Management*. Entails accurate configuration and backups of network elements like routers and switches, as well as network services and at least up to the network layer for application and database servers. Accurate and timely configuration of network elements reduces provisioning errors and time intervals within change management windows.

- *A = Accounting Management*. Involves tracking and policing of usage of network resources with respect to business quotas or customer entitlements. Aspects of network management regarding access control policies, network utilization with respect to business parameters, and monitoring service level agreement (SLA) compliance fall within accounting management.

- *P = Performance Management*. Deals with tracking performance of network elements and services, along with resource utilization. Tracking of network resource utilization, network/server performance, and data flows fall within the purview of performance management.

- *S = Security Management*. Includes the securing of information regarding the network and its users, providing access controls, as well as audit logging and security breach detection. The prior chapter was devoted explicitly to security, so we won't address security further in this chapter.

We'll discuss IPv6 network management considerations in the context to FCAPS, including corollary functions like inventory tracking, address management, configuration databases, and release and change management as well within appropriate contexts. In fact, we'll start with the "configuration" component, specifically inventory and address management, since these functions are critical to defining the scope for the other FCAPS functions. Your inventory of routers comprises the set of devices that you will monitor for faults or performance, for example.

7.2 NETWORK MANAGEMENT SCOPE

As with your overall IPv6 deployment plan scope, the portion of your network into which you are deploying IPv6 comprises that portion that must be manageable for IPv4 and IPv6 information and tracking. Each infrastructure or end user device, application, and transport network component within the deployment scope must be accounted for from a network management perspective. The place to start is by taking stock of the current composition of your target scope.

7.2.1 Network Inventory

The network inventory is a repository of every router, switch, access point, communications device server, printer, and end user device within the confines of "your network," or targeted scope thereof. This inventory is a key component of an

IPv6 deployment plan to enable identification of devices, operating systems and applications that natively support IPv6 or require modification or upgrades as we discussed in Chapter 4. For each device or network element, the following attributes should be tracked: vendor, make model, operating system and version, function(s) or application(s), device hardware modules, and network interfaces. Device identifier information should also be tracked including hostname(s), DHCP unique identifier (DUID), MAC addresses per interface, interface association identifier (IAID) per interface, IPv4 and IPv6 address(es) per interface. Device access information should be maintained securely and consists of information like secure shell (SSH) login identifiers and passwords, as well as SNMP community strings and passwords.

7.2.2 IP Address Inventory

The IP address management (IPAM) function intersects with the inventory function in terms of associating IPv4 and IPv6 addresses to each device currently permitted and on the network. IPAM also facilitates discovery of network devices using the IP network and can also assist with identifying new or moved devices on the network, potentially affecting network inventory. IPAM is generally broader than inventory management as it also comprises configuring DNS and DHCP servers with corresponding host domain names and IP address pools, respectively.

In fact, the IPAM function dovetails with the network topology in terms of mapping hierarchical address blocks for assignment in accordance with the topology. IPv6 requires hierarchical allocation as we discussed in Chapter 5 around address planning. Applying disciplined IPAM practices enables individual address assignments, router advertisements, and DHCP address pools to align with the hierarchical address plan, simplifying the address assignment process while retaining network addressing consistency. So the inventory management function provides a consolidated inventory of network devices with associated attributes, including IP addresses that link to the IPAM function, which itself maps IP address assignments to subnets and DHCP server(s) if a dynamic address, along with associated DNS naming information.

Generally, the device inventory before and after IPv6 deployment should be close to the same; that is, IPv6 deployment should not require the addition of hardware though it may necessitate replacement of some legacy network elements. One may choose to deploy additional hardware to isolate IPv6 servers during an initial "soak" period but this is certainly optional. Hence, an organization that maintained an accurate device and IP inventory repository prior to IPv6 deployment (i.e., as a result of the assessment phase) should be well positioned for the deployment and should be able to supplement the inventory and IPAM repositories with IPv6 subnet and address assignments per the IPv6 addressing plan.

7.2.3 The Management Network

Just because some or all of your routers are configured for IPv6 does not necessarily mean management information needs to be communicated via IPv6 transport. For example, polling of IPv6-related management information bases (MIBs) can be accomplished over IPv4 as can polling of IPv4-related information over IPv6. The major management application protocols used in IP networks today, namely SSH, Telnet, TFTP, syslog, ping, traceroute, and SNMP all support IPv6. While polling for information and alert detection may be performed using either protocol, connectivity, and reachability testing using tools like ping, traceroute or network services testing tools like dig (DNS lookup tool) should be run in the desired transport protocol to emulate clients' experiences as we shall discuss.

7.3 THE SIMPLE NETWORK MANAGEMENT PROTOCOL (SNMP)

SNMP is the *de facto* network management protocol for IP devices, at least infrastructure devices like routers, servers, printers, and so on. SNMP specifies the communications protocol for configuring and retrieving information from managed devices. The general architecture consists of a network manager that communicates using SNMP over IP to one or more managed devices via an agent that runs on each managed device. The agent has access to relevant data on the managed device and communicates to the network manager via SNMP. The information that is available for configuration and/or collection on a managed device is defined by the number and types of Management Information Bases (MIBs) it supports.

SNMP defines an overall information hierarchy for managed information while MIBs define the structure of information objects or variables for a given set of metrics. MIB-II is referred to as the current version of MIBs in use today. You can think of a MIB as a database table and each of its rows is an object identifier (OID). Each OID is uniquely identified numerically by its place in the standard SNMP object hierarchy. This allows any vendor management system to access a given variable at a standardized OID value.

The SNMP standard was initially developed prior to specification of IPv6 as a network protocol. Hence, MIBs defined for IP/ICMP, TCP, UDP accounted only for IPv4 address formats and information. With the development of IPv6 specifications, new MIBs were specified for IPv6, ICMPv6, TCP, and UDP. Since then, specifications have evolved to support both IPv4 and IPv6 together in terms of transport support and of data structures in MIBs, starting with the data structure of the IP address itself. In older versions of MIB-II, an IP address textual convention was defined as a 4-octet string, which applied a standard convention to all IP address-related object variables. RFC 4001 [98] defined the InetAddressType and InetAddress pair that together identify the protocol type and the corresponding IPv4 or IPv6 address, respectively. In this manner, object attributes conveying an IP address can be specified by type and the actual address.

In addition to unifying the textual conventions for IP addresses, SNMP now supports common MIBs for IP, TCP, UDP, and IP-FORWARD (routing information) instead of separate IPv4 and IPv6 versions of these MIBs. This is good news in helping to save time in configuring SNMP managers and managing "IP addresses" holistically, though several devices have vendor-specific and/or application-specific MIB information.

7.3.1 Configuration Management

The network inventory and IP address plan define the management scope. As we mentioned in the previous chapter on security, it's a good idea to periodically scan your networks to identify new or moved IP addresses or devices. For each managed device, configuration may be managed using a variety of configuration management tools. Such tools must support your chosen transport, IPv4, IPv6, or either and must be able to configure IPv6 parameters.

If you're planning to use IPv6 transport, certainly defining the mechanism for IPv6 address assignment is a requirement! You can utilize SLAAC, DHCPv6, or both, and consider using privacy options though not for infrastructure that generally requires reliable or static addressing. Use of an IPAM system can help reduce errors in managing IPv4 and IPv6 address space together and in most cases can automate provisioning of DHCP and DNS servers with corresponding address, domain name, and resource record information. Regardless, each entry in the network inventory repository should link to its assigned addresses and assignment methodology, along with other relevant required configuration or initialization parameters.

Configuring or viewing IPv6 addresses assigned on network devices requires management system support of IPv6 address parsing and displaying. Much like other applications that display or communicate using IPv6, support of IPv6 addresses is required. When assessing the capability of your current network management tools, this is certainly a key criterion.

7.3.2 Fault Management

Fault management entails monitoring of network links and devices, alerting, and troubleshooting toward problem resolution to keep the network running smoothly. SNMP MIB polling or SNMP traps are commonly utilized to monitor device status and to detect alert conditions. Those MIBs and traps that will be monitored and trapped on should be documented and support confirmed for each device being monitored. Visibility to and trap processing for these MIBs and traps must also be verified for the network management system(s) in use or planned.

Other vendor-specific forms of management notification may also be provided over IPv4, IPv6, or both. Once a monitored attribute varies beyond its "normal" range, proactive steps may be taken to identify the cause of such variance and to take any corrective action necessary to avert a larger network issue. Of course, "normal" is defined by having a track record of the values of the given variable being monitored by time of day and day of week in order to compute a running mean and reasonable variance. Depending on the variable being monitored and its implication on the network at large, thresholds on measurements can be tightened or graduated to provide info/warning/critical level notifications.

Upon initial deployment, thresholds may be applied more tightly to the expected mean in order to "hypermanage" the initial stages of IPv4/IPv6 operation, especially from a security monitoring perspective. Detailed logging and analysis should be performed of firewall processing to identify any attempts to subvert policies as discussed in Chapter 6. After a few months of smooth operation from a security and communications perspective in general, thresholds may be relaxed, though occasional "spot checks" may be warranted to review activity.

Monitoring of network occupancy, or what devices are on the network by their respective IP address(es) is important to verify proper address planning and assignment and to detect potentially suspicious or rogue devices. Periodic polling of router ARP tables or IPv6 neighbor tables provide a convenient means to detect this information, transient though it is.

Troubleshooting process documentation should be expanded to define steps to invoke when thresholds are exceeded or alerts detected to account for IPv6-related alerts and for IPv6 addressability to devices. Dual-stack devices unreachable in one protocol may be reachable in the other, and this can provide an effective means to detect address assignment, routing or device IP stack issues.

7.3.3 Accounting Management

Accounting management involves tracking of network assets. A large part of accounting management deals with tracking devices, IP address assignments, users, and applications. Porting the address tracking function to IPv6 is challenging due to the sheer magnitude of IPv6 address space within a subnet, which renders IPv6 discovery methods unrealizable. Polling routers' ipNetToPhysical SNMP table offers the best approach for tracking individual IPv6 address assignments from a central location. On-network probes such as nmap could also be used to perform multicast pings to elicit responses or other forms of passive discovery. Regardless of the collection mechanism, reporting results to the centralized IPAM system facilitates identification of new, removed, or moved devices on each subnet. If your IPAM system supports this form of discovery, you are ready to track IPv6 devices. Otherwise, request a roadmap date from your vendor.

7.3.4 Performance Management

Many performance management systems leverage SNMP for statistics collection, aggregation, and reporting, and given our prior discussion regarding the evolution and homogenization of SNMP support for IPv4 and IPv6, performance management systems should adapt to support IPv6 relatively easily. Perhaps the larger challenge for such systems is user interface data representation mingling IPv4 and IPv6 traffic information. On-network probes may also be used by performance management systems to "listen" for IPv6 traffic and associated flow-control TCP and ICMPv6 messages to detect traffic patterns and potential issues.

7.4 METHODS AND PROCEDURES

Most organizations document standardized methods and procedures (M&Ps) for provisioning, monitoring, testing, and diagnosing computing or network equipment. Such documents require updating with IPv6 deployment. While IPv6 deployment yields another thing that can go wrong in a network, it also provides the benefit of an alternative network layer route to a given device for troubleshooting. Device reachability issues over one protocol and not the other likely indicates routing or device stack issues. Among the key items to consider when updating M&P documentation, consider the following:

- Procedures for allocating address blocks and subnets, particularly for single IPv6 subnets or dual-stack IPv4-IPv6 environments.

- Procedures for provisioning or configuration of new devices may be effortless if you're using SLAAC or DHCPv6, but for manually addressed devices, provisioning procedures need to document the assignment of IPv4 and/or IPv6 addresses and associated parameters.

- Fault detection guidelines need to account for IPv6-related statistics and alerts as well as actions that need to be taken to isolate and resolve the fault.

- Troubleshooting steps need to incorporate steps to contact a given device over either or both IPv6 and IPv4.

- Accounting functions for discovery need to incorporate IPv6 neighbor table polling or use of other discovery tools such as nmap. Analysis of address assignment differentials between discoveries must consider SLAAC privacy extensions and the use of DHCPv6. Identification of unauthorized devices requires comparison of discovered host information with a repository of authorized DUIDs and/or MAC addresses for exception reporting.

- Performance management procedures must account for collection of IPv6 MIB statistics and resulting performance reports.

- Security systems monitoring procedures must account for IPv6 filtering guidelines presented in Chapter 6 with documented log review steps to help identify possible attacks and to validate security policy settings.

The testing prephase of production deployment affords a good opportunity for refining M&P documentation.

7.5 SUMMARY

The basic process for managing an IPv4/IPv6 network mirrors that of an IPv4 only network, but the scope of information must account for both protocols across all aspects of network management from configuration, fault, accounting, and performance management. Many current network management tools support both IPv4 and IPv6 information if not transport for information collection. Identifying such capabilities of your network management infrastructure was part of the overall assessment process described in Chapter 4. Based on any required upgrades and available resources, a prioritized list of remediation actions may be added to the overall IPv6 deployment project plan. This basic process is summarized in Figure 7-1.

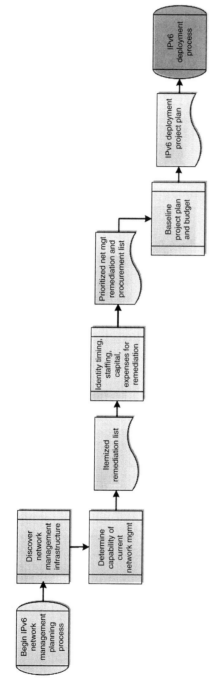

Figure 7-1. IPv6 network management planning process.

CHAPTER 8

MANAGING THE DEPLOYMENT

8.1 INTEGRATING PLANS

Building upon the planning work described in previous chapters, you are now prepared to consolidate plans for addressing, infrastructure modifications or additions, security policy updates, and network management. This consolidation enables you to further identify cross-functional dependencies and to map out all required tasks with respect to time frames and resource availability. In some organizations, the firewall person is the same as the network manager, so corresponding processes must account for this; in larger organizations, different teams may be responsible for different functions, so while more work can presumably be accomplished in parallel, more coordination among teams is required to manage dependencies and contingencies.

Bringing together constituent plans also enables identification of deployment test cases. Testing before production deployment is highly recommended if not absolutely required. Based on the necessary changes to infrastructure, address plans, network management, and security policies due to IPv6 deployment, the test plan should document the verification process to test adherence to network requirements. The testing phase enables characterization of IPv6 behavior on your planned infrastructure and its implications on planned security and network management updates. The subject elements of testing will comprise a subset of your network but should represent a reasonable facsimile of the scope of your deployment. Testing should cover dual protocol addressing, routing, data flow, outage simulations and detection, simulated security attacks, troubleshooting capabilities, and overall network monitoring and reporting.

Figure 8-1 illustrates the overall "unified" planning process incorporating the major planning functions for network, IP address planning, security, and network management. Processes for these constituent functions are illustrated in parallel in the figure, all feeding into the "baseline project and IP plan and budget" process. Here is where the overall plan comes together in terms of ordering tasks, identifying dependencies, and shopping list items. An overall refined budget may be prepared based on the shopping list as well as the time requirements for various resources. Appoint an overall project manager to conduct periodic status meetings, review progress, invoke contingency plans, and mitigate inter-organizational issues. Enlist project team members representing each functional area to participate on status meetings to provide reports on activity since the last meeting, new issues or costs, and any information or resource requirements of other team members.

IPv6 Deployment and Management, First Edition. By Michael Dooley and Timothy Rooney.
© 2013 by The Institute of Electrical and Electronics Engineers, Inc. Published 2013 by John Wiley & Sons, Inc.

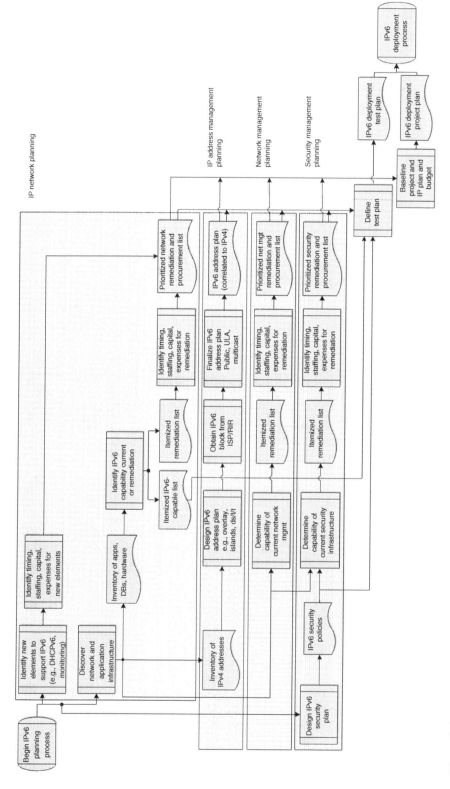

Figure 8-1. Overall unified planning process.

8.2 PROJECT MANAGEMENT

The goal is to baseline the overall project plan based on resources availability, including staffing and budget amounts that may be required. Once baselined, the project plan serves as the plan of record and the project team uses this document to monitor project status. The project plan helps identify upcoming deliverables and dependencies. Discussion at project team meetings should focus on deliverables due leading up to the meeting as well as those due in the coming interval until the next meeting, along with any issues potentially impacting meeting deliverable dates.

The project manager must consider such issues with the team and manage it, invoke contingencies or raise a jeopardy on the project to management. As such, the project team lead must possess a mixture of skills including organization, leadership, creativity, sound judgment, and flexibility. The project lead is responsible for the overall project and is accountable for:

- All planning aspects of the deployment project, including documenting and updating the project plan, posting project team and ad hoc issues meeting minutes, and communicating status regularly and on demand.

- Managing the project in keeping it progressing while identifying, articulating, and driving issues to closure.

- Monitoring progress with respect to task completion status, resource usage versus budget, issue status, and contingency plans.

- Maintaining teamwork among project team members, assuring each functional area is represented in presenting status, providing input and supporting discussion, and issue resolutions.

- Motivating the project team in accordance with the organization's culture to diligently complete respective member tasks without overtly humiliating team members.

- Resolving issues involving team resources to identify the cause, possible solutions, and workarounds, contingencies and associated impacts on schedule and cost, and driving to resolution.

- Communicating project status succinctly yet thoroughly on a regular basis as well as when project jeopardies arise.

Project team members must also be accountable for the functional area(s) they represent, which should include all impacted areas including network operations, engineering, network testing, customer/end user support, security, and network management. Ideally, each team member has authority to make decisions during the meeting to expedite issue resolutions without requiring excessive follow-up meetings, which can cause project delays. As we've seen throughout this book, the IPv6 deployment process is cross-functional and network wide. It's likely to have very high visibility so select your project team judiciously.

A well-documented project plan generally helps streamline the deployment phase, though unforeseen issues are inevitable. The general deployment process is

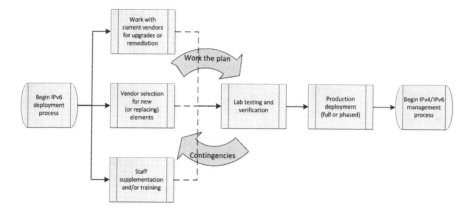

Figure 8-2. Deployment process.

illustrated in Figure 8-2. We illustrate this as involving three prongs, the first involving current vendors as needed to coordinate upgrades for IPv6 compliance, the second with new vendors for new network, IP management, security, or network management components, and the third with internal or consulting staff for assigning and managing tasks.

Depicted as an iterative process, the periodic project meeting affords the opportunity for "working the plan" to procure and deploy systems initially in the laboratory for testing, and to identify progress and issues, feeding back plan revisions and contingencies due to encountered obstacles. It's imperative that as inevitable issues arise, each is documented, discussed, and ideally resolved as quickly as possible. Resolution may range from a simple workaround to a major shift in plans, impacting resource and cost budgets. Regardless of scale, issues must be tracked through resolution, though those impacting organizational resources will likely involve approval from others in the organization. The project plan needs to be updated as well to reflect any resource changes, system or infrastructure substitutions, schedule slips or advances, or budgetary changes.

8.3 TESTING DEPLOYMENT

As mentioned earlier, IPv6 deployment needs to be qualified in a non-production or laboratory environment to minimize possible disruption with the production IPv4 network. While the project plan defines the implementation of network devices and systems, the test plan serves as the final gate through which these systems must pass before production deployment. In addition to identifying issues, the testing phase helps foster IPv4-IPv6 hands-on experience with respect to addressing and configuration of infrastructure, security, and management systems and to identify interworking issues. Testing of IPv4 and IPv6 together is recommended barring an IPv6 greenfield deployment.

Network error conditions and simulated security attacks should be staged for the laboratory testing phase to identify the response of network devices along with corresponding detection notifications from security and management systems. Tweaking of device or system parameters and retesting can facilitate convergence on the best configuration approach. In addition, documentation of the simulated condition with a mapping to how notifications and alerts are rendered in security and management systems and logs helps to build the knowledgebase of detected "symptoms" to possible network root causes.

Thus the test plan needs to incorporate input from all planning phases: IP network, IP addressing, network management, and security. Input to the test plan includes the itemized IPv6-capable infrastructure list and the planned remediation list together comprising the IPv4-IPv6 network infrastructure, along with the corresponding plans for IPv6 addressing, network management, and security. The security policies document updated for IPv6 also serves as valuable input to enable testing of planned infrastructure to policy adherence.

Issues identified during testing must be raised with the project team for discussion. Issues not immediately resolvable within the scope of the project may require involvement of vendors or require follow-up work, if an interim solution or workaround may be imposed. We recommend leaving the laboratory configuration intact to facilitate testing of upgrades, ongoing troubleshooting, and reproduction of production network problems for resolution.

8.4 PRODUCTION DEPLOYMENT

Completion of testing will likely yield an issues list identifying failed test cases, noted anomalies, and associated network impacts. The project team and possibly upper management need to determine whether any identified issues prohibit production rollout. If so, such blocker issues must be resolved directly or through use of an acceptable workaround. After blocker issues have been satisfactorily addressed, remaining issues should be documented in terms of scope and remediation, and if appropriate monitored for occurrence in the production network.

The production network should be closely monitored in any case immediately after initial deployment. Laboratory testing helps characterize the addition of IPv6 traffic, but reality in production often raises a surprise or two. Close monitoring of IPv6 traffic and security logs in particular are recommended. In a phased deployment approach, post-initial deployment phases will likely require less laboratory testing time, unless a new component is added to the network. After attaining a comfort level within the laboratory environment, a closely monitored deployment phase may ensue, implementing the various components to deploy IPv6 fully in production for the scope in question.

CHAPTER 9

MANAGING THE IPv4/IPv6 NETWORK

Deployment of IPv6 in accordance with a well-managed plan sets the stage for successful deployment and the beginning of ongoing post-deployment management of your IPv4/IPv6 network. Your IPv6 deployment may completely overlap the IPv4 network or perhaps share only a common segment of the network (e.g., Internet-facing only), while IPv4 still prevails throughout (for now). In addition, if you plan to deploy over multiple stages, each stage must be tested and rolled into production, which includes incorporation into the network management scope. Having prepared for the management of the network per Chapter 7, it's now time to reap the benefits of such careful planning to configure, monitor, troubleshoot, and manage the network.

Given that "the network" is still "the network" after IPv6 deployment, physical management scope likely changes little; however, procedurally, perhaps more so. From now on, methods and procedures (M&Ps) must account for IPv6 address planning, for IPv6 connectivity tracking, security and troubleshooting, and for monitoring and analysis of IPv6-related statistics. We'll discuss examples of these in this chapter.

9.1 COMMON NETWORK MANAGEMENT TASKS

Returning to the basic FCAPS functional categorization, we introduced in Chapter 7, we'll discuss some common management tasks, starting with "configuration," then move on to the other categories. In describing these tasks, we have stuck to the required steps. Your process may require additional documentation and approval steps.

9.2 CONFIGURATION MANAGEMENT

Configuration management is a fundamental network management function, and after initial deployment is primarily driven by technology or business initiatives such as adding (or modifying) a new device or new network service or opening a new branch office. In this section, we'll discuss common tasks required particularly related to managing IP address space and device configurations. These tasks relate to

IPv6 Deployment and Management, First Edition. By Michael Dooley and Timothy Rooney.

the day-to-day business-driven activities impacting the network planner with respect to moves, adds and changes for devices, subnets, new office locations, and so on. The output of the configuration management function is that each of the core elements of the network, from routers, switches, firewalls, and network services such as DHCP and DNS servers, is configured as necessary to perform their respective roles in the network. Other device-specific parameters generally would need to be configured as before, with the possible addition of IPv6 configuration information.

9.2.1 Network Allocation-Related Tasks

Let's consider an example where we need to plan for a new office location, whether a retail store, branch office, or new site that requires both IPv4 and IPv6 support. For the network planner, configuration management involves planning for address space allocation, assignment of IPv4 and IPv6 addresses for existing and new infrastructure devices (static), determination and assignment of other device addresses, implementation of security policies, and configuration of device-specific network information, including DHCP/DHCPv6 and DNS server configurations. Beyond allocation of IPv4 and IPv6 subnets[1], multiple subnets may be required if address space has been partitioned for per application, for example, VoIP addresses versus wireless per our addressing plan presented in Chapter 5.

Given your typical model or "template" for address allocation for the new site, identify the version (IPv4 vs. IPv6), type (VoIP vs. wireless, etc.), and size for each subnet required. Note that given the sheer capacity of a /64 IPv6 subnet, you may choose to allocate one IPv6 subnet for all services at the site to simplify your subnetting plan and simply configure multiple DHCPv6 pools, one per application, to support perapplication addressing. For each required subnet, identify a subnet address that is available, which rolls up with the address allocation plan for the given location and application, and assignment of the subnet in the IP address plan "database." Depending on your allocation strategy at this level of your network hierarchy, let's say you'd like to allocate the next available subnet for each type using a best-fit approach. This entails selecting the smallest available subnet for each type that meets or exceeds the required size.

In addition to identifying and recording each allocated subnet, the subnet allocation process requires provisioning of each subnet address on the appropriate router interface and configuring prefix options for IPv6 subnets, for example, setting or clearing the "M" and "O" bits in router advertisements to indicate availability of DHCPv6. When using DHCP/DHCPv6, "helper" (relay agent) addresses may also need to be configured in the local router(s). Some individual IP addresses on the subnet need to be assigned to infrastructure devices like routers and servers for each allocated subnet. Defining and updating DHCPv6 server configurations are also required to account for address pool(s) and corresponding DHCPv6 options and/or client class parameters needed for devices that will require DHCPv6 on the allocated subnet.

---

[1] If you plan to support IPv6 using tunneling or translation, an IPv6 subnet allocation may not be necessary, though this approach may require host configuration or translation gateway configuration, respectively.

Devices to be assigned addresses on the subnet, now and in the future, will likely require name resolution information in DNS. At a minimum, this information applies to a forward domain for domain name-to-IP address lookup and a reverse domain for the IP address-to-name lookup. This requires defining and updating DNS server configurations with domain updates (e.g., in-addr.arpa and ip6.arpa domain (s)) and resource-record updates for name servers and statically assigned addresses. Of course, these domains must exist or must be provisioned and configured on the respective DNS servers.

Depending on your domain topology, adding a new subnet to a location may utilize an existing zone, though this is not necessarily the case. A new domain may need to be defined and configured as a subdomain or as a new zone on the appropriate DNS servers. In the same way, the reverse domain corresponding to the subnet address may need to be added as well, unless higher layer in-addr.arpa or ip6.arpa zones will host the corresponding PTR resource records.

Consider impacts to your security policy based on the newly allocated networks and devices. Filtering access control lists may need to be expanded to enable devices on this subnet to traverse certain firewalls. DNS ACLs may also need to be updated to accommodate DDNS updates from servers or devices on each newly allocated subnet.

The subnet allocation process illustrates the tight interrelationship among address allocation, assignment, security and router policies, and DHCPv6 and DNS server configuration tasks. Depending on your business processes, subnets may be allocated or reserved prior to address assignment and network element configuration. Nonetheless, this complete set of steps will typically be required to bring a subnet into production:

- Identify free address space within the scope of the network topology where each subnet is needed.

- Allocate each subnet of the required size from the appropriate address space and record the allocation in the IP address plan.

- Update router configurations regarding the allocated network(s).

- Assign and provision manually assigned addresses for routers, servers, or other subnet infrastructure devices.

- Design and configure DHCP/DHCPv6 address pools as necessary to serve dynamic hosts on the subnet. This may require association of options, directives, and client classes based on requirements of devices planned for use of the address pool(s).

- Define new DNS domains as required to serve hosts on the subnet, define resource records for infrastructure or static devices within new or existing domains, and configure appropriate DNS servers[2].

- Consider security policy updates required to enable or limit reachability to/from each allocated subnet.

---

[2] In some networks, pre-seeding of resource records for DHCP addresses is required to permit users of these addresses to appear in DNS (e.g., to facilitate VPN connections, which require the presence of a PTR record) without performing dynamic DNS updates.

- Complete the allocation process by confirming provisioning and reachability of the subnet along with suitability of network and application performance, as well as by verifying corresponding DHCP and DNS configurations and those of other core network services such as NTP.

9.2.2 Adding a New Device

Adding a new device to the network involves configuring its IP address(es) or assignment methodology(ies), configuring security settings on the device, and setting application-specific parameters. Assigning, deassigning, and reassigning IP addresses to individual hosts are often the most frequent configuration management activity in many organizations. This is typically associated with deployment, redeployment, or decommissioning of devices, including routers, servers, printers, and the like. In terms of address assignment, the IP address inventory database should be consulted to identify an available IP address. It may be useful to ping each candidate IP address to be assigned just to verify accuracy of the inventory, though we'll discuss the process of overall inventory assurance as a separate task. The IPv4 and/or IPv6 address(es) to be assigned should then be denoted as assigned to the given device in the network inventory database. If you are using host-endpoint tunneling in support of IPv6 on this particular subnet, note the associated tunneled address within the inventory as well.

The physical IP address assignment may be performed by manually (statically) configuring the device via SLAAC or by using DHCP/DHCPv6. In the static assignment case, the assigned address must be configured directly on the device, so unless the IP address assigner is also responsible for the physical assignment, this process may entail an email or phone call to the device owner conveying the assigned IP address information to be entered. If SLAAC is enabled, the device will autoconfigure its IPv6 address; determining what address was selected will require local "console" access to display this or by polling the router's neighbor table. When using DHCP, an entry in the appropriate DHCP server(s) configuration file may be necessary to map the device's DHCP Unique ID (DUID) to the assigned IP address if a deterministic IPv6 address is required.

Most devices with IP addresses will require corresponding DNS resource records to enable reachability by name. Using the DHCP method of address assignment, the DHCP server can be configured to update a master DNS server upon assignment of the IP address. This update would affect the forward domain for domain name-to-IP address (A/AAAA) lookup and the reverse domain for the reverse (PTR) lookup. A similar DNS update task would be required if assigning the address manually. Updating DNS with this new host information may entail editing or updating the corresponding zone files on the server or by sending dynamic updates.

You may not want an autoconfigured device to update DNS on its own, at least on an enterprise network, though this may be suitable for a community or *ad hoc* network. Identifying the presence of a newly autoconfigured device to manually update DNS presents its own challenge! If such devices require resolution information in DNS, use of a router log or subnet snooping utility may be necessary to identify the IPv6 address.

Depending on the type of device being added, security policies configured on the device may include defining access control lists, configuring a host firewall, and/or initializing other preventive security measures such as antimalware software. If required, exposure to management systems may need to be initialized to enable ongoing configuring and managing of the device.

In summary, the task of adding a new device includes the following subtasks:

- Determine how the device will obtain its IP address: via manual configuration, SLAAC, or DHCP.
- If DHCP, determine if current address pools, if any, on the subnet have capacity to support the device; if not, configure an address pool of the corresponding DHCP type on the DHCP server along with necessary option parameters.
- If Manual DHCP (that is, the device is assigned a "static" address via DHCP), identify a free IP address within the subnet where the device is located and assign the address to the device by configuring the DHCP server to reserve or assign a Manual DHCP address for the device's DUID setting.
- If manually configured on the device, identify a free IP address within the subnet where the device is located and assign the address to the device. Have the assigned static IP address configured on the device manually. Select a nonmonotonically increasing (i.e., random) interface ID if possible.
- In all cases, update the IP address plan with the assigned address, whether a spreadsheet or other IP address management (IPAM) tool.
- Determine if DNS resource records need to be manually created and updated. This would generally be the case for statically assigned addresses. For DHCP-assigned devices, the DHCP server can be configured to perform dynamic updates, though in some cases where dynamic updates are not feasible or allowed by policy, manual updating of corresponding resource records may be required.
- Configure device security software and policies.
- Configure device management parameters if necessary.
- Verify completion of the address assignment process by pinging the address successfully and verifying its resource records in DNS. For devices assigned addresses via an address pool, verification may not be needed; however, if it is, the address may not be known *a priori*. Locating the device's MAC address or DUID in the DHCP lease file, followed by a ping of the corresponding address confirms its assignment in this case.

9.2.3 Deletion Tasks

Address allocation is a top-down process, with allocation of hierarchical blocks from your base deployment, from which subnets can be allocated, from with IP addresses can be assigned. Deletion of devices or address space requires the inverse operation and is necessarily bottom-up. Deleting an address block before the underlying blocks, subnets, and devices would strand these underlying elements.

9.2.3.1 Deleting Devices Deleting a device from the network is relatively straightforward: denote the device as deleted or pending deletion in the network inventory and the corresponding security and management systems as needed. This includes removing any M-DHCP entries from DHCP server(s) if appropriate, releasing the lease, and removing associated DNS resource records. However, care must be taken to assure the address has been relinquished by the device and that DHCP and DNS updates have been completed before assigning the address to another device. For example, simply deleting a lease on a DHCP server does not force the client holding that lease to relinquish it. The DHCP RECONFIGURE message was designed to force a DHCP client to enter the renewing state to enable a server to potentially NAK the client's attempt to renew the lease, thereby freeing the address. However, this has not been widely implemented as yet.

Denoting the address as in a state of "pending deletion" or something similar would alert other administrators not to assign that address to another device until confirmation is received of its availability. This confirmation process entails pinging the address, perhaps successively over several days, and confirming the deletion of its associated data in DNS and DHCP servers.

If the deleted device is itself a network element, ACLs or related information for the deleted IP address(es) will require some attention. For example, if removing a DNS server, its address should be removed from corresponding "allow-update" or related DNS ACLs.

9.2.3.2 *Deleting Subnets* Deleting a subnet may be required when closing a site or consolidating address space. Devices with IP addresses on the subnet to be deleted should be moved or decommissioned such that the subnet is free of address assignments (other than perhaps subnet-serving routers). After all IP addresses have been verified as free, the subnet may be reclaimed into the free address space for future allocation.

Upon freeing up of a subnet, it may be possible to join the freed space with a contiguous free address block, creating a larger free block for future assignment. Additional housekeeping tasks related to firewall and DNS ACL configurations should be considered with respect to deleted subnets, domains, ACLs, and resource records.

9.2.4 Address Renumbering or Movement Tasks

Moving or renumbering address blocks, subnets, or individual addresses essentially combines the allocation process with the deletion process. The allocation process, as described above, should be performed from a top-down perspective to allocate space to which underlying subnets and IP addresses will be moved. The deletion process frees up address space from the bottom up as addresses are moved to the target allocated space. In essence, the size of the scope of the addresses to be moved must be allocated to accommodate the addresses to be moved, temporarily doubling the address space associated with this set of devices. As addresses are moved, the former address space can be freed up, returning address allocations to previous levels.

9.2.4.1 Device Moves Moving a server or other device from an IP assignment perspective can be considered a combination of assigning IPv4/IPv6 addresses on the destination subnet and deleting the IP address on the current subnet after the move has completed. Depending on the method of address assignment and the type of move, different tactics can be used. The type of move relates to physical movement of a device to a different subnet (physical move) versus the reassignment of the IP addresses on the same or a different subnet (logical move or renumbering). A physical move of a nonmobile IP device, for example, a server will typically involve a power down and reboot, which affords more control of the timing of the address assignment process.

Physical Moves Physical moves imply powering down, moving, then powering up devices at the destination location. We will assume here that routers and switches are installed and configured at the destination location prior to moving other network devices. This approach helps minimize downtime that would otherwise be experienced with a complete "pick up and move" approach. For DHCP and DHCPv6-assigned devices, if an entire pool is being moved, the destination pools should be setup on a (same or different) DHCP server for each IP address type required. Make sure the routers serving the destination subnet are configured to relay DHCP packets to the DHCP server (s) configured with the new pool. You can also configure relays for DHCPv6 though well-known multicast addresses have been defined to obviate this requirement.

When moved devices power up at the new location, they will likely attempt to renew the most recent lease they possessed on the old subnet. The DHCPv6 server will issue a REPLY to each client's REQUEST message indicating that the respective lease cannot be renewed. The client will reinitialize and issue a SOLICIT packet to obtain a new lease. The DHCPv6 server obliges with an IPv6 address lease from the new destination pool. Once all devices have physically moved, the pools serving the old subnet may be decommissioned.

A Manual DHCP (M-DHCP) device is like a bootp device that receives the same IP address every time it transacts with DHCP. This requires a preconfigured 1:1 association of the device's DUID with a fixed IPv6 address in the DHCPv6 server configuration. Physical movement of a M-DHCP device entails creation of the M-DHCP ("host") entry in the DHCPv6 server serving the new subnet and deleting the entry on the former DHCPv6 server afterwards. If the same DHCPv6 server is being used, simply edit the IP address associated with the device's DUID. When the device powers up on the new subnet, it should follow a similar process described above, with reinitialization of the DHCPv6 process.

Moving a device that autoconfigures its IPv6 address will lead to the device detecting its new subnet upon boot via router discovery along with corresponding subnet policies including the availability of DHCPv6 services. If using SLAAC, the device autoconfigures its IPv6 address, then verifies its uniqueness through duplicate address detection. If using DHCPv6, the normal DHCPv6 process is followed to obtain an IPv6 address and associated parameters. In some cases (i.e., when the O bit is set and M is not set in the router advertisement), both autoconfiguration and DHCPv6 may be used.

Updating of DNS resource records may be performed by the DHCP server upon address assignment. This process can update the forward (A/AAAA) and reverse zone records (PTR). If SLAAC is supported and DNS updates can be trusted, end clients may be configured to update DNS automatically. The trust model is organization-dependent, and some organizations forgo DNS updates with the trade-off that such hosts will be unreachable by name. The other alternative is to use an IPAM system or manually update DNS with the dynamic host's A, AAAA, and PTR records.

Physical move of a manually configured device requires assignment of an address from the IP inventory repository and manually configuring the new IP addresses as it power up on the new subnet. At this point, the old address can be freed up in inventory, though an interim "pending delete" state may be useful in preventing pre-mature reassignment of the corresponding address prior to verification of address availability. DNS resource records should be updated as well to reflect the device's new IP addresses.

In all of these cases, the IP inventory should be utilized to identify available addresses on the destination subnet or pool, and to free up addresses on the old subnets as well as corresponding DNS resource records as device moves are confirmed. Any device inventory system that tracks IP addresses should likewise be updated.

Any ACLs or address-based filtering rules impacting moved devices also need to be updated, as does any address-related network management systems' polling configurations. Also any configuration files or applications which "hard code" IP addresses that are affected by the move must be updated.

Logical Moves   Logical moves are a bit more challenging as they do not necessarily involve a device reinitializing. For DHCP devices, address pools containing the desired destination IP addresses should be configured on the (same or different) DHCP server. The lease time for the current pools should be stepped down in advance of the move date. For example, if a normal lease time is 1 week, it should be lowered to 1 day for example during the week leading up to the move and to 2–6 h on the day of the move. A device may have renewed a weeklong lease just before you changed the lease time to days, so it will not attempt to renew until halfway through the week (or based on your DHCP T1 time option setting). Thus, if your nominal lease time is 2 weeks, ratchet down the lease time at most 2 weeks before the planned move. On the day of the move, set the lease time to a minimum[3] time if it's important that all devices move at nearly the same time. If move coincidence is not critical, leaving lease times on the order of hours should yield a complete move within a few hours.

In this scenario, it's recommended that the DHCP server perform DNS updates if possible to more closely map DNS information updates with address changes. Manual intervention for an "infinitely leased" IPv6 device may be necessary unless it adheres to lease renewal policies despite possessing infinite leases. Another option is to command the DHCPv6 server to issue a RECONFIGURE message to the client, instructing it to reinitiate the DHCPv6 process, if the client supports such reconfiguration.

---

[3] Minimum time can be on the order of minutes or hours depending on network traffic and server performance considerations. The shorter the lease time, the more DHCP packets will be sent but the more time-aligned the move of DHCP clients can be orchestrated.

Movement of manually addressed devices follows the same process as in physical movement. A set of destination IP addresses is assigned from the IP inventory, and each new IP address is configured on the device. Once confirmed, each old address can be freed up respectively. DNS resource records should be updated as well to reflect the device's new IP address.

Logical movement of an autoconfigured device can be performed by configuring the router serving the corresponding subnet to ratchet down the preferred and valid address lifetime values it advertises during the neighbor (router) discovery process. Shortening these timer values for the address prefix from which the device is being moved while introducing the new prefix with a "normal" address, lifetimes will enable autoconfigured devices to perform this logical move automatically. Once all devices have moved and the valid lifetime of the former prefix expires, the prefix can be removed.

9.2.4.2 Subnet Moves Moving a subnet could involve one of two results: movement of the subnet and its assigned IP addresses to another router interface, preserving the current address assignment or movement to another router or interface, requiring new subnet addresses. We'll include the subnet renumbering task with the latter case as it too results in a new subnet address though without necessarily moving the subnet to another router interface. The first case requires consideration of address space rollup within the hierarchy but generally consists of modifying and verifying router provisioning compliance with the addressing plan, updating affected security and filtering policies, and network monitoring systems, as well as updates to routing tables and DHCP relay addresses as necessary.

Movement of a subnet due to a physical move or a higher level renumbering generally requires a bit more work. A physical movement where devices are physically moved, for example, when an office is moved, is inherently disruptive. The destination subnet may be allocated and provisioned on the destination router interface, along with the other tasks described above related to reserving static addresses, updating DHCP/DHCPv6, DNS, firewall, and network management configurations. When each moved device plugs in, it will need to be manually readdressed with the new address and/or obtain a DHCP/DHCPv6 lease on a pool relevant to the subnet as described above for IP address moves. Autoconfigured devices will detect the new prefix for the subnet to which they are now attached via NDP and should autoconfigure a unicast IPv6 address accordingly for each such prefix. Logical subnet moves or renumbering likewise follows the logical IP address move process for each device.

After all devices have been moved from the old subnet to the new, the old subnet address spaces may be freed up following the delete subnet process.

9.2.5 Block/Subnet Splits

Splitting an address block entails the creation of two or more smaller-sized blocks from a given source block. Splits may be necessary to free up address space or even as a means of suballocation of address space. In the former case, the addresses within a subnet may be consolidated to the first half of the subnet, freeing up assignments in the second half. In this case, splitting the block yields an occupied subnet (first half) and a free subnet (second half). Some organizations have historically allocated regional blocks, then split them to assign subblocks and subnets lower in the address hierarchy. In some sense, this is a form of block allocation.

Be cognizant of DNS reverse zone impacts when splitting blocks. If DNS administrative authority for the two resulting subnets remains consolidated under one set of administrators, the original in-addr.arpa or ip6.arpa zone probably does not require modification. However, if a resulting split block or subnet will have its devices administered in DNS by a separate delegated authority, then the original reverse domain will require splitting as well. This entails creation of two reverse zones corresponding to the resulting split subnets and notification to the parent reverse zone administrator of the split in responsibility to properly delegate down the reverse zone tree to the proper set of DNS servers for authoritative information.

Splitting a block need not be restricted to only splitting in half, say a /60 into two /61s. A split may be used to carve out a /64 from a /60, though this is perhaps better performed using the subnet allocation process in general. Such a split would yield the required /64, and free space consisting of a /64, a /63, a /62, and a /61. In this example, we preserved large blocks following an optimal allocation strategy. Alternatively, we could have simply split our /60 into 16 /64s, which comprises the uniform allocation policy, as opposed to the as-needed "best-fit" allocation strategy.

In summary, the process of splitting a block is similar to that of allocating a block. The block to be split is successively divided until the desired block size is attained. Remaining free blocks are either retained or also split to the same size as the desired block to render a uniform block split. DNS implications on the reverse zone tree and administrative delegation must be considered. And keep in mind that each network resulting from the split results in an additional network and broadcast address.

9.2.6   Block/Subnet Joins

A join combines two contiguous same-sized address blocks or subnets into a single block or subnet. For example, blocks 2001:db8:0:2::/64 and 2001:db8:0:3::/64 could be joined to form 2001:db8:0:2::/63, as both /64s share a common 63-bit prefix. Note that this is not the case if one attempted to join 2001:db8:0:1::/64 and 2001:db8:0:2::/64, which is not a valid join. Why would one want to perform joins? Joins enable aggregation of larger blocks that can be allocated in the future. We saw an example of this in Chapter 5 in our discussion of sparse allocation to enable adding address space capacity without growing routing tables. Allocation requests can arise for any sized block or subnet, so aggregating block space also increases the probability that larger blocks are available for allocation as needed, which in turn minimizes networks requiring advertising in routing protocols.

Rolling up of joined blocks may also require an updating of DNS reverse zones to consolidate underlying device resource records into a "joined" reverse zone reflecting the resulting consolidated subnet as well as updating security filtering policies.

9.2.7 DHCPv6 Server Configuration

DHCPv6 server configuration is a key address management task that goes beyond address pool creation, movement, and deletion, though the extent of additional functions is constrained by the capabilities of the DHCPv6 server vendor. Key among DHCPv6 server configuration parameters are

- *DHCPv6 Prefix Pools.* Sets of IPv6 blocks for allocation to requesting routers for prefix delegation.
- *DHCPv6 Address Pools.* Address ranges and associated DHCPv6 options and server policies for dynamic, automatic, and manual DUID-based DHCPv6 clients.
- *Client Classes.* Parameter match values (e.g., vendor-class-identifier = "Avaya 4600") and associated allow/deny pools and DHCPv6 options and server policies.
- High availability parameter settings for split scopes (DHCPv6 failover is currently under study within the IETF).
- Configuration of server activities such as dynamic DNS updates and other server directives and parameters.

The actual server configuration syntax and interface will depend on the server type. For example, ISC DHCPv6 servers can be configured by editing the dhcp.conf file while Microsoft DHCP can be updated using a Windows MMC interface. Both of these and other DHCP vendors also provide command line interfaces or APIs to perform configuration updates. For these and other products, please consult your vendor's documentation.

Individual static IPv6 address assignments need to be recorded to assure uniqueness. Within allocated subnets, DHCPv6 address pools should be tracked to provide an overall view of address assignments within the subnet, whether statically or dynamically assigned. While tracking of individual DHCPv6 leases within a spreadsheet is not readily performed, recording of address pools within the spreadsheet or database should be performed at the least. This will help assure unique address assignments over time.

Such tracking is also necessary to correlate a given host's multiple addresses, for example, for dual stack. This consolidated address assignment data store would provide the known level of IP address inventory, and Figure 9-1 illustrates and example spreadsheet representation.

Notice in the figure the dual stack address assignment for the reserved device of IPv4 address 10.17.2.5. The IPv6 address consists of the subnet prefix concatenated with an interface ID that visually maps to the corresponding IPv4 address. The Interface ID is not a binary mapping of the IPv4 address, but a "visual" mapping such that the IPv4 address is easily distinguishable by sight. This address assignment method certainly helps map device addresses detected in logs or management systems to well-known or familiar IPv4 addresses, but it also exposes a potential security vulnerability. The vulnerability relates to allowing an attacker to target a given device of a known IPv4 address through its presumably more weakly defended IPv6 address.

Europe - West - Rome - VoIP subnet					
10.17.2.0/24	2001:db8:4af0:8812::/64				

IPv4 Address	IPv6 Address	Hostname	Device Type	Assignment Method	Hardware Address
10.17.2.1	2001:db8:4af0:8812:ca00:21ff:fe07:39f1	roma-core01	Gateway/Router	Manual	C8-00-21-07-39-F1
10.17.2.2	2001:db8:4af0:8812:ca00:22ff:fefe:a901	roma-core02	Gateway/Router	Manual	C8-00-22-FE-A9-01
10.17.2.3	2001:db8:4af0:8812:212:65ff:fe91:27	roma-ops01	Switch	Manual	00-12-65-91-00-27
10.17.2.4	2001:db8:4af0:8812:212:65ff:fe91:1eb1	roma-ops02	Switch	Manual	00-12-65-91-1E-B1
10.17.2.5	2001:db8:4af0:8812:10:17:2:5			Reserved	
10.17.2.6	2001:db8:4af0:8812:10:17:2:6			Reserved	
10.17.2.7	2001:db8:4af0:8812:10:17:2:7			Reserved	
10.17.2.8	2001:db8:4af0:8812:476a:1ff:fe00:d98	romops-print01	Printer	M-DHCP	45-6A-01-00-0D-98
10.17.2.9	2001:db8:4af0:8812:476a:1ff:fe20:3df0	romops-print02	Printer	M-DHCP	45-6A-01-20-3D-F0
10.17.2.10	2001:db8:4af0:8812:476a:1ff:fe01:65d1	romops-print03	Printer	M-DHCP	45-6A-01-01-65-D1
10.17.2.11	2001:db8:4af0:8812:476a:1ff:fe94:309e	romops-print04	Printer	M-DHCP	45-6A-01-94-30-9E
10.17.2.12	2001:db8:4af0:8812:476a:1ff:fe89:a20c	romops-print05	Printer	M-DHCP	45-6A-01-89-A2-0C
10.17.2.13	2001:db8:4af0:8812:476a:1ff:fe0a:a98b	romops-print06	Printer	M-DHCP	45-6A-01-0A-A9-8B
10.17.2.14	2001:db8:4af0:8812:476a:1ff:fe49:1fe	romops-print07	Printer	M-DHCP	45-6A-01-49-01-FE
10.17.2.15	2001:db8:4af0:8812:10d::78f3	opsfile41	Server	Manual	
10.17.2.16	2001:db8:4af0:8812:8021:776:d:1ce1	opsfile42	Server	Manual	
10.17.2.17	2001:db8:4af0:8812:1107:ca1:50ee:7b	opsfile43	Server	Manual	
10.17.2.18	2001:db8:4af0:8812:8e:320:dec1:90a:a8	opsfile44	Server	Manual	
10.17.2.19	2001:db8:4af0:8812::8e10:d878	opsfile45	Server	Manual	
10.17.2.20	2001:db8:4af0:8812:4:7dad:910:21a2	opsfile46	Server	Manual	
10.17.2.21-10.17.2.50				Reserved for net-servers	
10.17.2.51-10.17.2.254			VoIP Phones	D-DHCP	
	2001:db8:4af0:8812:ffff::/80			DHCPv6 pool	

Figure 9-1. Sample subnet inventory table for IP addresses.

9.2.8 DNS Server Configuration

Like DHCP, DNS server configuration is a critical network management function and is tightly linked with address allocation, assignment, moves, and deletions. These tasks discussed previously affect DNS domains, resource records, and possibly server configuration parameters. Key among DNS server configuration parameters are

- *Domains.* Adding, modifying, or deleting domains/zones on DNS servers.
- *Resource Records.* Adding, modifying, or deleting resource records, for example, AAAA and PTR types in particular.
- *Server, View, and Zone Configurations.* Setting and modifying option parameters affecting ACLs, server configuration, DNS64 configuration, and so on.

The actual DNS server configuration syntax will depend on the server type. ISC BIND servers can be configured by editing the named.conf and associated zone files on the server. DNS servers that support DDNS may also support resource record updates in this manner. The use of `nsupdate` or similar DDNS mechanism provides a means to perform incremental updates without having to manually edit zone text files and reload respective zones, for example, using rndc. DDNS updates apply to resource record adds/changes/deletes only, so any zone or server configuration parameter changes or zone additions or deletions would still require text file editing and reloading of named.conf and/or affected zones.

Given the direct relationship between IP addresses and reverse domains, hostnames and other host information, and the fact that DNS enables navigation by name instead of by IPv6 address, it's clear that DNS is a key ingredient for managing an IPv6 network. DNS provides the critical linkage between hostnames and IP addresses, making IP applications easier to use.

From an IP address management perspective, clearly reverse DNS domains have a direct association with IP address block and subnet allocations. These domains are derived directly from their corresponding IP addresses.

In keeping with the philosophy of centralizing IP address inventory, it follows that tracking hostnames and resource records associated with each IP address should be performed. Referring to our IP inventory spreadsheet in Figure 9-1, if the Rome office administers its own DNS zones, its administrators would need to manage zone files for rome.ipamworldwide.com (forward domain), 2.17.10.in-addr.arpa and 2.1.8.8.0.f.a.4.8.b.d.0.1.0.0.2.ip6.arpa. Within these zone files, resource record entries need to be maintained. For example, for host opsfile41 with IPv4 address 10.17.2.15, the following zone file entries must be made:

- rome.ipamworldwide.com. zone:

opsfile41	IN	A	10.17.2.15
opsfile41	IN	AAAA	2001:db8:4af0:8812:10d::78f3

- 2.17.10.in-addr.arpa. zone:

15	IN	PTR	opsfile41.rome.ipamworldwide.com.

- 2.1.8.8.0.f.a.4.8.b.d.0.1.0.0.2.ip6.arpa. zone:

3.f.8.7.0.0.0.0.0.0.0.0.	IN	PTR	opsfile41.rome.
d.0.1.0			ipamworldwide.com.

We need to assure that we properly transcribe this inventory information into the DNS server configurations. From this "database," we can derive the A, AAAA, and PTR records corresponding to each host. We could expand the columns on the spreadsheet to track additional resource records associated with given hosts such as CNAME, MX, and so on. In this example, we are entering the DNS information for a statically defined host, and this process should be replicated for each such host on the subnet. Hosts obtaining leases from a DHCP/DHCPv6 address pool or autoconfigured devices can update their hostname information in DNS via Dynamic DNS.

9.2.9 Prefix Renumbering

In the event of a change in service provider, which had provided provider-aggregate IPv6 address space for use within your network, the IPv6 prefix changes by necessity. RFC 4192 [99] describes the process for renumbering IPv6 networks. In order to minimize disruptions, deployment of the new prefix is required while the soon-to-be-deprecated old prefix is operational. This entails subnetting the new prefix successively down to the subnet level, enabling individual devices to autoconfigure, or be manually assigned IPv6 addresses from the new prefix prior to removing the old prefix, retaining connectivity. This process is similar to deploying IPv6 initially over an IPv4 network. Related steps include configuring router interfaces accordingly with subnet information and propagating routing updates for the new prefix, configuring security filters and ACLs to accommodate the new prefix, and configuring DNS servers with the respective reverse zone(s). In addition, any IPv6 addresses specified in applications, configuration files, DHCP option parameter values, and anywhere else need to be updated respectively to reflect the new prefix. Once the new prefix has been deployed, the network is effectively utilizing (at least) two prefixes. As when moving subnets and devices, addresses on the old prefix should be ramped down over time, for example, by shortening DHCP lease times and reducing router-advertised preferred and valid lifetime values. As devices transition to the new prefix, old prefix addresses become free, which roll up to freeing subnets and eventually blocks up to the entire prefix itself.

9.3 FAULT MANAGEMENT

Fault management encompasses not only fault detection, but also alert notification, trouble isolation capabilities, trouble tracking, and problem resolution processes. Monitoring of IPv6 network elements and servers for faults and events enables a proactive means of minimizing services outages and serves as an extension to current IPv4 monitoring processes. As we discussed in Chapter 7, IPv6 ideally requires an extension of current monitoring and fault management tools to support IPv6 transport, SNMP MIBs, log information, and related health and status data, as opposed to requiring use of new systems.

9.3.1 Fault Detection

Fault detection may be performed using a variety of methods depending on the capabilities supported by deployed network elements and servers. These range from proprietary polling or notification, to syslog scanning and/or forwarding, to SNMP polling, and trap detection by SNMP-based network management systems.

In addition to monitoring the state of network devices as reported by the devices, it's a useful to monitor services provided by these devices, especially critical DHCP, DNS, NTP, and other services. Monitoring the service simply entails send a message of the corresponding protocol and verify a proper response within a reasonable response time. For example, issuing a DNS query periodically to a server would enable detection of whether the DNS service is running and able to perform its role resolving DNS queries.

Monitoring of networking equipment and communications links is a common practice for general network monitoring and can provide insights to outages affecting the ability of clients to reach core networks servers. This added information can be very helpful in troubleshooting a particular problem or a fault. Fault correlation is the analysis of individual faults received from multiple network elements or management systems to help isolate the root cause of a set of faults. For example, faults from a layer 2 switch, a router, and a WAN access device can be analyzed collectively to suggest that these three faults are related and the likely root cause is a link outage.

Fault correlation is a common feature of large-scale network management systems. Whether fault correlation is performed automatically by a network management system or manually by comparing information from multiple systems, this process exposes a broader set of data for fault analysis with the goal of isolating a fault to a given server, link, or network element. Simple fault correlation of poll responses from a single device on its multiple IP addresses as a dual stack device can be helpful in identifying potential protocol and routing issues.

9.3.2 Troubleshooting and Fault Resolution

IPv6 introduces an additional layer in troubleshooting, which is a double-edged sword. It adds a layer of complexity in requiring identification and resolution of IPv6-related issues, but it also provides a secondary protocol access to a device for data collection and diagnosis.

9.4 ACCOUNTING MANAGEMENT

Accounting management basically intends to keep everyone honest. Are those assigned addresses still in use? Are any unassigned addresses actually being used? Did the new subnet get provisioned on the router yet? Thus, accounting management enables verification of successful configuration, as well as overall adherence to the IP network and addressing plan. Techniques for accounting management functions include discovery of IP addresses, router subnets, switch port mappings and device interface information, DNS resource records, and DHCP lease files.

Analysis of discovered information is necessary in order to compare this information with the IP inventory "plan of record." Such discrepancy reporting and comparison are difficult work, but provides a level of assurance of inventory accuracy. Without such a function, rogue users could access free service or otherwise infiltrate the network. In addition, planned network changes yet unimplemented may cause downstream process delays and violation of internal or external service level agreements (SLA) on provisioning intervals.

9.4.1 Inventory Assurance

Each of the common network management tasks we've covered so far relies on accurate device inventory to enable the allocation, deletion, and movement of subnets, devices, IP addresses, and corresponding routing and filtering configurations. Accuracy is absolutely essential for these address management tasks. But accurate inventory is also essential for general troubleshooting. Should a remote site be unreachable due to a network outage? It may be necessary to identify IP addresses, asset information, or other network-related data for devices at the site. Only by maintaining an accurate network inventory can such information be accessed when it may be needed most and when it cannot be obtained directly from the network.

In this section, we'll review steps you can take to assure the accuracy of your network inventory. This includes controlling who can make certain changes to certain IP and device information, to discovering actual network data, reconciling the actuals for the inventory, and finally reclaiming address space.

9.4.1.1 *Change Control and Administrator Accountability* As we've seen in reviewing these network management tasks, a change in network and IP address inventory often affect other network elements, including routers, security systems, DHCP servers, and DNS servers. If different individuals or teams manage these different elements, it's a good idea to convene a planning or change control meeting periodically or as needed to review and schedule upcoming planned addressing changes to keep those potentially affected by changes in the loop.

One way to help assure accuracy of network inventory itself is to limit write access to the inventory to those whom are authoritative for and keenly knowledgeable of the network topology and IP addressing plan. Using a single password-protected spreadsheet that the one and only network planner can modify is one approach to protecting the IP inventory from inadvertent or erroneous changes. However, for even modestly sized organizations, this approach is unwieldy. With the organization reliant on a single individual for the entire network inventory, the individual must work around the clock and should he or she leave the organization, recovery of access to the inventory may be very difficult unless a successor is groomed in advance.

Support of multiple simultaneous administrators is a key feature of most network management systems on the market, and most allow some level of scope control so that certain administrators can only perform certain functions on certain devices or portions of the network. Make sure your chosen system supports administrator logging should you need to investigate "who did what" on the system.

As important as disciplined multi-administrator scoped access to the network inventory is to delegating accountability, arbitrary changes to IP address assignments, DNS resource records, and device configurations can be made outside of the scope of the inventory. For example, manual configurations can be mistyped, subnets can be provisioned on the wrong router interface, and client or DHCP updates to DNS can all contribute to network inventory drift from reality. The inventory is a model of the network and address plan, and network management tasks rely on the accuracy of the plan. Therefore, additional "pulse readings" are required from the network itself. Periodically polling and comparing the actual configurations from the network with the inventory is key to assuring inventory accuracy.

9.4.1.2 *Network Discovery* A variety of methods are available to gather actual network data, from ping, to DNS lookups, to SNMP polls. Pinging enables detection of an occupant of an IP address and provides a basic method to determine which IP addresses are in use for comparison with the respective portion of the IP inventory though as we discussed in Chapter 6, it is not a realistic discovery solution in and of itself. Ping6 is a very useful in verifying IPv6 connectivity and addressing for a given target, but be aware that some routers or firewalls will drop ping packets or even some devices can be configured to ignore pings. Setting up remote ping agents to perform local pinging on command can help avert the router/firewall traversal issue.

Nmap, freely available at insecure.org/nmap, is a useful IP discovery tool. It combines several discovery mechanisms to gather a variety of information from devices connected to the IP network, including link local multicast pings, direct host pings, DNS lookups, and port scanning. When sweeping a subnet, Nmap can perform these tasks in one command, issuing a ping to each address, looking up a corresponding PTR record in DNS, and attempting connections to various TCP and UDP ports to identify the device's operating system. Ping results help identify IP address occupancy, DNS lookups help corroborate hostname-to-IP address mapping between DNS servers and the IP inventory, and port scanning can provide additional information about the type of device occupying each IP address.

SNMP is another means of discovering network inventory-related information. While most end devices like laptops or VoIP phones don't natively enable SNMP, most infrastructure elements like routers, switches and servers do. Of particular interest within router MIBs are the Interfaces, IP addresses, and Arp tables. If your infrastructure devices support MIB-II, the interpretation of these tables *should* be consistent across different products. Just be aware of minor variations, even among different products from the same vendor. The information in these tables enables collection of the interfaces and subnets per interface provisioned as reported by the router. This provides useful validation of inventory in general, but can also be polled when in the process of allocating, moving, or deleting subnets and devices.

Polling a router's Neighbor Discovery table, for example, the "neighbor" SNMP table can provide a definitive mapping of MAC addresses to IPv6 addresses for a given subnet. This approach provides a more effective means to perform IPv6 host discovery than brute force pinging. Once a list of subnet occupants is identified using this information, each individual host may be queried for further information; hence detailed IPv6 host discovery generally requires two steps: identify the set of hosts on the subnet, then cycle through each to obtain further details.

9.4.1.3 IP Inventory Reconciliation

Network discovery information provides a reality check on actual subnet allocations, IP address assignments, and associated resource records. By comparing discovered information with the IP inventory database, discrepancies can be identified and investigated. While this comparison may require "eyeballing" the differences between the inventory spreadsheet and the discovery output, the effort can prove beneficial for several reasons. For example, database discrepancies can be identified that may be the result of

- *Incorrect Router Provisioning.* Incorrect subnet, mask, router interface, and so on.
- *Incomplete Router Provisioning.* Planned change not yet implemented.
- *Device Reachability Issue.* If a device should be at a given IP address and no response is received. This could result from a device outage, a transient outage (reboot), address reassignment, or network unreachability.
- *Incorrect IP Address Assignment.* Manually configured address is incorrect or device obtains a DHCP address from an unintended pool or address.

- *Actual IP Address Assignment.* In some decentralized scenarios, the installer of a device on the subnet may select an IP address; discovery can be used to update the IP inventory accordingly.
- *Incomplete IP Address Assignment.* All aspects of the assignment process, whether manual or DHCP, are incomplete. This issue is particularly applicable to manually assigned addresses where manual effort is needed to configure the assigned IP address and to update DNS.
- *Rogue Device Presence.* An unknown or unauthorized device has obtained an IP address. This provides an effective postaccess control mechanism to complement and audit a network access control solution.

In addition to detecting discrepancies, analyzing discovery information can confirm completion of allocation or assignment tasks, as well as delete tasks. Discovery data is indispensable when moving blocks, subnets, and IP addresses. Since moves require allocation of the new address(es), movement, then deletion of the old address(es), confirmation of move completion is essential prior to deleting the old address(es) from the IP inventory. These addresses should not be deleted before the move completes, so they are not unknowingly reassigned to other devices or subnets prior to their actual relinquishment.

In summary, network discovery is essential to assuring the accuracy of the IP inventory. It is also beneficial to monitoring provisioning or assignment progress and time frames, managing the completion of tasks requiring multiple related subtasks, and detecting incorrect assignments as well as potentially rogue devices.

9.4.2 Address Reclamation

Another benefit of network discovery and reconciliation discussed above is the detection of device reachability issues. If a server has been provisioned and has historically responded on a given IP address, but now no longer does so, such an event should stimulate further investigation. If there were no plans to move or decommission the device or there are no network problems reaching other devices on the subnet, the device may be suffering an outage, may be rebooting, may have been moved or disconnected or may have been readdressed. If the server is providing critical services or applications, you should be monitoring its status via a network management system that can corroborate the outage theory and trigger corrective actions. If the IP address is discovered on the next attempt, perhaps it was simply rebooting. If it does not respond for the next *n* attempts, perhaps it is no longer physically (or at least electrically!) there. Unfortunately people don't always inform the IP planning team that a device has been removed or moved elsewhere, even in the tightest of organizations. A quick phone call to the site to check on the device's status may prove fruitful, but it's often difficult and time-consuming to identify the device's "owner" to verify status.

Nevertheless, the key point to assessing the possible fate of the device is that it may take multiple discovery attempts to determine if a device was there and no longer is, suffered a transient outage or disconnect, or was borrowed and has now been returned. Tracking a succession of discovery attempts may be difficult. A running log or spreadsheet can be used to log discrepancies or "missing" IP addresses as they are (not) detected. Reviewing this log over time may help determine if an IP address recorded as in use actually isn't.

In reviewing such a log, if a given IP address had been successfully discovered until a month ago, when it was last reachable after so many attempts, for example, 30, it may be confirmed as available for future assignment, or *reclaimable*. The concept of reclaim entails identifying IP addresses that are denoted as in-use in the IP inventory, but are in reality not in-use, nor have they been in-use in recent history. Analyzing multiple discovery results provides a more robust sample set on which to base a reclaim decision, essentially deleting the device from the inventory and freeing it up for assignment to another device. While a valuable function for managing IPv4 networks, the reclaim feature is of limited value outside of manually configured IPv6 addresses. Most devices will likely use DHCPv6 or SLAAC with privacy extensions.

Besides providing robust confirmation of a device deletion from the IP inventory, reclaim may likewise be applied to subnets. When moving or deleting a subnet, it's generally advisable to verify that all IP address occupants have been deleted and are no longer using IP addresses on the subnet[4]. Analyzing discovery results from all addresses on a given subnet can provide assurance that the subnet may be deleted. But like IP address reclaim, multiple sample sets provide more robust confirmation of the reclaimable disposition. Just keep in mind that you'll rarely see zero responses on a subnet, at least while it's still provisioned on a router interface, so you'll want to check successive discovery results ignoring routers, switches, and perhaps other device types.

9.5 PERFORMANCE MANAGEMENT

Performance management involves monitoring network performance and that of key network elements. It's useful to track critical element hardware statistics such as CPU utilization, memory, disk, and network interface input/output (I/O). Such monitoring enables tracking of the hardware's ability to manage the capacity of services running on the device. Trending analysis in this regard is beneficial as well to enable proactive planning of future hardware procurements to enable load distribution among more servers.

9.5.1 Services Monitoring

Monitoring of uptime and hardware statistics is certainly critical to staying on top of core services status, but you may also want to monitor the protocol functionality of these devices. For example, monitoring the DNS service helps assure adequate DNS horsepower to meet the demands for name resolution, and to help identify any exception conditions. Measuring from the client perspective to validate application functionality requires the periodic issuance of a DNS or NTP query or DHCP SOLICIT packet and measuring the response time for receipt of a proper response[5].

---

[4] Ignoring the router IP address's occupancy, since it will typically identify itself on the subnet.

[5] As mentioned in the fault management section, the absence of a response may indicate a services outage and should be investigated if it persists.

This application test could originate from services probes deployed in various locations to generate these "synthetic transactions," and measure and store response time results. Analyzing historical data from different probes can provide keen insight into DNS/DHCP/NTP services and network performance.

9.5.2   Application Performance Management

While services support the network with such functions as address assignment and name resolution outside the data path, monitoring of in-band infrastructure is likewise critical to staying on top of overall network health and performance. This includes not only monitoring of health and performance status of infrastructure devices such as switches, routers, and load balancers, but also application "flows" through your network. Supporting a view of the user experience with applications accessed across your network enables proactive detection of issues and simpler diagnosis and resolution of reported problems.

Adding IPv6 to a network should not necessarily impact application performance. However, use of tunneling or translation within the network could hinder the user experience especially on high volume segments. Try to set aside resources during the testing phase prior to production deployment to characterize potential performance implications of planned tunneling, translation or even dual stack implementations. This will help you determine which approach may best serve the needs of your network users and also help with building a knowledgebase of potential performance issues that may arise along with possible resolution paths.

9.5.3   Auditing and Reporting

Most management systems in general provide some level of auditing of "who did what" and varying levels of reporting. These functions, which could just as easily be categorized under Accounting Management, enable administrators to track and troubleshoot activity and to convey status information in report format. Auditing of IP address usage, that is, who had a given IP address at a certain point in time is valuable information when troubleshooting a network issue or investigating potential illicit activity. Likewise, if you are attempting to track the history of IP address occupancy for a given device, reporting by hardware address is also beneficial.

Performing such auditing without a network management system may be difficult except for the smallest of networks. Processing iterative dumps of server and infrastructure logs and alerts over time are necessary. This process enables tracking of configuration status and performance for troubleshooting, change control and auditing.

Common reports of interest for IP address planning include the following, though your system may provide different or additional reports.

- *Network Asset Report.* Itemized report of network elements and services along with configuration summary information.
- *Address Assignment Report.* Summary of assigned addresses by subnet or block as current snapshot and/or history.

- *Address Discrepancy Report.* Highlights of discrepancies between the IP inventory and discovered IP address information.
- *Services Performance Report.* Summary and details of network services protocol messages by type and/or client and server key metrics summary.
- *Application Performance Report.* Summary and details of application response time and load, and application server key metrics summary.
- *Audit Reports.* Administrator activity, by subnet, by device, by hardware address, by router, by server.

9.6 SECURITY MANAGEMENT

Chapter 6 is devoted to security policies that you should consider for implementation in your IPv4/IPv6 network. Once operational, firewalls and other security systems must be monitored to detect possible attacks. Monitoring of filtered packets enables identification of attacks or attempts to use services not offered, for example, Mobile IPv6. Responding to end user complaints regarding remote access could require loosening of certain policies, though close monitoring after such a change is recommended to detect possible attackers leveraging the new opening. If you have periodic security reviews, IPv6-related results and analysis need to be added to the agenda.

9.7 DISASTER RECOVERY/BUSINESS CONTINUITY

Business continuity practices seek to maintain the operation of the organization in the face of a major outage. A major outage or "disaster," implies that the sheer magnitude of the outage goes beyond a handful of servers or network devices. Automated and manual procedures must be documented in advance to reconfigure or redeploy resources to maintain operation of the network and applications, or at least the critical services and applications. Core network elements and services should be deployed in redundancy configurations to provide network continuity in the event of a router, server, application, or link outage.

Continuity of network operations will likely require deployment of additional network elements, management systems, and databases. Deployment of multiple active databases or primary/backup configurations will depend on your selected vendor for each component. Vendors implement a wide variety of approaches to facilitate redundancy such as full database copies and transfer, multimaster databases that require some level of network partitioning, to deployment of database replication technologies using storage area networks or SQL or LDAP replication capabilities. Operations tasks required to perform a disaster recovery will likewise vary per vendor.

CHAPTER *10*

IPv6 AND THE FUTURE INTERNET

The Internet has experienced tremendous success since its initial widespread commercial adoption in the 1990s. The Internet Protocol has proven scalable, robust, and extensible, which is a testament to the vision and foresight of its inventors. And there's no end in sight to its continued success. As we discussed in Chapter 1, the compound average growth rate (CAGR) over the last decade has averaged 18% worldwide. And continued investment in wireless communication infrastructures particularly in developing countries promises to spur increasing Internet demand.

Such Internet success has ultimately led to the exhaustion of available IP addresses for Internet communications. The only solution to support continued Internet growth is IPv6. Fortunately, IPv6 technology has existed for over a decade and is relatively mature and broadly implemented by a wide variety of vendors and communication devices. With IPv6 deployment, the Internet is now a hybrid IPv4-IPv6 network, and the relative density of IPv6 users and traffic will continue to grow. IPv6 is the only fuel available to satisfy the ever-increasing demand for Internet access and organizations desiring to communicate with this growing set of users will need to deploy IPv6.

10.1 TECHNOLOGY ENABLERS

Certainly Internet address capacity to support Internet access to new users is a critical IPv6 benefit, but IPv6 has several new features that facilitate new thinking on Internet applications and the evolution of the Internet in general. Key features among these are SLAAC and improved mobility support. Coupled with IPv6, this set of technology improvements provides the raw material for development of pervasive Internet access for people and things:

- IPv6 (SLAAC and mobility in particular);
- computing device improvements in terms of miniaturization, multimedia capability, computational power, and cost;
- power-conserving, opportunistic, secure, and air interface-efficient wireless communications protocols;

IPv6 Deployment and Management, First Edition. By Michael Dooley and Timothy Rooney.
© 2013 by The Institute of Electrical and Electronics Engineers, Inc. Published 2013 by John Wiley & Sons, Inc.

- management software that enables parsing of voluminous input and sensor feeds to filter and store data for automated actions or human consumption.

These technology improvements will continue producing smaller, more powerful smart phones, tablet computers, and other portable user devices. They will also help drive the enabling of Internet connectivity for "things." A key research topic today explores the future "Internet of Things" (IoT). The IoT consists of such devices or sensors that gather data about people, places, and things for aggregation, processing, and reporting.

The capability of anywhere, anytime communications with anyone or anything affords the opportunity for Internet users to better track and more efficiently utilize resources that can help reduce costs, preserve the environment, and provide peace of mind. Organizations seeking to capitalize on these technologies can develop and offer smart[er] services and products. Example applications include:

- *Smart Applications.* Provides a centralized view of yet unrealized volumes of data for more intelligence resource management and customer service such as:
  - *Smart Grid.* Dynamic matching of electricity, water, gas, etc., supply with demand, reducing resource waste, and saving consumers on utility bills.
  - *Smart Cars.* Diagnostic and usage sensors within an automobile for performance reporting, troubleshooting and customer notification of worn components, and recommended service check-ups as well as automated crash detection and reporting.
  - *Smart Homes.* Remote monitoring of premises, remote control of power, heating/cooling, lighting, entertainment, and access.
  - *Smart Cities.* Dynamic traffic management with traffic light controls, message boards for communicating alternate routes and improved energy utilization.
- *Municipal and Industrial Surveillance and Monitoring.* Physical access control and monitoring, environmental monitoring for extreme conditions (e.g., natural disaster, fire, floods), structural monitoring, and traffic monitoring.
- *Field Applications.* Fleet management, dispatch, and vehicle telematics.
- *Healthcare.* Remote monitoring of a patient's vital signs, diagnostics and medication administration, "body area networks," monitoring of stringent storage environments, e.g., for plasma, organs.
- *Industrial.* Factory line monitoring, diagnostics, resource control, supply chain management, process monitoring, and control leveraging improved accessibility that wireless provides.
- *Military.* Battlefield ad hoc networks with various soldier sensors reporting status updates to military command.
- *Consumer.* Location-aware services for tracking children or pets as well as marketing (find the nearest shop), electronic payment via digital identification, gaming, and other consumer services.

10.2   THE INTERNET'S DARK SIDE

With any enabling technology, especially one growing in scale and power in terms of personal daily use and increasing dependence on Internet access, possibilities to constrain access arise. For example, many organizations today limit certain Internet traffic inbound and outbound. This "censorship" has been and continues to be enforced by some governments, ISPs, and content providers. Device manufacturers that control the content and application delivery supply chain may likewise constrain access to sites or applications. Broadband providers and ISPs may shape traffic in accordance with subscription fees, counter to "net neutrality" principles of equal treatment per IP packet [100].

As devices proliferate that provide access to information through sensors, cameras, and other forms of information aggregation, empowered organizations may impose controls on free access to this information. As the price of storage hardware continues to decrease, the opportunity exists for organizations with access to this "surveillance" data to aggregate it, profile it, and act upon it for better or for worse.

In one view of a utopian world, every person might have "equal access" to every tidbit of information published on the Internet. But when one thinks about having one's own information, such as photographs, personal information, and banking data freely available, we can quickly conclude that some limits are necessary. The constraint line becomes blurred however along multiple control levels of personal, corporate, service provider, and government. One would like to believe that information published on the Internet with the intent of enabling global access would indeed be globally available, while information intended for a limited scope would not be available outside that scope. Neither of these scenarios can be guaranteed.

In all of these scenarios, this constrained access to Internet information is generally irrelevant to the protocol version in use on the Internet and in fact is "nothing new." This threat to personal freedom applies to both IPv4 and IPv6.

10.3   THE INTERNET'S BRIGHT FUTURE

Despite dark forces that pervade most aspects of society on-line or otherwise, we are optimistic about the future Internet and its role in making the world a smaller place by fostering global communications, automating, and remotely controlling elements of daily life, and generally improving quality of life. And IPv6 with judicious allocation provides a keystone technology to support this role.

10.3.1   Living Smarter

Forthcoming smart homes, smart energy, and smart cars promise to give consumers the ability to better control utilization of energy, water, and communications facilities, automate maintenance functions, and provide better information and diagnostics related to cars, home appliances, and resource consumption. These "self-reminding" efficient technologies can reduce worry and lower costs, while reducing environmental resource demands.

10.3.2 Keeping Track

Keeping an eye on the house, the kids, the pet, or an elderly relative is becoming more affordable and easier to implement. Internet accessible surveillance cameras enable visual access and recording while wearable or otherwise attached sensors can be used for location tracking. The latter application would be welcome by parents of young children and pet owners!

10.3.3 Extensible Healthcare

With patients returning home from hospitals nearly immediately after medical procedures, emerging remote patient diagnostics and healthcare technologies will enable location-agnostic tracking of vital signs and other metrics. Alert notifications of metric readings beyond acceptable thresholds can be used to trigger follow-up. These techniques may also be used for less stringent everyday monitoring applications as well.

10.3.4 Public Safety

For public safety applications, such as those for police, ambulance, and fire rescue, the quicker relevant information can get to nearby personnel for action, the better. Leveraging sensor data, surveillance cameras, or other triggers, information can be dispatched to nearby officers for action. This also applies in disaster preparedness, recovery, and relief operations.

10.3.5 Credit Cards of the Future

As IPv6 helps to fuel smartphone growth all over the world, new uses of these devices will be enabled such as using smartphones in place of credit cards. There is a huge issue today with identity theft and the fraudulent use of credit card data gleaned during innocent transactions over the Internet. What if credit cards were replaced with some technology that is not so easy to duplicate? We have already witnessed the transition from cash to debit/credit cards, and the move from debit/credit cards to the smartphone is analogous to using a virtual credit card.

Jermome Svigals known as the "father of the credit card" predicts that within the next 10 years the smartphone will surpass plastic credit cards as the primary payment vehicle. In his book, *Bank on Your Smartphone* [101], he predicts that retail banking is evolving into a new era that is centered on handheld mobile smartphones connected to the Internet. Although there are other protocols besides IPv6 that will be used to perform the actual financial transactions, the proliferation of the smartphone will be one of the key drivers behind this evolution, and IPv6 will help to fuel the broader adoption of smartphones worldwide.

10.3.6 Consumer Applications

Location-aware applications coupled with profile-aware information can be used by retail enterprises to opportunistically send "coupons" or selective advertisements to users as they travel near a retail store. Some may view this as intrusive, however, and a bit too "big-brother-ish" but if you're thinking about a cup of coffee and a message appears adverting a discount on a latte just a block away, you may find it irresistible!

Another potential application that could leverage all of this home, car, and health sensor information being collected is one used by insurance companies for assessing premiums based on measured use as well as for detecting root causes of accidents or incidents.

10.4 CONCLUSION

The set of sample applications presented in this chapter is merely scratching the surface in terms of applications and opportunities for better living in an increasingly networked world. As with every benefit, there are caveats, but as technology continues to press on with smaller, cheaper, more-integrated, and most of all, IPv6-networked, devices, access to information will rise to unprecedented levels and effective management application software will be needed for analysis, reporting, and alerting as needed.

IPv6 READINESS ASSESSMENT BOILERPLATE REVISION 1

This boilerplate document outlines the IPv6 Readiness Assessment for a given organization. It is used to collect and provide a central repository for the information needed to access the current state of IPv6 readiness. An electronic version of this boilerplate is available for you to download and use from http://www.ipamworldwide.com.

A.1 IP ADDRESSING

This section outlines the current IP address plan.

Functional area	Item	Block address	Usage/ utilization	Assessment	Next steps
IPv4 address space					
	ARIN root block allocation				
	RIPE root block allocation				
	APNIC root block allocation				
	LACNIC root block allocation				
	AfriNIC root block allocation				
	RFC 1918 root block allocation				
IPv6 address space					
	ARIN root block allocation				
	RIPE root block allocation				
	APNIC root block allocation				
	LACNIC root block allocation				
	AfriNIC root block allocation				
	ULA root block allocation				

A.2 PROCESSES AND PEOPLE

This section outlines the assessment criteria for processes, practices, and people.

Functional area	Item	IPv6 ready or certified?	Next steps to incorporate IPv6
IT management processes			
	Process 1		
	Process 2		
Security processes			
	Process 1		
	Process 2		
Staff readiness			
	Network architect 1		
	Network engineer/analyst 1		
	Network technician 1		
	IT help desk staff 1		

IPv6 Deployment and Management, First Edition. By Michael Dooley and Timothy Rooney.
© 2013 by The Institute of Electrical and Electronics Engineers, Inc. Published 2013 by John Wiley & Sons, Inc.

Functional area / Item	Item ID	Current vendor	Current version	Current hardware & OS	OS IPv6 capable?	Function IPv6 capable?	Assessment: check one			IPv6 specific limitations	Additional units required	Next steps to IPv6 capability
							Item fully IPv6 capable	Item IPv6 capable with upgrade	Item NOT IPv6 capable			
Network services												
DHCP												
DNS												
NTP/SNTP												
Radius/Diameter												
FTP												
TFTP												
Rsync												
SMTP/POP/IMAP												
HTTP												
Other												
Network infrastructure												
Routers												
Core switches												
Distribution/edge switches												
Load balancers												
Application servers												
Firewalls												
SAN/NAS storage systems												
Wireless access points												
IP telephony servers												
Other												
End user/end point systems												
Desktop/laptop/workstation												
Tablet/PDA												
Smart phone												
Other hand held device												
Printer												
Point of sale device												
CPE device												
Other												
Software applications												
Business application 1												
Network mgmt application 1												
OSS application 1												
Customer/partner systems/links												
Partner system 1												
Partner system 2												

BIBLIOGRAPHY

1. Internet World Stats. *Internet Usage Statistics.* Internet World Stats. [Online] Miniwatts Marketing Group, June 30, 2012. [Cited: January 19, 2013.] http://www.internetworld stats.com/stats.htm.

2. Kim, Y., Kelly, T., Raja, S. *Building Broadband: Strategies and Policies for the Developing World.* s.l.: World Bank, January 2010.

3. Netcraft. 2012*archives*. Netcraft. [Online] http://news.netcraft.com/archives/2012/.

4. Hubbard, K., Kosters, M., Conrad, D., Karrrenberg, D., Postel, J. *Internet Registry IP Allocation Guidelines.* s.l.: IETF, November 1996. RFC 2050.

5. International Monetary Fund.*World Economic Outlook (WEO).* October, 2012.

6. *Eastern Europe continues to move up the broadband and IPTV league tables,* Press release, London, UK: Point Topic Ltd., October, 2012.

7. The World Bank. *GDP Growth.* The World Bank. [Online] [Cited: January 21, 2013.] http://data.worldbank.org/indicator/NY.GDP.MKTP.KD.ZG.

8. RIPE NCC. *IPv6 Enabled Networks.* RIPE NCC. [Online] http://v6asns.ripe.net/v/6? s=_ALL;s=_RIR_APNIC;s=_RIR_AfriNIC;s=_RIR_ARIN;s=_RIR_LACNIC; s=_RIR_RIPE_NCC.

9. Kim, E., Kaspar, D., Vasseur, JP. *Design and Application Spaces for IPv6 over Low-Power Wireless Personal Area Networks (6LoWPANs).* s.l.: IETF, April 2012. RFC 6568.

10. Delgrossi, L., Berger, L., ed., Internet Stream Protocol Version 2 (ST2) Protocol Specification - Version ST2+, s.l.: IETF, August, 1995, RFC 1819.

11. Rooney, T. *IP Address Management Principles and Practice.* Hoboken, NJ: Wiley, 2011.

12. Deering, S., Hinden, R. *Internet Protocol, Version 6 (IPv6) Specification.* s.l.: IETF, December 1998. RFC 2460.

13. Protocol Numbers. *IANA.* [Online] http://www.iana.org/assignments/protocol-numbers/ protocol-numbers.xml.

14. Kawamura, S., Kawashima, M. *A Recommendation for IPv6 Address Text Representation.* s.l.: IETF, August 2010. RFC 5952.

15. Hinden, R., Deering, S. *IP Version 6 Addressing Architecture.* s.l.: IETF, February 2006. RFC 4291.

16. Kohno, M., Nitzan, B., Bush, R., Matsuzaki, Y., Colitti, L., Narten, T. *Using 127-Bit IPv6 Prefixes on Inter-Router Links.* s.l.: IETF, April 2011. RFC 6164.

17. Internet Assigned Numbers Authority (IANA). *Internet Protocol Version 6 Address Space.* www.iana.org. [Online] [Cited: October 12, 2012.] http://www.iana.org/ assignments/ipv6-address-space/ipv6-address-space.xhtml.

IPv6 Deployment and Management, First Edition. By Michael Dooley and Timothy Rooney.
© 2013 by The Institute of Electrical and Electronics Engineers, Inc. Published 2013 by John Wiley & Sons, Inc.

193

18. Hinden, R., Deering, S., Nordmark, E. *IPv6 Global Unicast Address Format*. s.l.: IETF, August 2003. RFC 3587.

19. Hinden, R., Haberman, B. *Unique Local IPv6 Unicast Addresses*. s.l.: IETF, October 2005. RFC 4193.

20. Haberman, B., Thaler, D. *Unicast-Prefix-based IPv6 Multicast Addresses*. s.l.: IETF, August 2002. RFC 3306.

21. Park, J.-S., Shin, M.-K., Kim, H.-J. *A Method for Generating Link-Scoped IPv6 Multicast Addresses*. s.l.: IETF, April 2006. RFC 4489.

22. Conta, A., Deering, S., Gupta, M., Eds. *Internet Control Message Protocol (ICMPv6) for the Internet Protocol Version 6 (IPv6) Specification*. s.l.: IETF, March 2006. RFC 4443.

23. IANA. *Internet Control Message Protocol version 6 (ICMPv6) Parameters*. IANA. [Online] http://www.iana.org/assignments/icmpv6-parameters.

24. Deering, S., Fenner, W., Haberman, B. *Multicast Listener Discovery (MLD) for IPv6*. s.l.: IETF, October 1999. RFC 2710.

25. Vida, R., Costa, L. *Multicast Listener Discovery Version 2 (MLDv2) for IPv6*. s.l.: IETF, June 2004. RFC 3810.

26. Crawford, M. *Router Renumbering for IPv6*. s.l.: IETF, August 2000. RFC 2894.

27. Crawford, M., Haberman, B., Eds. *IPv6 Node Information Queries*. s.l.: IETF, August 2006. RFC 4620.

28. Rooney, T. *Introduction to IP Address Management*. IEEE Press/Wiley, 2010.

29. Narten, T., Draves, R., Krishnan, S. *Privacy Extensions for Stateless Address Auto-configuration in IPv6*. s.l.: IETF, September 2007. RFC 4941.

30. Microsoft. *IPv6 Address Autoconfiguration*. www.microsoft.com. [Online] [Cited: October 19, 2009.] http://msdn.microsoft.com/en-us/library/aa917171.aspx.

31. Johnson, D., Deering, S. *Reserved IPv6 Subnet Anycast Addresses*. s.l.: IETF, March 1999. RFC 2526.

32. Loughney, J., Ed. *IPv6 Node Requirements*. s.l.: IETF, April 2006. RFC 4294.

33. Chown, T. *Use of VLANs for IPv4-IPv6 Coexistence in Enterprise Networks*. s.l.: IETF, June 2006. RFC 4554.

34. Thaler, D., Draves, R., Matsumoto, A., Chown, T. *Default Address Selection for Internet Protocol Version 6 (IPv6)*. s.l.: IETF, September 2012. RFC 6724.

35. Wing, D., Yourtchenko, A. *Happy Eyeballs: Success with Dual-Stack Hosts*. s.l.: IETF, April 2012. RFC 6555.

36. Durand, A., Ihren, J. *DNS IPv6 Transport Operational Guidelines*. s.l.: IETF, September 2004. RFC 3901.

37. Chown, T., Venaas, S., Strauf, C. *Dynamic Host Configuration Protocol (DHCP): IPv4 and IPv6 Dual-Stack Issues*. s.l.: IETF, May 2006. RFC 4477.

38. Huston, G. *The ISP Column*. www.potaroo.net. [Online] May 2012. http://www.potaroo.net/ispcol/2012-05/notquite.html.

39. Rooney, T. *IPv4-to-IPv6 Transition and Co-Existence Strategies*. Santa Clara, CA: BT INS, Inc., March 2008.

40. Blanchet, M., Parent, F. *IPv6 Tunnel Broker with Tunnel Setup Protocol (TSP)*. s.l.: IETF, February 2010. RFC 5572.

41. Huitema, C. *Teredo: Tunneling IPv6 over UDP through Network Address Translations (NATs)*. s.l.: IETF, February 2006. RFC 4380.

42. Thaler, D., *Teredo Extensions.* s.l.: IETF, January, 2011, RFC 6081.

43. Ibid.

44. Thaler, D., Krishnan, S., Hoagland, J. *Teredo Security Updates.* s.l.: IETF, September 2010. RFC 5991.

45. Bound, J., Toutain, L., Richier, J.L. *Dual Stack IPv6 Dominant Transition Mechanism (DSTM).* s.l.: IETF, October 2005. draft-bound-dstm-exp-04.txt.

46. Baker, F., Li, X., Bao, C., Yin, K. *Framework for IPv4/IPv6 Translation.* s.l.: IETF, April 2011. RFC 6144.

47. Li, X., Bao, C., Baker, F. *IP/ICMP Translation Algorithm.* s.l.: IETF, April 2011. RFC 6145.

48. Bao, C., Huitema, C., Bagnulo, M., Boucadair, M., Li, X. *IPv6 Addressing of IPv4/IPv6 Translators.* s.l.: IETF, October 2010. RFC 6052.

49. Huang, B., Deng, H., Savolainen, T. *Dual-Stack Hosts Using "Bump-in-the-Host" (BIH).* s.l.: IETF, February 2012. RFC 6535.

50. Tsuchiya, K., Higuchi, H., Atarashi, Y. *Dual Stack Hosts using the "Bump-in-the-Stack" Technique (BIS).* s.l.: IETF, February 2000. RFC 2767.

51. Lee, S., Shin, M.-K., Kim, Y.-J., Nordmark, E., Durand, A. *Dual Stack Hosts Using "Bump-in-the-API" (BIA).* s.l.: IETF, October 2002. RFC 3338.

52. Bagnulo, M., Matthews, P., van Beijum, I. *Stateful NAT64: Network Address and Protocol Translation from IPv6 Clients to IPv4 Servers.* s.l.: IETF, April 2011. RFC 6146.

53. Tsirtsis, G., Srisuresh, P. *Network Address Translation - Protocol Translation (NAT-PT).* s.l.: IETF, February 2000. RFC 2766.

54. Aoun, C. Davies, E. *Reasons to Move the Network Address Translator—Protocol Translator (NAT-PT) to Historic Status.* s.l.: IETF, July 2007. RFC 4966.

55. Leech, M., Ganis, M., Lee, Y., Kuris, R., Koblas, D., Jones, L. *SOCKS Protocol Version 5.* s.l.: IETF, March 1996. RFC 1928.

56. Kitamura, H. *A SOCKS-based IPv6/IPv4 Gateway Mechanism.* s.l.: IETF, April 2001. RFC 3089.

57. Hagino, J., Yamamoto, K. *An IPv6-to-IPv4 Transport Relay Translator.* s.l.: IETF, June 2001. RFC 3142.

58. Vincent, M. *Vin's World.* Vin's World. [Online] http://vinsworldcom.blogspot.com/2011/12/cat-with-10-lives.html.

59. Rooney, T. *Service Provider IPv6 Deployment Strategies.* s.l.: BT INS Inc., 2011.

60. Yamagata, I., Shirasaki, Y., Nakagawa, A., Yamaguchi, J., Ashida, H. *NAT444.* s.l.: IETF, January 2011. draft-shirasaki-nat444-03.txt.

61. Donley, C., Howard, L., Kuarsingh, V., Chandrasekaran, A., Ganti, V. *Assessing the Impact of NAT444 on Network Applications.* s.l.: IETF, October 2010. draft-donley-nat444-impacts-01.txt.

62. De Clercq, J., Ooms, D., Prevost, S., Le Faucheur, F. *Connecting IPv6 Islands over IPv4 MPLS Using IPv6 Provider Edge Routers (6PE).* s.l.: IETF, February 2007. RFC 4798.

63. De Clercq, J., Ooms, D., Carugi, M., Le Faucheur, F. *BGP-MPLS IP Virtual Private Network (VPN) Extension for IPv6 VPN.* s.l.: IETF, September 2006. RFC 4659.

64. Despres, R. *IPv6 Rapid Deployment on IPv4 Infrastructures (6rd).* s.l.: IETF, January 2010. RFC 5569.

65. Townsley, W., Troan, O. *IPv6 Rapid Deployment on IPv4 Infrastructures (6rd)— Protocol Specification.* s.l.: IETF, August 2010. RFC 5969.

66. Rooney, T. *IP Address Management Principles and Practice.* Hoboken: IEEE Press, 2011.

67. Wu., J., Cui, Y., Li, X., Xu, M., Metz, C. *4over6 Transit Solution Using IP Encapsulation and MP-BGP Extensions.* s.l.: IETF, March 2010. RFC 5747.

68. Durand, A., Droms, R., Woodyatt, J., Lee, Y. *Dual-Stack Lite Broadband Deployments Following IPv4 Exhaustion.* s.l.: IETF, August 2011, RFC 6333.

69. Internet Society. *Internet Society.* [Online] http://www.internetsociety.org/news/internet-society-number-resource-organization-and-regional-internet-registries-reinforce.

70. Netformx Discovery. *Netformx.* [Online] http://www.netformx.com/discovery.

71. HP DDMI. *HP.* [Online] http://www8.hp.com/lamerica_nsc_carib/en/software/software-product.html?compURI=tcm:246-936991.

72. OPNET NetMapper. *OPNET.* [Online] http://www.opnet.com/solutions/network_management/netmapper.html.

73. IANA. *Number Resources.* www.iana.org. [Online] [Cited: October 20, 2009.] http://www.iana.org/numbers/.

74. AfriNIC. AfriNIC Home Page. *www.afrinic.net.* [Online] [Cited: October 20, 2009.] http://www.afrinic.net/.

75. APNIC. APNIC Home Page. *www.apnic.net.* [Online] [Cited: October 20, 2009.] http://www.apnic.net/.

76. ARIN. ARIN Home Page. *www.arin.net.* [Online] [Cited: October 20, 2009.] http://www.arin.net/.

77. LACNIC. LACNIC Home Page. *www.lacnic.net.* [Online] http://www.lacnic.net/.

78. RIPE NCC. *RIPE Network Coordination Centre Home Page.* www.ripe.net. [Online] [Cited: October 20, 2009.] http://www.ripe.net/.

79. Huitema, C. *The H Ratio for Address Assignment Efficiency.* s.l.: IETF, November 1994. RFC 1715.

80. Durand, A., Huitema, C. *The Host-Density Ratio for Address Assignment Efficiency: An Update on the H Ratio.* s.l.: IETF, November 2001. RFC 3194.

81. Rooney, T. *IPv6 Addressing and Management Challenges.* Santa Clara, CA: BT INS, Inc., March, 2008.

82. Blanchet, M. *A Flexible Method for Managing the Assignment of Bits of an IPv6 Address Block.* s.l.: IETF, April 2003. RFC 3531.

83. Wasserman, M., Baker, F. *IPv6-to-IPv6 Network Prefix Translation.* June, 2011. RFC 6296.

84. Bates, T., Rekhter, Y. *Scalable Support for Multi-home Multi-provider Connectivity.* s.l.: IETF, January 1998. RFC 2260.

85. Abley, J., Lindqvist, K., Davies, E., Black, B., Gill, V. *IPv4 Multihoming Practices and Limitations.* s.l.: IETF, July 2005. RFC 4116.

86. Huston, G. *Architectural Approaches to Multi-homing for IPv6.* s.l.: IETF, September 2005. RFC 4177.

87. Nordmark, E., Bagnulo, M. *Shim6: Level 3 Multihoming Shim Protocol for IPv6.* s.l.: IETF, June 2009, RFC 5533.

88. ISO/IEC. *Information Technology—Open Systems Interconnection—Basic Reference Model: The Basic Model,* second edition. Genera, Switzerland: ISO/IEC, November 1994. ISO/IEC 7498-1:1994(E).

89. Internet Protocol Version 6 Address Space. *Internet Assigned Numbers Authority.* [Online] October 29, 2010. [Cited: April 12, 2012.] http://www.iana.org/assignments/ipv6-address-space/ipv6-address-space.xml.

90. IPv6 Global Unicast Address Assignments. *Internet Assigned Numbers Authority.* [Online] August 27, 2008. [Cited: April 12, 2012.] http://www.iana.org/assignments/ipv6-unicast-address-assignments/ipv6-unicast-address-assignments.xml.

91. Davies, E., Mohacsi, J. *Recommendations for Filtering ICMPv6 Messages in Firewalls.* s.l.: IETF, May 2007. RFC 4890.

92. Krishnan, S., Woodyatt, J., Kline, E., Hoagland, J., Bhatia, M. *A Uniform Format for IPv6 Extension Headers.* s.l.: IETF, April 2012. RFC 6564.

93. Chown, T. *IPv6 Implications for Network Scanning.* s.l.: IETF, March 2008. RFC 5157.

94. Levy-Abegnoli, E., Van de Velde, G., Popoviciu, C., Mohacsi, J. *IPv6 Router Advertisement Guard.* February 2011. RFC 6105.

95. Davies, E., Krishnan, S., Savola, P. *IPv6 Transition/Coexistence Security Considerations.* s.l.: IETF, September 2007. RFC 4942.

96. Bhatia, M., Manral, V., Lindem, A. *Supporting Authentication Trailer for OSPFv3.* February 2012. RFC 6506.

97. Savola, P., Patel, C. *Security Considerations for 6to4.* s.l.: IETF, December 2004. RFC 3964.

98. Daniele, M., Haberman, B., Routhier, S., Schoenwaelder, J. *Textual Conventions for Internet Network Addresses.* s.l.: IETF, February 2005. RFC 4001.

99. Baker, F., Lear, E., Droms, R. *Procedures for Renumbering an IPv6 Network without a Flag Day.* s.l.: IETF, September 2005. RFC 4192.

100. The Economist. *The Future of the Internet—A Virtual Counter-Revolution.* The Economist. [Online] http://www.economist.com/node/16941635.

101. Svigals, J. *Bank on Your Smartphone.* Xlibris, 2012.

INDEX

IPv6 Deployment and Management, First Edition. By Michael Dooley and Timothy Rooney.
© 2013 by The Institute of Electrical and Electronics Engineers, Inc. Published 2013 by John Wiley & Sons, Inc.

IEEE Press Series in
Network Management

The goal of this series is to publish high quality technical reference books and textbooks on network and services management for communications and information technology professional societies, private sector and government organizations as well as research centers and universities around the world. This Series focuses on Fault, Configuration, Accounting, Performance, and Security (FCAPS) management in areas including, but not limited to, telecommunications network and services, technologies and implementations, IP networks and services, and wireless networks and services.

Series Editors:
Thomas Plevyak
Veli Sahin

---

1. *Telecommunications Network Management into the 21st Century*
   Edited by Thomas Plevyak and Salah Aidarous
2. *Telecommunications Network Management: Technologies and Implementations*
   Edited by Thomas Plevyak and Salah Aidarous
3. *Fundamentals of Telecommunications Network Management*
   Lakshmi Raman
4. *Security for Telecommunications Management Network*
   Moshe Rozenblit
5. *Integrated Telecommunications Management Solutions*
   Graham Chen and Quinzheng Kong
6. *Managing IP Networks: Challenges and Opportunities*
   Thomas Plevyak and Salah Aidarous
7. *Next-Generation Telecommunications Networks, Services, and Management*
   Edited by Thomas Plevyak and Veli Sahin
8. *Introduction to IT Address Management*
   Timothy Rooney
9. *IP Address Management: Principles and Practices*
   Timothy Rooney
10. *Telecommunications System Reliability Engineering, Theory, and Practice*
    Mark L. Ayers
11. *IPv6 Deployment and Management*
    Michael Dooley and Timothy Rooney